forms of writing
a brief guide and handbook
Fourth Canadian Edition

Kay L. Stewart

Marian Allen
Grant MacEwan Community College

PEARSON

Prentice
Hall

Toronto

National Library of Canada Cataloguing in Publication

Stewart, Kay L. (Kay Lanette), 1942–
    Forms of writing: a brief guide and handbook / Kay L. Stewart, Marian E. Allen.—4th ed.

Includes index.
ISBN 0-13-122893-5

    1. English language—Rhetoric. 2. English language—Rhetoric—Problems, exercises, etc. I. Allen, Marian, 1945– II. Title.

PE1408.S762 2005   808'.042   C2003-907167-7

0-13-122893-5

Vice President, Editorial Director: Michael J. Young
Executive Acquisitions Editor: Jessica Mosher
Marketing Manager: Toivo Pajo
Supervising Developmental Editor: Suzanne Schaan
Production Editor: Richard di Santo
Copy Editor: Claudia Forgas
Proofreader: Sharon Kirsch
Production Coordinator: Anita Heyna
Page Layout: Janet Zanette
Art Director: Julia Hall
Cover and Interior Design: Miguel Acevedo

    4 5   09 08 07 06 05

Printed and bound in Canada.

Credits
Page 133: "Warren Prior" from *Under the Ice* by Alden Nowlan, 1961. By permission of Claudine Nowlan.
Page 145: "Please Don't Eat the Animals" by Kerry Bowman as printed in *The Globe and Mail,* July 7, 2003, A11.
Page 157: "A 55-Million Ride—Worth Every Cent" by Paul Sullivan as printed in *The Globe and Mail,* July 7, 2003, A13.

To the memory of
Jeanette Thornton
Jack Rogers

Preface
to the Fourth Edition

Our Approach

Our approach in *Forms of Writing* rests on this assumption: good writing results when you know your purpose, your audience, your subject, and the conventions of your chosen form. We focus on three main purposes for writing—to explain, to persuade, and to share personal experience—and show how your purpose influences the strategies you choose in writing for a particular audience. This emphasis on purpose and audience gives you a basic orientation that helps you to understand the conventions of a wide variety of forms, such as personal essays, research papers, and business letters.

This book works well in communications courses, introductory and advanced writing courses, and English courses with a writing component. Many students keep the text as a reference for writing in other courses and on the job.

This edition retains the basic organization of the previous editions. We have, however, updated the material and revised sections to make the book easier to use.

Features of the Text

- An overview of the writing process

- An extensive section on developing writing strategies and the critical thinking that informs them

- Short chapters with easy-to-follow guidelines for many different types of writing, with samples

- Checklists for evaluating your own or your classmates' writing

- Explanations of sentence structure, grammar, punctuation, and mechanics with Exercises and Answer Keys

Organization of the Text

- Part 1, The Writing Process, gives you an overview of all the steps in completing a writing assignment, from defining your purpose and audience to revising and proofreading.

- Part 2, Developing Your Writing Strategies, introduces you to principles of paragraph structure and methods of developing paragraphs—such as analysis, definition, and evaluation—that you may use in many forms of writing.

- Part 3, Writing Essays, provides guidelines for the types of writing you are most likely to do in college and university courses, including essays on literature and research papers.

- Part 4, Business Writing, covers the kinds of business writing that most people do, whatever their occupation—letters of application and résumés, memos, emails, brief reports, and promotional material.

- Part 5, Proofreading: The Final Touches, explains accepted practices in grammar and punctuation so that you can meet your readers' expectations for clarity and precision in language.

- The appendices cover material you may need to consult frequently: guidelines for formatting, using quotations, and documenting sources. Tips on writing exams, a Glossary of grammatical terms and Answer Keys for exercises are also included.

- Up-to-date Web Links at the end of each part direct you to online resources offered, in most cases, by Canadian and US colleges and universities.

Changes in the Fourth Edition

- Chapter 4, Writing Better Paragraphs, has been expanded to include sections on Choosing Appropriate Language and Improving Your Style to facilitate early attention to these aspects of writing.

- New examples illustrate many types of paragraphs and essays discussed in parts 2 and 3.

- Chapter 14, Research Papers, has been substantially revised to clarify the process of doing research and writing, to update information on conducting electronic searches, and to emphasize the necessity of documenting sources.

- Part 4, Business Writing, has been updated and expanded to include guidelines for writing memos and emails as well as tips for preparing for job interviews. New sample résumés and application letters demonstrate proven strategies for finding a job.

- Points of grammar and usage have been clarified in the handbook section, especially in areas of concern to students whose first language is not English, and exercises replaced.

- Appendices A, B, and C have been reorganized to provide easier access to MLA and APA styles of documentation.

- New exercises appear throughout.

- Web Links and material on conducting computer-aided research have been updated.

Other Resources

- *Instructor's Manual* includes suggested course outlines, classroom activities and exercises, teaching tips, and suggestions for further reading.

Good writing!

Acknowledgments

We wish to thank again all those who contributed to the previous editions; this text also owes much to you.

Throughout, we have relied heavily on work done by students in various courses. Where we had permission to do so, we have named them. Named and nameless, we thank them all for entrusting their writing to us. Special thanks to Sharon Cornelius for allowing us to use her research paper.

This edition has profited greatly from the expertise of colleagues at Grant MacEwan College. Ilona Ryder brought her sharp mind and keen eye for detail to the task of revising and updating the material on research papers and documentation. Susan Lieberman put her extensive knowledge of business communications to work in updating Part 4. We appreciate their speed, thoroughness, and cooperation. Thanks also to Arlene Davies-Fuhr, who provided us with material of particular relevance to students whose first language is not English. Marilyn Nikish's timely word processing made our task easier. We also thank Mary Braun, a student in Library Science at the University of Alberta, for updating the Web Links. Marian would like to thank Barbara North, Chair of the English Department, and Peter Mitchell, Dean of Arts and Science at Grant MacEwan College, for their support and encouragement.

We would also like to thank the following colleagues who made suggestions for this edition: Sharon Brown, Sir Sandford Fleming College; Maureen Engel, Athabaska University; Martha Finnigan, Durham College; and Valerie Spink, Grant MacEwan Community College.

Thanks too to those at Pearson Canada who have worked with us on this edition: Marianne Minaker, Andrew Simpson, Richard di Santo, Claudia Forgas, Sharon Kirsh, and Judy Dunlop. Special thanks to the design team for the new look.

To Chris and Laurie, who offered encouragement and endured neglect while we completed this project, our heartfelt appreciation.

Kay Stewart
Marian Allen

CONTENTS

PART 3: WRITING ESSAYS

PART 4: BUSINESS WRITING

PART 5: PROOFREADING: THE FINAL TOUCHES

APPENDICES

Appendix D: Writing Essay and Short-Answer Exams

Appendix E: Glossary of Grammatical Terms   **348**

Appendix F: Answer Keys

Index   **373**

PART 1

THE WRITING PROCESS
AN OVERVIEW

As the Industrial Revolution marked the nineteenth century, so the Communication Revolution marked the twentieth. We can now pop a DVD into a player, download from a computer database, send a text message to a cellphone. These new technologies, far from reducing the need for good writing skills, have increased them. Someone, somewhere, must write the script for the DVD, the entries in the database, the urgent email message. In the twenty-first century, that person may be you.

You can more easily meet the varied and changing demands made on your writing skills if you understand the basic steps that many successful writers take in completing a piece of writing.

What we offer is a blueprint: you may find your writing process much less clearcut and tidy. You may discover that you spend more time and energy on some steps than on others, depending on the writing project and your creative style. The writing process is not a rigid structure for you to impose on your writing, but a general plan to help you shape an idea into a written piece. Use the steps to guide you; make the process your own.

CHECKLIST | *The Writing Process*

1. What is your **subject** for this piece of writing?

   _____

2. What is your **purpose**?
   To explain what/how/why _____
   To change readers' opinions about _____
   To persuade readers to _____
   To share personal experience about _____

3. Who is your **audience**? _____

   _____

4. What does your **reader profile** suggest about your audience's needs and expectations?

   _____

5. a. Which method(s) of **gathering material** have you used?

   _____

   b. Do you have **enough material** to achieve your purpose?

   _____

6. What **focus** have you chosen for your subject?

   _____

7. Have you written a **draft** to clarify your thoughts?

   _____

8. Have you used an **outline** to organize your material?

   _____

9. Have you **revised** your draft for content and organization?

   _____

10. Have you **proofread** your writing to improve your style?

   _____

11. Have you **proofread** your writing for errors?

   _____

12. Have you presented your writing in an appropriate **format**?

   _____

CHAPTER 1

IDENTIFYING YOUR PURPOSE AND AUDIENCE

In most writing situations, you know the subject you are to write about, such as poverty in Canada or workplace injuries. You may also know the form your writing should take: an essay on poverty, a report on injuries. You may be less aware of the specific kinds of writing possible within these forms and the strategies for using them effectively. This book will introduce you to a broad range of forms and strategies.

Every piece of writing, whatever its subject and form, is shaped by its purpose and audience. The first question to ask yourself is about your purpose: What do I want this piece of writing to do? The second is about your audience: Who will read it?

1a Defining Your Purpose

In this book, we will focus on three broad purposes for writing: to explain, to persuade, and to share ideas and experiences. The first purpose leads to **expository writing,** the second to **persuasive writing,** and the third to **personal writing.** Your understanding of your purpose and audience will influence your choice of form and methods of development, your relationship to your readers, and your choice of language and style.

Writing to Explain

Your writing is expository whenever your main purpose is to provide information, to explain how something works or how something is done, or to explain the meaning of concepts, historical events, works of art, and so on. As these examples suggest, in expository writing your emphasis is on your subject, rather than on your audience or on you as a writer. You and your readers are like observers peering through a microscope and trying to see the same thing on the glass slide.

3

Writing to Persuade

The central question of all persuasive writing is, *What is good?*—good for one person, a group, a nation, humanity, or the planet. Your purpose is to convince others of your vision of what is good. You may want to persuade your readers to share your attitudes and beliefs, or to act on those beliefs. To accomplish your goal, you have to consider how to appeal to your audience. In the interplay among writer, subject, and audience, the emphasis in persuasive writing shifts toward the audience.

Writing to Share Personal Experience

Personal writing gives you the chance to discover what you think and how you feel about ideas and experiences, and to share these discoveries with others. However, your subject is not always something that happened to you—you may also write about your reactions to the world around you. Nor does personal writing always have to be the serious business of revealing your innermost thoughts and feelings. You, the writer, are on centre stage, and you may therefore choose to present yourself as comic or tragic, satiric or romantic, serious or slightly mad.

Examples

To illustrate differences in these types of writing, we will consider three paragraphs on the same subject: shoplifting. The first comes from an expository essay on what causes people to shoplift.

Sample Expository Writing
Purpose: To Explain Behaviour

The most basic question about shoplifting is this: Why do people steal? According to a security guard for Sears, the reason is not need: "In all the time I've worked here, and of all the arrests I've made, and I've made over 400 arrests, not once, not once was it out of need." Most shoplifters who are caught have more than enough money with them to pay for the item and many have credit cards as well. So why do they steal? According to Bill Cheung at The Bay, the peak seasons for shoplifting are September and January–February, when new school terms begin. Presumably, at

4

the beginning of the term, students look at the clothes or toys their peers have and want them. Children and adolescents, it seems, shoplift to fit in.

—Amanda Thompson

This paragraph illustrates the principal features of much expository writing. The writer explains why some people shoplift without stating her opinion about the behaviour. She presents her information and analysis as objectively as possible, referring to shoplifters as *people* and *students,* for example, not as *thieves* and *juvenile delinquents.* In this way, she keeps the focus on her subject, not on her opinions about the subject or on her own personality.

Sample Persuasive Writing
Purpose: To Change Opinion or Behaviour

Contrary to the popular view, most shoplifters do not steal because they are poor. A longtime security guard for Sears, who has arrested more than 400 shoplifters, points out that "not once" had the person stolen out of need. Shoplifters usually have more than enough money with them to pay for the stolen goods, and they often have credit cards as well. They may tell themselves that the stores are so rich they will not miss this little eraser/tube of lipstick/makeup case/radio/stereo/jacket. But it is not the stores that pay; honest customers pay through higher prices. There is thus no reason to be lenient with shoplifters. They are as guilty of theft as the person who steals a wallet from a locker room or a CD player from a car, and should be treated accordingly. If we turn a blind eye to shoplifting, we are not only condoning a crime, but also sentencing ourselves to pay the penalty.

Here the writer's purpose is not to explain some possible reasons for shoplifting, but to persuade readers to change their attitude, and possibly their behaviour, toward shoplifters. In contrast to the neutral language of the expository paragraph, the writer uses emotionally charged words and phrases (*honest, guilty, lenient, condoning, sentencing*). This language focuses attention on the attitude that the writer wants readers to adopt.

Sample Personal Writing
Purpose: To Share Personal Experience

I was thirteen at the time, in a new school, and desperate to make friends. For the first few weeks, everyone ignored me. Not that all my classmates were friends with each other. At lunch hour and after school they divided into groups and alternately ignored and insulted each other. I was afraid that if I didn't make friends soon, they would stop ignoring and start insulting me. So one day, I followed a gang of five or six into the mall at lunch. As they straggled through The Bay, I kept several feet behind, stopping every now and then to gaze intently at leather briefcases or umbrellas so they wouldn't think I was being pushy. When they clustered around the jewellery counter, I ducked down the next row. And there in front of me were bags and bags of candy, ready for Hallowe'en. Without thinking, I grabbed one and stuffed it under my jacket.

This writer invites us to share the isolation, fear, and desire to belong that led to shoplifting a bag of candy. The story carries us along and makes us part of the events. Even though we may disapprove of the theft, we are drawn into the writer's subjective experience.

The first question to ask yourself about any writing situation, then, is *What is my purpose?* In some writing situations, you may be free to choose your own purpose. If you wanted to write an article on grizzly bears for a general interest magazine, for instance, you could choose to explain the grizzly's habits, to argue for better protection for this endangered species, or to share your own adventures in grizzly country.

In many school and work situations, however, your purpose will be given or implied. An assignment that asks you to write a persuasive essay on capital punishment defines your purpose. A manager who asks you to write a report on the branch office assumes that you will explain the problems, not air your frustrations in trying to compile the data.

1b Defining Your Audience

Defining your purpose is the first step in writing; the second is defining your audience. Just as your style of speaking changes as you move from the poolroom to the classroom, so your style of writing changes with your audience. Are you writing for readers who already know a great deal about your subject, or for those who know nothing at all? For educated adults, or for elementary schoolchildren? Considering the needs of your audience will help you decide, for instance, how much background information to give and whether to use a formal or an informal style.

Making Reader Profiles

You can develop a clearer sense of your audience by asking yourself these questions.

1. **Who** will read this piece? A specific person, such as a supervisor? A group of people with similar interests, such as *Star Trek* fans? A group of people of varying ages and backgrounds, such as newspaper readers?

2. What **attitude** will my reader(s) probably bring to this piece of writing? Interest and enthusiasm? Hostility and defensiveness? Critical detachment?

3. How much **knowledge** will my reader(s) already have about my subject? What information do I need to provide?

4. What **expectations** will my reader(s) have about the way this piece is written? Is there a specific format I should follow?

Answering these questions will give you a **reader profile:** a general sense of your audience's needs and expectations. Keeping this reader profile in mind as you write or revise will help you communicate more effectively. If you give some thought to what a potential employer looks for in a letter of application, for example, you can tailor your application to match those expectations.

You will find suggestions on how to adjust your writing style for different audiences in Choosing Appropriate Language (4f).

Exercise 1.1

Choose two of the following subjects. Using the example of writing articles on grizzly bears as a guide (see p. 6), show how each subject could be the basis for three pieces of writing with different purposes: one expository, one persuasive, and one personal.

Example: Subject—Bicycles

Expository: to explain how to choose a bike
Persuasive: to persuade cyclists to obey traffic regulations
Personal: to share my experience cycling from Jasper to Banff

- budgeting
- extreme sports
- bodybuilding

- access to postsecondary education
- needs of people with disabilities
- *The Lord of the Rings*
  (the book or the movies)

Exercise 1.2

Choose one piece of writing from your response to Exercise 1.1 and make a reader profile for one of the audiences below.

- a magazine for elementary schoolchildren

- a newspaper

- an e-zine devoted to that subject

- a television newscast

- an instructor

- an employer

Exercise 1.3

Using the same piece of writing you chose for Exercise 1.2, make a reader profile for a different audience from the list above.

Exercise 1.4

Briefly explain the major similarities and differences in the way you would write the piece for the two audiences you have chosen, based on your reader profiles.

CHAPTER 2

GATHERING MATERIAL

Good writing, whether it's a job application letter or a term paper, begins with strong content focused around a central point. The following techniques will help you generate ideas, collect information, and find a focus.

Brainstorming

2a Brainstorming

Brainstorming allows you to capture your spontaneous responses to your subject. Put a key word from your writing task in the centre of a blank page. Allow yourself to free-associate—what ideas, examples, questions, memories, or feelings spring to mind? Surround your key word with notes, without rejecting anything. If you were preparing a report on the need for life skills courses in high school, for instance, you might end up with a brainstorming diagram something like this:

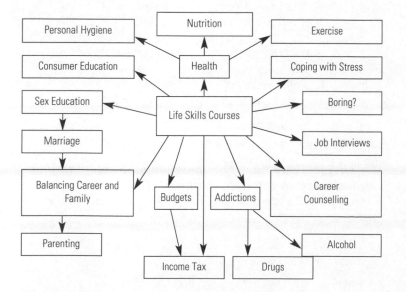

9

With so many ideas to consider, you can find a fresh angle on your subject or choose material of special interest to your readers. Brainstorming guarantees that you won't run out of things to say.

2b Freewriting

Many people discount their most creative ideas, intuitions, and memories before they start. To get around this internal censor, try **freewriting.** Write continuously about your subject for five or ten minutes, without stopping to correct or criticize. If you run out of things to say, write something like "I can't think of anything to say" and keep writing. Do not hesitate over words, make corrections, or stop to think. After ten minutes, look over what you've written and sum it up in a sentence. If your summary suggests new ideas, freewrite for another ten minutes.

2c Asking Discovery Questions

There are three ways to use this technique.

1. ***Start with the journalist's five Ws and an H: Who, What, When, Where, Why, and How.***

   Answering these questions will give you information that your reader is likely to need in any situation. If you were writing a problem-solving report on theft from gym locker rooms, for instance, you might ask questions like these: Who reported the thefts? Who investigated? What was stolen? When? Where—men's or women's locker room or both? How did the thieves gain access to the articles? What changes would reduce the incidence of theft?

   If you are writing on an unfamiliar topic, you may need to do research to answer even these basic questions.

2. ***Ask questions based on methods of developing your ideas (see chapters 5, 6, and 7).*** For an essay on drug addiction, for instance, you might ask questions such as these:

   • How is addiction defined?

   • What are the stages of addiction?

   • What are the causes? the effects?

- Can I classify drug addicts?

- How does drug addiction compare with other kinds of addiction?

- Is there a story I could tell about drug addiction?

- How could I describe the behaviour typical of addicts?

- How do social factors contribute to drug addiction?

- What are the strengths and weaknesses of current drug treatment programs?

- What analogy would help to explain the difficulties in overcoming drug addiction?

- What examples would support my points?

3. *Ask questions specific to the appropriate academic discipline or area of inquiry* (for examples, see the questions for analyzing imaginative literature, pp. 131–132, and the questions for evaluating an argument, pp. 156–157).

2d Keeping a Journal

Keeping a **journal** can be an excellent way of gathering ideas and information for a long-term writing project. Use your journal entries to reflect on issues, respond to your reading, collect relevant newspaper or magazine items, note questions to pursue, and record your progress. When the time comes to write your essay, you will have lots of material and original insights.

2e Finding a Focus

You have defined your purpose and audience. You have gathered ideas and information about your subject. Now you have so many ideas and so much information that you don't know what to include and what to leave out. You need a **focus.**

To define a focus for your writing, link your purpose and audience with one or more aspects of your subject. For a short piece, you may choose to discuss one aspect in detail. For a longer piece, you may include several. Suppose, for example, that your subject is car auctions and that your purpose is to explain some aspect of this subject to newspaper readers. For a short piece, you could focus on how cars are sold at auctions.

11

For a longer piece, you might also explain why people buy or sell cars there.

Writing your focus at the top of your paper when you begin your draft will remind you of the aspects of your subject you need to cover.

Exercise 2.1

Make a brainstorming diagram for one of the following subjects.

- current trends in music
- public figures you admire (or dislike)
- traffic fatalities
- use of natural resources
- genetic engineering
- your favourite/least favourite type of movie

Exercise 2.2

Choose a different subject from the list above and generate material for an essay by freewriting or by asking discovery questions.

Exercise 2.3

Using the material you have generated in Exercise 2.1 or 2.2, show how you could focus your material for five different purposes and audiences.

Example: Subject—Life skills courses
(see brainstorming diagram, p. 9)

Purpose: to persuade teachers that preparing for job interviews by role-playing should be a part of every life skills course.

CHAPTER 3

Drafting, Outlining, and Revising

Strategies for drafting and revising vary from form to form. For a brief letter, you may simply type out your request, proofread for mistakes, and seal it in the envelope. A letter of application, a report, or an essay will require a more careful consideration of content, organization, and style.

Strategies also vary among writers. Some writers discover their main point in the process of writing a draft, and then make substantial changes in content and organization. Others plan what they want to say, either in their minds or in an outline, to ensure their first draft has a main point and a clear pattern of organization. Revision for these writers may consist of smoothing out sentences and improving word choice. Many writers fall in between these extremes.

We will discuss various methods of using fast-drafting and outlining so that you can choose the method that best suits you and your writing task.

3a Fast-Drafting

If you decide to write a fast draft to help clarify your thinking, set a fixed period—usually an hour or two. Using the material you have gathered through brainstorming (2a), freewriting (2b), or asking discovery questions (2c), write a complete draft. Don't let yourself get bogged down. If you have trouble with the introduction, for example, either leave some space and come back to it later, or write your statement of focus and go on from there.

When you reread, you may find that your main point has surfaced near the end and that you need to restructure. Making an outline of your draft will help you decide how to reorganize your material.

3b Making an Outline

An outline shows you at a glance the main divisions of your paper and the relationships among major points, minor points, and details. Making an outline thus helps you to classify your material and detect gaps in it.

There are several points in the process of drafting and revising at which you might find an outline useful. Some writers like to make a **draft outline** before they write. For this kind of preliminary outline, use your statement of focus as a guide to your main points. Under each main point, jot down the details you will need to include.

Other writers use a **revision outline** to clarify the organization of their ideas. After writing a draft, they make an outline showing the main point and supporting details in each paragraph. The outline will reveal problems in content and organization: paragraphs that need to be combined or divided, points that need further explanation, and topic sentences that could be improved, for example. You may find a revision outline useful for evaluating the structure and completeness of your piece.

You can also make a **formal outline** of your final version to accompany a lengthy report or research paper. Put your thesis— the main point of your piece—at the top of the page. List your major points with Roman numerals, your subpoints with capital letters, and details with Arabic numerals. The format of your outline should resemble the one below.

Sample Formal Outline

Thesis Because shoplifting has become so widespread, methods of identifying and apprehending shoplifters have changed.

    I. Extent of the problem
       A. Type of goods stolen
         1. From novelty stores
         2. From department stores
       B. Amount stolen annually

    II. Types of shoplifters
       A. Professionals
       B. Amateurs

    III. Reasons for shoplifting
       A. Need
       B. Desire to fit in
       C. Thrills

    IV. Methods of detection
       A. Following suspects
       B. Using one-way mirrors and closed-circuit television

As you can see, each level of the outline (Roman numerals, capital letters, Arabic numerals) represents a division of the level above. For this reason, you should have at least two items at each level (if you have an A, you must have a B; if you have a 1, you must have a 2). Each item at a particular level must be an equivalent subdivision of the level above. For example, *Need, Desire to fit in,* and *Thrills* are equivalent items under *Reasons for shoplifting.* This equivalence will be more obvious if you make items at each level grammatically parallel (see Faulty Parallelism, 18e).

3c Revising and Proofreading

Revision is one of the most important parts of the composing process, and often the most time-consuming. So give yourself plenty of time. When you have written a draft, evaluate the content and organization according to the appropriate checklist(s): for paragraphs, p. 18; for essays, p. 92; for business writing, p. 192. Make any necessary revisions.

Then read your work aloud to get a sense of how it sounds to another reader. If some sections seem wordy, monotonous, or stilted, consult the relevant sections of chapter 4.

Next, proofread carefully for typos and errors in grammar and punctuation. For more information on these aspects of writing, see the checklist for Proofreading (p. 224) and the relevant sections of part 5.

Finally, make sure that you have presented your work in the appropriate format. You will find examples in appendix A, Format Conventions; appendix B, Documentation: MLA System; and appendix C, Documentation: APA System.

Exercise 3.1

Using your material from Exercise 2.1 or 2.2, fast-draft an essay. Then write a paragraph on the process. How well did fast-drafting work for you? Were you able to continue writing or did you get stuck? Did you begin with a thesis statement or did a main point emerge as you wrote? Did you come up with new ideas or examples?

Exercise 3.2

Using material from Exercise 2.3, make a draft outline. Put your statement of focus at the top of the page as a guide to your main points. Under each main point, jot down the details you will need to include. Then write a paragraph on the process. How well did making a draft outline work for you? Could you more easily see how to organize your material? Did the outline reveal areas where you needed more ideas or information? Or did the process seem mechanical and boring?

Exercise 3.3

Make a formal outline of either the Sample Literary Research Paper (14f) or the Sample Non-Literary Research Paper (14g).

Web Links

- Directory of Academic Internet Resources—listings of best Internet sites for each subject.

  www.academicinfo.net

- York University Pre-writing Strategies Online Tutorial—an excellent resource that provides techniques and strategies for writing essays.

  www.yorku.ca/tutorial/prewriting

- Writers on the Net—classes, tutoring, mentoring, and writers' groups. Free newsletter.

  www.writers.com

- Canadian-Based Publications Online—articles and abstracts from newspapers, magazines, and trade journals.

  www-2.cs.cmu.edu/Unofficial/Canadiana/ CA-zines.html

- Drew University Writing Program Web Resources—good material on peer critiques as well as links to search engines, writing centres, and other resources.

  www.users.drew.edu/~sjamieso/Webresources.html

PART 2

DEVELOPING YOUR
WRITING STRATEGIES

CHECKLIST | *Paragraphs*

	OK	NEEDS WORK
1. Is your purpose clear?	☐	☐
2. Have you chosen an appropriate method of development?	☐	☐
3. Does the topic sentence state the main point?	☐	☐
4. Are the details adequate?	☐	☐
5. Are the details relevant?	☐	☐
6. Is the paragraph a readable length (not too long or too short)?	☐	☐
7. Have you used effective transitions?	☐	☐
8. Have you chosen language appropriate to your purpose and audience?	☐	☐
9. Is your writing varied, concise, and stylistically interesting?	☐	☐

CHAPTER 4

WRITING BETTER PARAGRAPHS

Paragraphs are the building blocks of writing. Introductory paragraphs lay the foundation; concluding paragraphs provide the capstone, or finishing touch. In between are the middle paragraphs, each one discussing one aspect of your subject (one point in an analysis, one step in a process, one event in a narrative). Each middle paragraph is thus both a self-contained piece of writing and a part of a larger structure.

In this chapter we focus on general strategies for writing paragraphs. You will find detailed guidelines for developing paragraphs for particular purposes in the following chapters: chapter 5, Methods of Sharing Personal Experience; chapter 6, Methods of Explaining; and chapter 7, Methods of Persuading.

4a Topic Sentences

The purpose of a topic sentence is to make the main point of your paragraph obvious to your reader. You will therefore need to figure out exactly what idea you want to develop in each paragraph and state that idea in a sentence. This topic sentence then controls the content of your paragraph, helping you decide which details to include and which details you can leave out.

Here is an example of what can go wrong if you write a paragraph without figuring out a topic sentence:

> Some people regard physical fitness as a means to physical health and well-being. They believe that vigorous exercise strengthens the heart and lengthens life. Unfortunately, these exercise enthusiasts tend to monopolize all the equipment in a fitness centre. Other people exercise to make themselves more physically attractive. They want to reshape their bodies to fit the model that society presently holds as representative of physical perfection. I see both young and middle-aged women struggling to create a body that is genetically impossible for them. Still others are more interested in exercise clothes than in exercise itself. They wear the latest fashions in running shoes, jogging suits, and headbands, but they would never work out for fear that sweat might ruin such expensive gear.

19

The writer's main point seems to be that people have various reasons for wanting to be part of the fitness scene, but the paragraph drifts into comments on the use of exercise equipment and unrealistic goals for physical appearance. Beginning the paragraph with a good topic sentence would help the writer to stay on track, as in this revised version:

> For various reasons, people want to be, or want to appear to be, part of the fitness scene. Some people regard physical fitness as a means to physical health and well-being. They believe that vigorous exercise strengthens the heart and lengthens life. Other people exercise to make themselves more physically attractive. They want to reshape their bodies to fit the model that society presently holds as representative of physical perfection. Still others are more interested in exercise clothes than in exercise itself. They are attracted to the latest fashions in running shoes, jogging suits, and headbands, but they would never work out for fear that sweat might ruin such expensive gear.

As you can see, knowing the main idea you want to develop will help you to determine which details are relevant to your paragraph.

In actual writing situations, however, you may need to begin with the details you have collected and then figure out what point you can make with them. Suppose, for example, that you were writing an essay on how the misuse of antibiotics is endangering people's lives. One paragraph of this essay could focus on the dangers of not finishing a prescription. Your notes for such a paragraph might look like this:

- "Superbugs" are bacteria that don't respond to antibiotics.

- These bacteria remain alive after a person has taken antibiotics for just two of the seven days of a prescription.

- Antibiotic-resistant bacteria survive because they have evolved through the process that Charles Darwin described as "survival of the fittest."

- These bacteria have mutated and are now strong enough to resist antibiotics and to make you sicker.

- You can now infect other people with these antibiotic-resistant bacteria.

- Diseases that have become more difficult to treat include staph infections, strep infections, and tuberculosis.

By reading through this list of details, you can see that they develop one point: by not finishing a prescription for antibiotics, people are endangering both their own lives and the lives of everyone around them. A paragraph stating that point in the topic sentence and using the details above to develop it could look like this:

The common practice of not finishing a prescription for antibiotics is endangering people's lives. It's true that after you've taken antibiotics for 48 hours, most of the bacteria are dead and you are probably feeling a lot better. The problem is that some bacteria are still alive; moreover, they are alive because they have mutated into antibiotic-resistant "superbugs." These stronger bacteria will make you sicker than you were before you started your prescription; unfortunately, you may not be able to find any antibiotic that will make you better. Even if you recover, you may now be a disease carrier—not actively sick yourself but capable of infecting others with serious illness. Staph infections, strep infections, and tuberculosis are among the diseases you could easily pass on to others because you have not taken all of your prescribed medication.

Exercise 4.1

Read through the following list of details. Figure out what main point you could make about these details and state that idea as clearly as you can in a topic sentence. Underline your topic sentence. Then write the body of the paragraph, including only the details that fit with the point you make in the topic sentence.

- You can choose from lots of different kinds of housing, such as single-family dwellings and multiple-family dwellings (duplexes, townhouses).

- Consider the proximity to work, schools, and shopping.

- The number of bathrooms, bedrooms, and size of yard may also be important.

- Small children and pets, especially cats, may find moving traumatic because they dislike a change in surroundings.

- Having a new house built is more expensive than buying an existing home.

- Owning a home is an opportunity to express creativity in home decorating.

- You may find that there is a discouraging gap between what you want in a home and what you can afford.

Exercise 4.2

Read the following paragraph. In it, the writer attempts to pin down an aspect of his father's influence on his life. See if you can figure out the writer's main point. State that point as clearly as you can in a topic sentence. Then rewrite the paragraph, eliminating any irrelevant details.

> I must have gone out with Father many times: to the movies, to the pub (where I sat on the bench outside drinking pop), to football and hockey games. Always I had a sense of extreme pleasure and pride. Our dog Whiskers would sometimes tag along, and I enjoyed throwing sticks for him to retrieve. My father and I also had lots of personal fun and games. He would toss a football and I would pretend that I was the heroic receiver speeding away from fierce Argonaut defencemen. Or I would stand between two horse chestnut trees in the Crown Inn Gardens pretending that I was the Canadien goalie waiting for Father's speeding puck, exulting in every spectacular save, every reckless plunge between flashing blades. "Great save, Lorenzo!" my father would shout. These trees have now been cut down to enlarge the parking lot. My fun was intensified by my father's own leaps of mind. He was never flamboyant in any of this; instead, he maintained a simple, involved plausibility.

4b   The Body of the Paragraph

As we have seen, topic sentences make a point that you can then develop through more specific points and details. If your paragraph lacks specific details, you will have trouble explaining your ideas and convincing your readers that the ideas are valid. Consider the following example.

> **Cyclists who ignore the rules of the road are a danger to themselves and others.** Most motorists hate and fear cyclists. When I see how cyclists ride anywhere they want on the road, I wonder what they are protecting inside their helmets.

This paragraph consists of three generalizations that make the same point, rather than one topic sentence with general statements and specific details to support it. Think of the topic sentence as a major point in an outline (see Making an Outline, 3b). To develop a major point, you move down to a subpoint and the specific details that support it.

The topic sentence about cyclists, for example, suggests two subpoints to be explained further. Which rules of the road do cyclists ignore? How do they endanger themselves and others by ignoring these rules? You would develop the body of the paragraph by explaining these subpoints and providing examples and other specific details to illustrate each one.

If you have trouble developing your ideas, you may need to clarify your purpose: Is your aim to explain something? to persuade your readers to change their opinion or behaviour? to share your experiences or perceptions? You can then choose an appropriate method (or methods) of development discussed in the next three chapters. The guidelines in these chapters will help you improve the content of your paragraphs.

Whichever method(s) of development you choose, you will probably need to provide examples to illustrate your main points. For suggestions on using examples more effectively, see Giving Reasons and Examples (7a).

Exercise 4.3

List several subpoints and examples you could use to develop each of the following topic sentences.

1. Fast food chains could help to combat rising levels of obesity.

2. My home town has changed for the better (for the worse) since I was a child.

3. Rates for car insurance should be based on driving performance, not age.

4c Paragraph Structure

There are two basic ways of organizing information in a paragraph. You can begin with your topic sentence and then fill in the reasons, examples, and other details that provide evidence to support it, or you can begin with these details and examples and gradually lead your reader to the main point you want to make about them. The first method places immediate emphasis on your main point, whereas the second emphasizes the process of thinking and feeling that led you to it. You can see the difference between these two basic ways of organizing information in the following examples.

23

Sample Paragraph: Topic-Sentence–First Arrangement

Working nights in a convenience store introduced me to a side of my neighbourhood I hadn't known before. One surprise was the discovery of neighbours who emerged from their homes only after midnight, but the night lives of people I had met before were also surprising. I discovered that old Mr. Moses, with whom I had exchanged perhaps twenty sentences in the past ten years, was a talkative insomniac, addicted to corned beef sandwiches at 3 a.m. He had been an intelligence agent with an amazing career, which he unfolded in successive nightly instalments. And then there was Mrs. Anderson. I had always imagined her to be one half of a happily married older couple, but twice in the first month I worked at the store, Mrs. Anderson met a man (who was definitely not her husband) and disappeared into the night. I was beginning to see new meaning in the term "convenience store."

Sample Paragraph: Details-First Arrangement

Before I started working in one, a convenience store was just a place to go when you ran out of milk late at night. I hadn't realized that I had many nocturnal neighbours who emerged from their homes only after midnight. More surprising, however, were the night lives of people I knew. Old Mr. Moses, with whom I had exchanged perhaps twenty sentences in the past ten years, turned out to be a talkative insomniac, addicted to corned beef sandwiches at 3 a.m. In nightly instalments, he unfolded his amazing career as an intelligence agent. And then there was Mrs. Anderson. I had always thought of her as one half of a happily married older couple, but twice in the first month I worked at the store she met a man (who was definitely not her husband) and disappeared into the night. Working nights in a convenience store introduced me to a side of my neighbourhood I hadn't known before.

Note: Do not end a paragraph with the topic sentence for the next paragraph. While your intention may be to provide a transition, you will only confuse your readers.

Exercise 4.4

Write a paragraph on any subject that interests you. Begin with your topic sentence. Then rewrite the paragraph, putting the details first and ending with your topic sentence. Underline your topic sentences in each paragraph.

4d Paragraph Divisions

By dividing your material into paragraphs, you signal that all the information in a particular paragraph relates to one aspect of your subject. In this way, you help your reader to understand how you have organized your material. Paragraph divisions that seem random—because paragraphs run on for pages or consist of only a sentence or two—will confuse your reader.

Readers find excessively long paragraphs difficult to understand and uninviting to read. Normally, you should be able to discuss one aspect of your subject adequately in about half a page. If you need more room to develop your ideas, subdivide your paragraph. Instead of trying to discuss several effects of taking a summer school course in one paragraph, for example, focus each paragraph on one effect, such as the effect on your relationship with your family.

You may occasionally use a one-sentence paragraph to signal a transition or to emphasize a point. But a series of short paragraphs can confuse readers; they lose the sense of how the paragraphs relate to each other and to the piece of writing as a whole. If several short paragraphs discuss only one aspect of your subject, you can simply combine them. More often, however, paragraphs are short because they do not provide enough reasons, details, and examples to explain one aspect of your subject. You will find many methods of developing paragraphs discussed in chapters 5, 6, and 7.

4e Transitions

As you move from sentence to sentence and paragraph to paragraph, you constantly present your readers with a mixture of known information (terms and ideas you have already introduced) and new information. You can emphasize the continuity between known and new information by these stylistic devices.

1. *Use transitional words and phrases.*

The transitions in the list below can help your readers to understand how you have organized your material, making it easier for them to move from one point to the next in your writing. (The terms listed before each semicolon are less formal; those listed after the semicolon are more formal.)

NARRATION   first, next, then, last, as soon as, early the following morning, later that day; in the beginning, in the end

DESCRIPTION	nearer, farther, on the right, on the left, at the top, at the bottom, to the east, beside, between, above; adjacent to
CLASSIFICATION	one group, another kind, a third type; one subcategory, moreover, furthermore
EXAMPLE	for example, for instance; to illustrate, a case in point
PROCESS ANALYSIS	first step, second step, next stage, final stage
SYSTEMS ANALYSIS	one component, another part, the most important element
CAUSAL ANALYSIS	one reason, a final reason, the most important effect, although, because, despite, however; therefore, nevertheless, consequently, as a result, thus, if/then, provided that
DEFINITION	one meaning, another meaning, the most relevant meaning; primary meaning, secondary meaning
COMPARISON	and/also, but/too; in comparison, in contrast, similarly; just as/so too, not only/but also, neither/nor
EVALUATION	a practical advantage, a logical inconsistency, another legal aspect, from a moral perspective, an aesthetic weakness

If you compare the following paragraphs, you will see how transitions can dramatically increase the clarity of your ideas and the flow of your writing.

Sample Draft Paragraph without Transitions

I had been working as a carpenter for five years. I injured my back. I needed to find a different sort of job. I had always been interested in starting my own business. I decided to take business courses at a community college. I was uneasy about taking college courses. My writing skills needed work. I got a D on my first essay. I was discouraged and considered dropping the course. My instructor asked me to speak with her. She explained how I could improve my essay and gave me a chance to revise it. I decided to stay in the course and pursue my dream of a new life.

Sample Revised Paragraph with Transitions

After working as a carpenter for five years, I injured my back. **As a result of this injury,** I needed a different kind of job. I had always wanted to start my own business, **so** I decided to take some business courses at a community college. I was, **however,** uneasy about taking college courses. English, **for example,** scared me **because** I knew my writing skills were weak. **When** I got a D on my first essay, I was discouraged and considered dropping the course. **Then** my instructor asked me to come in and speak with her. **During this interview,** she explained how I could improve my essay and gave me a chance to revise it. **Because of this encouragement,** I decided to stay in the course and pursue my dream of a new life.

2. *Repeat key words or phrases.*
Repeating a key word lets your readers know you are still talking about the same subject. If you introduce synonyms, readers may think you are offering new information. For example, in this short paragraph, the many synonyms for *bear* and *hunting partner* distract attention from the main subject, the father.

> Dad was fearless. Once when he and a hunting partner were tracking deer in the foothills, they surprised a wounded bear in a thicket. When the maimed animal knocked his friend down, Dad struck the brute with an empty rifle, distracting the angry monster long enough for his companion to get up and shoot the beast.

The paragraph reads much more smoothly when fewer terms are introduced:

> Dad was fearless. Once when he and a hunting partner were tracking deer in the foothills, they surprised a wounded bear in a thicket. When the bear knocked George down, Dad struck it with an empty rifle, distracting it long enough for George to get up and shoot it.

3. *Use personal pronouns to refer to subjects you have previously named.*
Pronouns (*he, she, it, they*), like repeated terms, signal known information; in the example above, the pronoun *it* refers to the bear.

27

4. ***Put the idea you plan to discuss next at the end of the sentence.***

Link sentences by repeating the last word(s) of one sentence at the beginning of the next or by using a synonym and a demonstrative pronoun (*this, that, these, those*).

> British suffragettes challenged the existing system first through marches on Parliament, then through civil disobedience. When civil disobedience failed, they turned to property damage.

> British suffragettes challenged the existing system first through marches on Parliament, then through civil disobedience. When these measures failed, they turned to property damage.

5. ***Use sentence structure to indicate logical relationships.***

To show that two or more sentences contain equivalent points (as when you are giving a list of reasons, examples, or actions), use **parallel sentence structure** (see Faulty Parallelism, 18e).

FIRST SENTENCE	Slander may involve . . .
SECOND SENTENCE	It can also be . . .
THIRD SENTENCE	It is quite often . . .

When you move from a general point to a specific detail, or vice versa, signal the shift by changing your sentence structure.

GENERAL POINT	To be blunt, slander is an ugly, malicious lie about someone. [The sentence begins with an introductory modifier.]
SPECIFIC EXAMPLE	It may involve . . . [The sentence begins with a subject and verb—change in sentence structure.]

If you compare the following paragraphs, you will see how these devices achieve continuity and dramatically increase the flow of your writing. The material is from a personal essay on the writer's experiences with judo.

Sample Draft Paragraph

Bullies always have their little rituals. They go through a talking phase with a new kid who might be tough. If they aren't sure, they leave subtle threats and go away. After this little talk they hammer an opponent who reveals a weakness. They try to make friends with the "mark" who appears too formidable. I was skinny and scared, and so bullies always beat me up.

Sample Revised Paragraph

When bullies encounter a "mark" who might be tough, they go through little rituals. First they talk to him. If this talk reveals a weakness in their opponent, they hammer him. If they still aren't sure, they leave subtle threats and go away. If he appears too formidable, they make friendship gestures. But when the new kid is skinny and scared, like me, there is no ritual. It's all fists.

—Dan Martin

Exercise 4.5

Write a paragraph describing one of the items below. Be sure to use transitional devices that allow your reader to visualize spatial relationships among the things you describe.

- a room where you live or work
- a painting
- the view from your window
- a favourite place

Exercise 4.6

Improve the following paragraph by adding transitions and revising sentences to show how the events are related in time.

> For fifteen years Boots, our barn cat, and Alice, our spaniel, lived together outside, inseparable friends. Alice died. Boots was inconsolable. We moved Boots inside the house. We rarely saw her. She slept all day and sneaked to her food dish at night. My husband was making his lunch. He accidentally dropped a piece of cheese. Boots was nearby. Boots dove in and devoured it. The next morning my husband had the cheese in his hand. Boots started talking cat language. The morning ritual continued. Boots was trained to wait for her cheese until my husband was sipping his morning coffee. She followed him everywhere, including the bathroom. Boots began to make friends with the rest of the family. She is over her depression.
>
> *—Adapted from an essay by Darcy Colwell*

Exercise 4.7

Improve the following analysis paragraph by adding transitions and revising sentences to show cause-and-effect relationships among ideas.

> There are a number of reasons for the rise in customer complaints against our department store. We have not been living up to our promises. We have a sale. Usually several items advertised in our flyers remain on back order. Often the selection of available items is

29

very poor. Customers complain that the store is poorly laid out. Aisles are blocked by overflowing display tables and unpacked boxes. Trying to get from one department to another becomes an exercise in frustration. Finding particular merchandise is difficult. Customers have to wrestle with clothes jammed onto racks or struggle with linens stuffed into shelves. The store is chronically understaffed. Service is slow and at times nonexistent. Customers are annoyed at having to wait too long for assistance and at standing in crowded lines at sales counters. We must solve these problems as quickly as possible.

You will find reminders about using transitional words and phrases with specific methods of development in chapters 5, 6, and 7.

4f Choosing Appropriate Language

4f

Choosing Appropriate Language

Some writers use informal language in writing that requires more formal diction. Others adopt a formal vocabulary so completely that their writing becomes stilted. Still others coast along, using words that are safe but dull. Paying attention to the words you use will help you remedy these problems.

Understanding **levels of language** will help you choose words appropriate for your purpose and audience. Consider these words meaning *poor:*

Formal	Standard	Informal
impecunious, destitute, poverty-stricken, poor, hard up, broke, busted		

These words illustrate what we mean by levels of language, with "big words" such as *impecunious* and *destitute* at the formal end of the scale; colloquial and slang terms such as *hard up* and *busted* at the informal end; and the standard vocabulary of public writing and speaking in the middle (*poverty-stricken, poor*). Most of the words you use in writing for college or university should come from a standard vocabulary. For more suggestions on formal and informal writing, see below.

Formal Writing

When you are writing academic essays, keep these suggestions about word choice in mind. (Similar guidelines apply to business writing. See Business Style, 15a.)

1. *Aim for a serious, knowledgeable, and businesslike tone, but avoid sounding stuffy or pompous.*

In general, choose standard words rather than more formal terms (*need* rather than *necessity, uses* rather than *utilizes*). Emphasize key points by selecting words from the slightly formal range (*poverty-stricken* or *destitute,* but not *impecunious*).

2. *Use specialized terms only when necessary.*

Part of what you learn when you study psychology, sociology, and other academic disciplines is the language that specialists in the field use in talking and writing to other specialists. In an essay discussing Freud's theory of the unconscious, for example, you would use Freud's terms *id, ego,* and *superego.* There are no other words that would precisely convey the meaning of these concepts.

But when a specialized vocabulary is used inappropriately, it is called *jargon.* Jargon obscures meaning rather than making meaning more precise. When jargon combines with an unnecessarily formal vocabulary, writing can become almost unintelligible, as in the examples below.

NOT   As the precepts of individual psychology are ultimately reflected in social psychology, the psychic impairment experienced by the student as part of the educational process will be augmented within the context of the social environment.

BUT   Since students carry their perceptions of themselves into the larger social world, any damage to their self-esteem will become more severe when they leave school.

NOT   Management will access the input of all interested parties, prioritize their responses, and introduce modifications to the terms of the proposal accordingly.

BUT   The manager will ask all interested parties for their reactions to the proposal, review their responses, and make changes accordingly.

3. *Avoid slang and colloquial expressions.*

many rather than *a lot of*
an acquaintance rather than *a guy I know*

4. *Avoid clichés.*

Clichés serve a useful purpose in spoken language, but in formal writing they may suggest that the writer is treating the subject superficially, as in this example:

> Undoubtedly, there is pressure for change from within the country. The number may be small but every little bit helps.

5. *Use contractions sparingly.*

Some readers object to contractions in formal writing; others don't. If you use an occasional contraction to keep from sounding too stiff, make sure you use the apostrophe correctly (see Apostrophes, 22h).

6. *Use* I *and* you *sparingly.*

Don't distract your readers from your subject by constant references to yourself: *I think, I feel, I believe, it seems to me that.* When it is appropriate to use *I,* use it rather than substituting *one* or *this writer.*

NOT	It seems to me that this anthology is unsuitable for the high school curriculum.
NOT	In the opinion of this writer, this anthology is unsuitable for the high school curriculum.
BUT	This anthology is unsuitable for the high school curriculum.
OR	Although other reviewers consider this anthology suitable for the high school curriculum, I disagree.

Similarly, avoid using *you* in formal writing to mean *people in general.*

NOT	The university's marking system can be frustrating when all of your professors have their own scale within the scale.
BUT	The university's marking system can be frustrating when professors have their own scale within the scale.

Exercise 4.8

Comment briefly on the effect of jargon and big words in the following paragraph, taken from a research paper on the back-to-basics movement in education. Then rewrite the paragraph in simpler, more concrete language.

> The teacher I interviewed perceived her role as a socializing agent with a humanistic approach. She added that although students lacked skills to handle grade five curriculum, her priority was to allow student-directed activities in a safe environment free of negative labelling. Correcting exams and clerical tasks presented a strain on her role. She felt psychology was the most beneficial course she had taken at university: she taught many children experiencing stress from broken families or families who did not share time.

Exercise 4.9

Underline inappropriate word choices in the following paragraph, adapted from a research paper on impaired driving. Then rewrite the paragraph so that the diction is more appropriate for the subject and audience.

> Kathy Stechert's research on drunk driving (1984) has suggested some prevention techniques that you should consider when entertaining guests in your home: serve lots of food; provide non-alcoholic beverages; don't pressure guests to drink, water down drinks when guys are consuming too much alcohol. Don't let guests leave the house if they're tanked; ask them to wait until they've sobered up or to stay overnight. If they make a fuss and insist on leaving, drive them home. It is really amazing that many people don't think about what could happen after guests leave the party. It doesn't take a genius to see that these measures would help reduce drunk driving.

Informal Writing

For personal and persuasive writing intended for a general audience, follow these guidelines:

1. ***Try for the friendly, engaged tone of one person talking to another.***
That means choosing most of your words from the standard to slightly informal range (*poor, hard up*). Choose short, common words over longer synonyms.

possess = own, have	automobile = car
retain = keep	residence = house
purchase = buy	difficulties = troubles

2. *Use more formal words to create suggestive images, humour or satire, and subtle shades of meaning.*

the undulations of the wheat
the writer was lionized in London, lampooned in L.A.
serpentine streets

3. *Choose concrete nouns over abstract nouns and specific nouns over general nouns.*

Abstract nouns name qualities (*friendship, heroism*) or concepts (*the state, conservatism*). **Concrete nouns** name things we can perceive through our senses (*your friend, the brain*). **General nouns** apply to a class of things (*adolescents, buildings*) rather than to a single, specific thing (*the teenager who works at The Bay, the CN Tower*). Abstract and general nouns keep your reader at a distance.

4. *Use first- and second-person pronouns (**I, you**), where appropriate, to establish a personal relationship with your reader.*

5. *Use occasional contractions, colloquial expressions, or slang terms, if appropriate to your subject and audience.*

6. *Choose* **active verbs** *over* **state-of-being verbs** *and* **verbs in the passive voice.**
By changing **state-of-being**, or **linking**, verbs (*is, seems, exists, has, contains, feels*) to active verbs, you can often make a vague general statement into a precise, vivid image.

NOT	She *has* short brown hair. Her face *is* round.
BUT	Her short brown hair *cups* her round face.
NOT	I *felt* angry.
BUT	I *throbbed* with anger.
OR	I *stalked* out of the room.

Verbs in the **passive voice** may take the energy out of your writing:

NOT	The winning goal was scored by me.
BUT	I scored the winning goal.

To see how changing the diction can improve a piece of writing, compare the following versions of a paragraph on the perils of sailing. In the first, the formal language makes the danger seem remote.

Sample Draft Paragraph

Of course there are those who endure the elements as necessitated to earn a living. Traditionally they are the men of the sea. Sailors maintain many fears in terms of the elements. For instance, atmospheric electricity playing around the mast might cause a fire. To the sailor's peril, ice can cover the rigging, leaving the ship top-heavy and in danger of "turtling." Thrashing waves and Titanic swells can consume both craft and crew.

In the revised paragraph, the simpler language, active verbs, and concrete nouns create a vivid image of a ship in danger.

Sample Revised Paragraph

Sailors have traditionally earned their living by enduring the dangers of the elements. Sailors fear the blue haze of St. Elmo's fire encircling the mast, and its acrid smell of burning. They fear the surge that rises twelve metres above the mizzen and the waves that slam the hull from every direction. The wind, as it sings through the stays, charts a new course without aid of a compass, without earthly reason. But at no time is a sailor's job so perilous as when the wind chill plunges the mercury to minus thirty-five and droplets of mist condense on the supercooled rigging. Then layer upon layer of ice forms. When an ice-laden ship gets top-heavy, no amount of praying will keep it afloat. The captain's call goes out: "The gyros are toppling."

—*Chris Paterson*

Exercise 4.10

Underline word choices in the following paragraph that you find ineffective for a personal essay. Then rewrite the paragraph using more vivid language.

> Chuck is, simply put, a mean person. One would not say that he is a sadist, exactly. He is not of the character to pull the wings off flies, albeit he does on occasion step on ant hills. He merely loves practical jokes—mean-spirited practical jokes. One time a small, plastic-wrapped packet of cloves was left by Chuck on the desk of a fellow student named Ramona. Attached to the packet with tape was a note

that read, "Cloves make an effective breath freshener." Ramona was, with justification, mortified and offended. On other occasions, sample bottles of deodorant and acne medication have been left on classmates' desks. One could say that these tactics work to undermine a person's self-confidence. Chuck also has an inconsiderate mouth. In the recent past, on the day we were being photographed for the yearbook, Jerry Johnson wore a new suit. Hiding behind his most sincere smile, Chuck told Jerry, "Jer, my man, that suit really suits you, ha, ha. I donated one just like it to the Sally Ann last week." I used to laugh at Chuck's peccadilloes, until this morning. As we were walking out of math class, the teacher directly behind us, that insensitive Chuck enunciated clearly, "Ken, I wish you would not say those things about Mr. Mueller. I think he is a fine teacher." I am planning how to asphyxiate Chuck in his sleep. The deed will definitely be done with malice aforethought.

Commonly Misused Words

Choosing words from the appropriate range of formal and informal expressions is one way to ensure that your writing serves your purpose and meets the expectations of your audience. Another way is to check for words and expressions that many writers confuse or misuse. Here is a partial list. You will find others in Exercise 4.12 below. For problems with *its/it's, their/there/they're,* and *your/you're,* see Possessive Pronouns (21c).

A Lot

A lot is an informal expression meaning *many, much,* or *a great deal of.* Avoid *a lot* in most writing. When you use it, spell it as two words.

I have **a lot** of work to do this weekend.

All Right

All right should be spelled as two words. *Alright* is incorrect and should not be used.

"**All right**," the coach agreed reluctantly, "you can miss the practice Thursday afternoon."

Allude/Elude

Use *allude* when you mean *refer to,* as in an allusion to the Bible or to Shakespeare.

In his opening comments, the guest speaker **alluded** to Hamlet's indecision.

Use *elude* when you mean to *avoid* or *escape*.

The wary old wolf managed to **elude** the hunter.

Among/Between

Use *between* when you are referring to two things.

Divide the candy **between** the twins.

Use *among* when you are referring to more than two.

Share the food **among** all the refugees at the shelter.

Amount/Number

Use *amount* to refer to things considered as a mass (*a large amount of work, a small amount of money*). Use *number* to refer to things that can be counted (*a large number of people, a small number of desks*).

A large **amount** of money is missing.
A large **number** of bills were stolen.

Bored with

Use *bored with* (never *bored of*) to mean *wearied with dullness*.

She is **bored with** her courses this year.

Hanged/Hung

Use *hanged* as the past tense of the verb *to hang* when you are referring to a person.

The convict **was hanged** at dawn.

Use *hung* when you are referring to objects.

Her latest painting **was hung** in the city gallery.

Hopefully

Hopefully is an adverb meaning *full of hope*. It is used correctly in this sentence: *The sales representative knocked **hopefully** at the door.*

Do not use *hopefully* to mean *I hope* or *perhaps*.

| NOT | Hopefully, we'll be able to meet next week. |
| BUT | Perhaps [or I hope] we'll be able to meet next week. |

Lead/Led

The past tense of the verb *to lead* is *led*.

Yesterday he **led** the band in the Earth Day parade.

Less/Fewer

Use *less* with mass nouns (*less unemployment, less hunger*) and *fewer* with countable nouns (*fewer courses, fewer assignments*).

I'm having **fewer problems** this year.
I'm having **less difficulty** this year.

Lie/Lay

The principal parts of the verb *to lie* (to recline) are *lie, lay, lying,* and *lain.*
The principal parts of the verb *to lay* (to place) are *lay, laid, laying,* and *laid.*
Be careful not to confuse these verbs.

NOT	She **lays** on the chesterfield all afternoon.
BUT	She **lies** on the chesterfield all afternoon.
NOT	He **laid** in the sun for half an hour.
BUT	He **lay** in the sun for half an hour.

Like/As

Use *like* as a preposition. Use *as* to introduce a clause.

She was witty and informal, **like** any good master of ceremonies.

She was witty and informal, **as** any good master of ceremonies should be.

Loose/Lose

Loose is usually an adjective or adverb (*loose change, loose clothing, let loose*).

38

Occasionally *loose* is used as a verb meaning *to set free* (*He loosed the dog on the intruder*). Don't confuse *loose* with *lose* (to misplace).

He often **loses** his way when he is in a strange city.

I can only give you a **loose** translation of that phrase.

Take Part in/Partake of

To take part in something is *to join* or *to participate. To partake of* is *to have a share of something* (usually a meal).

Hamlet refused to **take part in** the wedding festivities.

Would you be willing to **partake of** our simple meal?

Exercise 4.11

Here are ten sets of commonly confused words. For each word, give a brief definition and then use the word in a sentence that clearly distinguishes its meaning from the word(s) with which it is often confused. Use the entry for *take part in/partake of* (above) as a guide.

- affect/effect
- allusion/illusion
- cite/sight/site
- defer/differ
- disinterested/uninterested
- elusive/illusory
- flaunt/flout
- principal/principle
- than/then
- thereby/therefore

Exercise 4.12

Correct all the usage errors in the following sentences. Some sentences have more than one error.

1. Archaeologists have uncovered what they believe is the principle residence of Colonel John Butler in Niagara-on-the-Lake. Butler lead his Loyalist Rangers in numerous raids into New York State during the American War of Independence.

2. Although you have put on a few kilos, you still weigh considerably less then your father.

3. During a chinook some people suffer from headaches or depression; others are not effected at all.

4. Louis Riel was hung at Regina on November 16, 1885.

5. "Help, I'm loosing my balance!" yelled Jack.
   "Are you alright?" Jill called after him as he tumbled down the hill.

6. Rip is laying under the maple tree, apparently disinterested in everything around him.

7. By the middle of the movie, a lot of the patrons were bored of the trite plot and one-dimensional characters. In fact, a considerable amount of people had already left the theatre.

8. Like I said before, I usually trust my own judgment, but this time I'll differ to your greater experience.

9. Mother divided the candy equally between all the children.

10. Hopefully, we will be able to catch David Copperfield's special on television. He is a master of allusion.

4g Improving Your Style

Style is the result of all the conscious and unconscious choices you make as you write, including choices about the words you use, the kinds of sentences you construct, the length and structure of your paragraphs. So you already have a style—in fact, you likely have many styles you shift among as you write for different purposes and audiences.

But perhaps you would like your writing to flow more smoothly, to be more concise, or to have more flair. If so, you will find numerous suggestions below.

Improving Your Sentence Structure

Keep your sentence structure consistent with your purpose and audience. To create a conversational tone in personal essays and other informal types of writing, use occasional sentence fragments (see Fragments, 18d) and avoid sentence patterns that require formal punctuation such as semicolons and colons. For more formal writing, avoid using sentence fragments and informal punctuation such as dashes and exclamation marks.

Reading your work out loud, to yourself or to a classmate, will help you determine whether your writing "flows." If in places the rhythm of your sentences seems jerky, monotonous, or at odds with the effect you want to create, try varying your sentence patterns or sentence length.

Varying Sentence Patterns

Most of your sentences are likely to follow the first pattern below: subject + verb + modifier. But if all your sentences fall into this pattern, your writing is likely to become monotonous. You can use the other five sentence patterns to create emphasis, to mimic the process of thinking, or to engage your readers more directly.

The Loose Sentence: Subject + Verb + Modifier

> The team never won, no matter how hard the players tried.

This sentence illustrates the most common sentence pattern in English, and the one most easily understood by readers: subject + verb + modifier. Since the most emphatic position in the sentence is normally at the end, this sentence would lead naturally into a discussion of how hard the players tried.

The Periodic Sentence: Modifier + Subject + Verb

> No matter how hard the players tried, the team never won.

Because we have to wait for the subject and verb, this sentence pattern creates interest and suspense. It also throws heavy emphasis upon the team's inability to win, and thus would prepare readers for a discussion of the reasons for its lack of success or for examples of its failures.

The Embedded Sentence: Subject + Modifier + Verb

> The team, no matter how hard the players tried, never won.

Here, subject and verb are separated by a lengthy modifier. Because this sentence pattern slows the reader down, it effectively imitates the process of thinking through a problem or situation. The modifier also shifts the emphasis to the beginning of

41

the sentence. As readers, we might therefore expect to explore less obvious aspects of the team that would account for its lack of success.

Sentences Employing Parallelism

There are two ways to use parallelism in sentences.

- Join two or more closely related clauses with a coordinating conjunction or semicolon. (This pattern is also called a **balanced construction.**)

You can allow your anxieties to rob you of sleep and satisfaction, or you can plan your time wisely and then enjoy your free time thoroughly.

—Wendy Amy

- Arrange a series of words, phrases, or clauses in order of increasing importance.

Friends listen to you babble, tell you honest opinions when you prefer lies but need the truth, tell you *I told you so* at annoying times, defend your reputation from others, and generally mother, father, grandparent, and sibling (brother or sister) you.

—Amanda Thompson

Rhetorical Questions

How many times have you waited in the rain or snow for a bus that is ten minutes late? How many times has a surly bus driver snapped an answer to your innocent question? How many times have you stood for half an hour in a bus crammed with people?

—Cheryl Lewis

Uncommon Constructions

- Use paired conjunctions (*both/and, neither/nor, not only/ but also*) to link ideas.

Neither fear of failure nor desire for glory drove her to practise that trumpet hour after hour.

- Use a noun clause as the subject.

That he would win the election was certain.

Varying Sentence Length

To create rhythm and emphasize important points, use a combination of short sentences (ten words or fewer), long sentences (thirty words or more), and medium-length sentences.

Short sentences are effective for rendering abrupt actions, giving directions, stating main points, and creating emphasis.

ABRUPT ACTIONS	She stopped.
DIRECTIONS	First, stop the bleeding.
MAIN POINTS	One cause of high unemployment is government policy. [Essay topic sentence]
	Safety violations have increased 10 percent over last year. [Report topic sentence]
EMPHASIS	He loved no one.
	The war was over.

Long sentences are effective for expressing continuous action, giving a series of details or examples, and creating a sense of closure.

CONTINUOUS ACTION	After discovering Jack's country address, Algernon assumes his friend's secret identity and poses as wicked Ernest Worthing for his meeting with Cecily, Jack's sheltered young ward; but when they meet for the first time, the worldly, cynical Algernon is momentarily confounded by the sophisticated wit of "little" Cecily.
DETAILS	According to the criteria for student loans, students are considered to be financially independent only if they have no parent, guardian, or sponsor; are married or a single parent; have been out of secondary school for four years; or have been in the labour force for twenty-four months.
CLOSURE	In the final analysis, the losers are not merely those who have been jailed for insider trading, nor the firms whose reputations have been sullied, nor the stock-

holders who have lost money; the losers are all those who have lost confidence in the integrity of the stock market.

Exercise 4.13

The following paragraph sounds choppy because it is written almost entirely in short, simple sentences. Rewrite the paragraph to improve the rhythm, using several of the techniques discussed above.

4g

*Improving
Your
Style*

> Being your own boss has its down side. I learned the hard way. One summer I decided to go into business for myself. I was tired of my usual part-time jobs. I was tired of the long hours and low pay at the fast-food restaurants and laundries I'd worked at in the past. I decided to strike out on my own. I started up the Domestic Bliss Home and Pet Care Service. It was a house-sitting service for clients away on vacation. I contracted to water plants, take in mail and newspapers, and feed pets. This last responsibility soon proved the most challenging. One of my charges was Baby. Baby was lonely. She was affectionate. She was untrained. She was a twenty-five kilogram Golden Retriever who leapt into my arms with joy every time I stepped into her house. Another of my charges was the Queen of Sheba. She was an overstuffed Persian cat with surgical steel claws capable of slicing through even the thickest denim. Another of my charges was Jabberwocky, the parrot, who had apparently committed to memory *A Complete Dictionary of the Vulgar Tongue*. I spent a month cleaning up accidents and cleaning up litter boxes. I longed to be back in uniform behind a counter serving up chicken and fries. I completed the contracts with my current customers. I said farewell to all my furry and feathered friends. I closed the door on Domestic Bliss.

Being Concise

In good writing, every word counts. Pruning the deadwood—words, phrases, and sentences that are not essential to your purpose—clarifies your meaning and makes your writing easier to read.

To make sure that every word counts, many writers set a goal of cutting their writing by 10 percent. If you tend to be wordy, you may want to set your goal higher. Here are four practical suggestions:

1. *Eliminate unnecessary repetition of words and ideas.*

Often whole sentences merely repeat a previous point.

REPETITIOUS PHRASE	Formerly, women's clothes were much more restrictive in the past.
REVISED	Women's clothes were much more restrictive in the past.
REPETITIOUS SENTENCES	Macbeth seems shaken by the witches' announcement that he will become king. He is uneasy when they tell him he is destined to gain the throne.
REVISED	Macbeth seems shaken by the witches' announcement that he will become king.

2. *Reduce phrases, clauses, and sentences.*

Reduce phrases to single words (*in a short time = shortly; a lot of = many* or *much; at this point in time = now*).

Reduce clauses beginning with *that, which,* or *who* to words or phrases.

NOT	the person who owns the store
BUT	the store owner
NOT	at the position that I was assigned
BUT	at my position
NOT	*School Violence,* which is another study of this problem
BUT	*School Violence,* another study of this problem
NOT	The magazine is designed for women who are from 25 to 50 years of age.
BUT	The magazine is designed for women aged 25 to 50.

3. *Rewrite wordy constructions.*

NOT	It is a fact that the car has been stolen.
BUT	The car has been stolen.
NOT	What this means is that profits are down.
BUT	This means that profits are down.

4. *Eliminate unnecessary modifiers.*

WORDY   The small, sporty-looking red car just left
                              us in the dust.

BETTER   The red sportscar left us in the dust.

To see how being concise can make your meaning clearer, consider these two versions of a paragraph from an essay on the importance of options in the school curriculum.

Sample Draft Paragraph

There are a lot of other courses that are very important to children growing up today. Courses such as home economics, industrial education, accounting, and computer courses help children function better in the outside world—whether in the job market or in the home. These courses enable the children to be able to learn about a wide variety of things. Students today learn about health and nutrition, they learn about first aid, how to look after a home (boys as well as girls), they learn how to look after a vehicle, and even how to budget themselves and to do their own taxes. [103 words]

Sample Revised Paragraph

Many other courses are also important to today's adolescents. Courses such as home economics, industrial education, accounting, and computer science help them function better in the home as well as in the job market. These courses enable students to learn about health and nutrition, first aid, and home maintenance. Students also learn how to look after a vehicle, how to budget, and how to do their own taxes. [68 words]

Exercise 4.14

Underline unnecessary words, phrases, and sentences. Then rewrite the paragraph in 200 words or fewer. Do not leave out any ideas.

At the base of the argument for an education based on facts lies a dangerous assumption: that a person with a good grasp of general knowledge has the will and the means to examine information critically to determine whether it is true and valid. Realistically, most people who get through school by memorizing information lack either the ability to think critically or the desire to think critically. A simple science fair project conducted by a junior high school student exposes people's failure to think critically and make reasoned judgments. At the Greater Idaho Falls Science Fair in April 1997, the student presented a presentation about the dangers of dihydrogen monoxide. The student asked people to sign a petition to have the chemical banned because of its harmful effects. The harmful effects included the statements that "accidental inhalation can cause death" and that dihydrogen monoxide "is a major component of acid rain." Of fifty people asked, forty-three supported elimination of the chemical, six people were undecided, and one person recognized that dihydrogen monoxide is the chemical term for H_2O. That is, dihydrogen monoxide is water. Clearly, these people did not analyze the situation effectively. The mental habits that enable people to make sound judgments are not inherent. Educators cannot expect that an individual will use his mind to reason, analyze, and make sound judgments simply because that person has a solid base of facts and knowledge. [235 words]

Adding Interest

Enliven your writing by using quotations and other kinds of allusions, dialogue, and figurative language.

Quotations

Use familiar quotations—proverbs, lines from songs, advertising slogans, sayings of famous people, well-known bits of poetry and prose—to make an emotional appeal and to create a sense of shared experience. You don't need to give complete bibliographical information for quotations used in passing, but do put them in quotation marks and identify the source.

> When you are backpacking through Europe, your money will start to dwindle and you will feel moments of fear and desperation. As *The Hitchhiker's Guide to the Galaxy* so wisely advises, "Don't panic."
>
> —*Lori Yanish*

Allusions

An allusion is a casual reference to a figure, event, or document from history, literature, mythology, popular culture, or religion. Allusions help to establish your authority as a writer by indicating the breadth of your knowledge or experience. They may also have a strong emotional impact because they evoke shared experiences.

> Like Caesar, he came, he saw, he restored order where confusion reigned. —*Chris Carleton*

Her hopes, like Miss Havisham's wedding cake, had been eaten away.
—*Chris Carleton*

I suspected life at Stephanie's house might be just like life at Dick and Jane's. —*Suzanne Cook*

Dialogue

Use dialogue for dramatic effect. Direct speech allows you to show what happened rather than merely to tell the story. It also gives variety to your writing by introducing other voices.

My parents were glued to a small black and white television in room #107. I wandered into the room and tugged on my mother's skirt until she lifted me into her lap. "Look, it's Neil Armstrong," she said as she directed my gaze at the small screen. "He's about to walk on the moon."

—*Mario Trono*

Figurative Language

Figures of speech create vivid mental images for your readers. Use them to sharpen your descriptions and to convey your attitude toward your subject. Try your hand at the five types illustrated below: simile, metaphor, personification, hyperbole, and irony. Avoid clichés (*dead as a doornail*) and mixed metaphors (*flooded with an iron resolve*).

A clock, hanging like a sign of doom over my head, showed the lateness of the hour [simile]. —*Terri Dana*

We are nothing but a jar full of flour beetles, continually eating and reproducing [metaphor]. —*Cheryl Lewis*

The unruly maple holds fast to her golden gown [personification]. —*Lillian Darling*

Those demonic savages, those cruel, sadistic, verminous beings, those bus drivers, have persisted in their heinous acts [hyperbole]. —*Amanda Thompson*

Mr. Simpson would pretend to drive into Miss Merril's little BMW just to terrify her in a neighbourly way [irony]. —*Alex Cheung*

Exercise 4.15

Rewrite a paragraph from one of your personal essays so that it includes two or more of the devices discussed in this section.

Exercise 4.16

Using the specific suggestions in Improving Your Style as a guide, evaluate the stylistic strengths and weaknesses of the following paragraph.

> As I returned home from interviewing my new client, I could not stop thinking about Jane. She had done nothing unusual during the interview. In fact, if I had not read her chart she would have appeared like the babysitter next door, except smarter. I felt that, for my own peace of mind and the safety of society, Jane should be wearing a tattoo on her forehead that said "psychopath." Inside I felt entirely unclean. The only emotion that came through clearly was fear. She was not someone who made me feel afraid for my personal safety, but she made me feel afraid for the world. She challenged the way I had categorized the world up until then. Jane was a woman with no mental illness, no deficits of intelligence or social skills, and apparently no conscience. She tortured and killed toddlers. She terrified me.

Exercise 4.17

Evaluate the stylistic strengths and weaknesses of two paragraphs of your own writing: one from an academic essay and one from a less formal piece. Then revise the paragraphs.

CHAPTER 5

METHODS OF SHARING PERSONAL EXPERIENCE

As newspapers, magazines, and television networks have discovered, readers and viewers have a seemingly insatiable interest in others' personal lives. You too can enliven your writing by adding personal touches from your own or someone else's experience. In this chapter you will learn how to tell stories that illustrate your point; how to describe people, places, and things so that they come alive; and how to use analogies that convey your feelings and attitudes.

5a

Telling a Story

5a Telling a Story

Telling stories is one of the main ways we make sense of our lives for ourselves and share our world with others. Funny stories, heroic stories, romantic stories—they all have something to say about who we are. The stories we keep hidden—stories about our fears, our failures, our struggles—are often the ones that, when told, connect us to others. To see how you can develop these stories into personal essays, see chapter 10.

Short personal narratives are often used to enliven other kinds of writing. An article criticizing cuts to health care, for instance, may begin with a story about a patient who died while awaiting surgery. It is these personal narratives we will focus on in this section. You will find examples of narration combined with analysis in the samples that illustrate causal analysis (6d), plot summaries (12c), and expository essays (11b).

Here are some suggestions for writing personal narratives.

• *Choose a single meaningful event with a definite beginning and end.*

The event may be part of a larger story that you could write about in a personal essay. For instance, you might write a narrative paragraph about one adventure with a friend that could later form part of a longer essay exploring your relationship with this friend more fully.

- **Decide what point you want to make about this event.**

Did your adventure, for example, teach you something about taking risks or about taking precautions? about trust or about self-reliance? You could state this point explicitly in a topic sentence, or you could allow it to emerge implicitly from the way you tell the story.

- **Decide how to organize your paragraph.**

To heighten suspense, you can give events in chronological order, with your point emerging at the end. Or, if you want to emphasize your reflections on the incident, you could begin with your point and then tell the story.

- **Use transitions to help your reader follow the sequence of events.**

Show how events are related in time by using terms such as *first, next, then, last; in the beginning, in the end; soon, later, as soon as, meanwhile;* and by referring to specific times, days, months, seasons, and dates.

- **Select details that will create in readers a response similar to your own.**

Recording small details is one way to individualize your stories. In writing about a familiar situation such as attending a circus, for example, you might make the experience fresh for your readers by comparing the fake tears of a clown with the real tears of a child who drops an ice-cream cone.

- **Choose words that make the experience vivid for your reader and convey your attitude toward the event.**

For more on word choice, see Choosing Appropriate Language (4f).

- **Include your thoughts, feelings, and judgments about the event.**

Direct statements about thoughts, feelings, and judgments help readers understand the significance of details. For example, you might begin or end a series of seemingly random and contradictory ideas with the statement *I was confused.*

Sample Personal Narrative

This narrative paragraph creates suspense through its precise details, expressions of feeling, and chronological arrangement of events. The image in the last two sentences implicitly makes the writer's point about overcoming fear. These two sentences therefore serve as the topic sentence for the paragraph. A paragraph such as this would make a good introduction to a personal essay.

Others have ascended the incredibly high platform, seemingly thousands of feet above the pool. More than one has returned by the wet ladder, a sensible choice in my mind. Why then is my foot on the first rung? It is colder and slicker than would appear. My feet leave the safe ground and propel me towards the high roof of the pool. Partway up I consider turning back. Yes. But another below has decided to follow, and I must reach the top before turning around. Halfway up, I guess, but I dare not look down lest my arms and legs freeze in terror. I keep my eyes focused on the ladder, only inches from my nose. The last step comes into view. With dangerously stiff muscles and complete lack of grace or courage, I plant my feet on the concrete slab. I see my wet footprints and decide to look at nothing else. With the slap of feet an older boy makes his entrance onto this platform in the sky. He passes, grinning at me, and in one quick fluid motion he disappears over the edge. I hear nothing, nothing, then a faint splash. Something deep inside me snaps and I follow suit. Crazy. Stupid. Stop! I'm in the air, hand clasped tight over my nose as I shut my eyes. Dear God, I'm drowning. I must be at the bottom of the pool. Frantically kicking, I break the surface. It's hard to wipe this maniac smile off my face. Perhaps once more.

—Ken Miller

Exercise 5.1

Identify a quality you particularly like or dislike in yourself or someone else. Then write a narrative paragraph about an incident that reveals this quality.

Example: a roommate's stinginess—refusing to share nachos and pizza while we watched the Grey Cup.

Exercise 5.2

Choose a significant experience in your life (such as a birth, death, marriage, divorce, move, accident, achievement, or failure). Use brainstorming to help you recall the small but meaningful incidents you associate with the experience (such as riding in an ambulance). Choose one of these incidents with a definite beginning and end, and write a narrative paragraph that shows its significance.

Example: Experience—changing schools in the middle of grade four. Event—failing a math test on my first day. Significance—always feeling an outsider at school.

5b Describing a Person, Place, or Thing

When you describe people, places, or things, you attempt to translate into words how they look, sound, feel, smell, move, or taste. The language you use to describe something will depend upon your purpose and audience. A geographer writing a scientific article about the Canadian Shield would describe Northern Ontario differently than would a real estate agent selling holiday properties. Someone writing a personal essay about growing up in the bush would offer a third perspective on the same landscape, one coloured by the intensity and selectivity of childhood memory.

In personal writing, you want your reader to share experiences—such as your father's delight in reading bedtime stories, your fear as you walk down a deserted street at night, your love-hate relationship with an unreliable car. As these examples suggest, descriptions are like snapshots of significant moments in which you capture your attitude toward a person, place, or thing. You convey your attitude by selecting details that work together to create a dominant impression of your subject. If you wanted to show your father's delight in bedtime reading, for example, you would ignore the note of exasperation that crept into his voice if you interrupted too often, and instead describe his excitement as he "became" different characters in *Peter Pan*.

Vivid descriptions of people, places, and things are central to most personal essays, as you can see from the sample essays in chapter 10. Descriptive paragraphs also make good introductions for expository and persuasive essays. For example, you might begin a persuasive essay on the importance of parental involvement in children's learning to read with a paragraph describing your father reading. A descriptive paragraph like this adds human interest to discussions of general issues. For an example, see the sample expository essay on child poverty (11b).

Follow these guidelines for writing descriptive paragraphs:

- *Choose a subject that you are very familiar with or that you can observe while you write.*

It is surprisingly hard to remember the kinds of detail that will bring your paragraph to life—the colour of a friend's eyes, the sound of wind through trees, the smell of a school room. If you choose to describe something from memory, try closing your eyes and putting yourself into the scene before you write about it.

- **Decide what dominant impression you want to convey about your subject.**

A good description is not merely a catalogue of features: "My cat is a Siamese with the usual blue eyes and dark grey ears." It creates a *dominant impression* by giving details that convey a particular quality of your subject: a kitten's playfulness, an aunt's stubbornness, the peacefulness of a landscape.

- **Focus your paragraph.**

To help you *describe* rather than give examples, focus on the details of your subject at a particular time or performing a particular action. For instance, you could vividly *describe* a kitten's playfulness—how it looks, moves, sounds—by focusing on how it acts in front of the mirror. Without this focal point, you might give many examples of a kitten's playful behaviour without describing any of them in enough detail to be interesting.

- **Select details that contribute to the dominant impression you want to convey.**

Include a broad range of sensory details—not just how something looks, but also how it sounds, feels, tastes, smells, moves.

- **Arrange the details in a spatial order with the most important detail last.**

Choose an arrangement that reflects how you as an observer would perceive your subject: in a panoramic sweep from left to right; from close up to farther away, or vice versa; or from the most obvious feature to the least obvious.

- **Show how objects are related in space.**

Use transitional words such as *nearer, farther; on the right, on the left; at the top, at the bottom; to the east, to the west.*

- **Begin or end with a point about the person, place, or thing you are describing.**

"My cat is very playful" is a descriptive generalization, but it is not an interesting point about the kitten's behaviour. You could make a more interesting point about the transitory nature of youth and playfulness. You could state this point explicitly in a topic sentence: "Watching my kitten play, I remember how I used to make faces at myself in the mirror, not realizing that the scowls of childhood would settle into the lines of middle age." Or you could let it emerge implicitly through your description: "Each day the kitten tires of the game more quickly, and soon we will both pass the mirror without a glance."

In the following paragraph from a personal essay, the writer tells us almost nothing about the physical appearance of a teacher who "shocked me so much that I experienced a marked change in my attitude towards school and the subject of English." Instead, he chooses details that show how Mr. Wellington's surroundings reflect his vulnerability, and then makes this point in a topic sentence at the end.

Sample Personal Description

Mr. Wellington was neither neat nor tidy. The chaos of his room seemed to echo the sound of someone saying, "Hang on, it's in here somewhere. I just put it down yesterday. I'll find it." The walls were covered from top to bottom with posters, but not a single one was hung straight. His desk was inhabited by masses of paper that had somehow gathered there as if attracted by a "paper magnet." Surrounding his desk was a whole herd of dictionaries, including a condensed version of the *Oxford English Dictionary*, which required a magnifying glass to peer into the depths of its compiled wisdom. Mr. Wellington would frequently consult these books in efforts to stop the arguments waged against him about the meanings of words in the poems we analyzed in class. Throughout all this activity, his coffee cup was never to be seen detached from his hand. I cannot blame him for needing a cup of coffee to carry him through to the next period. It was his coffee cup that made him look human, vulnerable—not like the other teachers, who were not human but "teachers." Perhaps it was his vulnerability that inspired confidence, even though he was surrounded by what looked like ineptitude.

—*Steve Marsh*

Exercise 5.3

Make a list of the sensations you experience as you eat something, such as an ice-cream cone or a slice of pizza. Use all of your senses. Arrange your list so that a point emerges from your description.

Describing a Person, Place, or Thing

Exercise 5.4

Write a descriptive paragraph about one of the following:

• a person who has had an impact on your life

• a place where you feel safe (or unsafe)

• an object to which you have a strong attachment

Exercise 5.5

Sit for half an hour in a public place—on a bus, in a mall, in church, at a hockey rink—and make notes about what you see, hear, and smell. Then write a descriptive paragraph about the place as a whole, one or more people in it, or a particular object. Be sure to select details that convey a dominant impression and make a point about your subject.

5c Using Analogies

Attitudes and emotions are difficult to describe without falling into clichés and generalities. Analogies allow you to translate inner experiences into vivid images that your readers can share. Consider, for example, the different attitudes suggested by these metaphors:

> Life is an exhilarating ride on a roller-coaster.

> Life is "a tale told by an idiot, full of sound and fury, signifying nothing" (*Macbeth*).

Each of these metaphors could be developed into an analogy by exploring the similarities it suggests. These analogies would tell us much more about the writer (or character) than would statements such as "Life is great" or "Life sucks."

To write an effective analogy, follow these steps:

• ***Make a list of metaphors or similes comparing your subject with a variety of things that are different in appearance, form, or kind but similar in behaviour.***

Overcoming an addiction is like

—salvaging a wrecked ship

—weaning a baby

—saying goodbye to an old friend

- **Choose the metaphor or simile that best fits the attitude or experience you want to convey.**

  x—salvaging a wrecked ship [does not acknowledge the pleasurable aspects of the addiction]

  x—weaning a baby [suggests we "grow out of" addictions]

  ✓—saying goodbye to an old friend

- **Develop your metaphor or simile into a paragraph by exploring the similarities it suggests.**

What is it like to say goodbye to an old friend? There's the memory of good times and bad, the desire to hold on and the need to let go. This analogy, by emphasizing the positive aspects, may help readers who do not share the addiction to understand why it is hard to give up.

In the following example, the writer helps readers understand the debilitating effects of an unfamiliar health problem by comparing it to a more familiar condition.

Sample Analogy

Think back to the most persistent flu or cold you have ever had. Remember that day when the virus was at its worst, you know, around day two, three, or four. You wished you could remove your head from your body, and you were too exhausted to remove it even if you could have, and it was all you could do to get up and drink some juice and maybe take a cold tablet before you collapsed back into bed. Add to it: sides so tender and sore that when someone touches you, you yelp in pain; kidney infections so extreme you are doubled over as you walk and cannot right yourself. Add food allergies to most of the foods you used to eat with no problem, including a complete intolerance for sugar. Add chemical sensitivities so extreme that walking past a running vehicle, passing through a smoky room, or standing near an acquaintance wearing hairspray or perfume can result in muscle convulsions or an unexpected mood swing, severe headaches or more fatigue. Add seizures or blackouts. These are some of the physical symptoms experienced by the more than 250,000 people in Canada who suffer from Myalgic Encephalomyelitis, otherwise known as Chronic Fatigue Syndrome.

—Patti Skocdopole

Exercise 5.6

Complete each of the following similes.

1. Looking for a job is like _____ .

2. Finding your way around an unfamiliar
   city is like _____ .

3. Visiting the dentist is like _____ .

4. Going on a blind date is like _____ .

Exercise 5.7

Make a list of the similarities suggested by two of the similes in Exercise 5.6.

Exercise 5.8

Choose one of the similes in Exercise 5.7 above and write a paragraph developing that analogy.

Review Exercise 5.9

Write a paragraph about a hard-to-communicate experience or feeling, using at least two of the methods discussed in this chapter: narration, description, and analogy. For example, you might convey the intensity of your feelings about your first car by both describing the car and developing an analogy with Aladdin's magic carpet.

CHAPTER 6

METHODS OF EXPLAINING

When your purpose is to explain, your focus is on your subject and what your readers need to know to understand your subject. In this chapter we will discuss four ways of explaining: **classifying,** which groups your material into manageable chunks; **comparing,** which highlights similarities and differences; **defining terms and concepts,** which lets your reader know what you are talking about; and **analyzing,** which shows how parts of your subject relate to the whole.

This chapter will give you practice in using these methods to explain a subject within a single paragraph. Paragraphs of explanation often occur within pieces of writing whose primary purpose is to persuade or to share personal experience. If you were writing a personal essay about a custom unfamiliar to many Canadian readers, for example, you might devote one or more paragraphs to explaining its history or its function within your culture. To see how to extend these methods into longer pieces of writing, see chapters 11 and 12.

6a Classifying

When you classify, you organize facts and ideas into categories and subcategories. That means you start with a general category, such as *customers*, and divide the category into specific types or kinds. You might, for instance, divide *customers* into these types: *the impatient, the rude, the apologetic, the businesslike, the indecisive*. These subcategories allow you to explain the general characteristics shared by many individual people. You can also classify abstract concepts. For example, you could divide the category *effects of unemployment* into subcategories such as *economic effects, social effects*, and *psychological effects*.

If you were writing an essay, you could make classification your principle of organization and devote a paragraph or more to each of your subcategories as shown in the following diagram.

Classification can also provide a systematic method of organizing material as you move from generalizations to specific

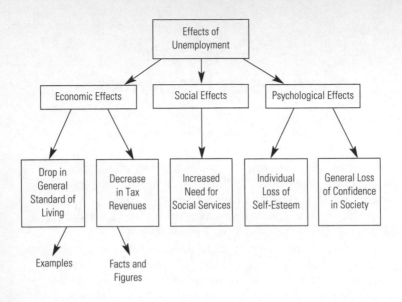

Effects of Unemployment → Economic Effects, Social Effects, Psychological Effects

Economic Effects → Drop in General Standard of Living, Decrease in Tax Revenues

Social Effects → Increased Need for Social Services

Psychological Effects → Individual Loss of Self-Esteem, General Loss of Confidence in Society

Drop in General Standard of Living → Examples

Decrease in Tax Revenues → Facts and Figures

6a

Classifying

details in individual paragraphs. If your classification is easy to follow, you can present a great deal of information in a short space.

For this reason, classification paragraphs make good overviews of material you will then explain in more detail, and good summaries of material you have already covered. They are also handy for making humorous points and points that don't need much development, as in the sample paragraph that follows.

Here are suggestions for writing classification paragraphs:

- *Choose a general category that you know enough about to divide into two to four subcategories.* (For example: customers, coffee bars, rock bands, Stephen King novels).

- *Decide on a principle of classification, and state this principle at the beginning of your paragraph.* A principle of classification tells you how to divide things into groups. For instance, you could group restaurant customers according to age groups, or attitudes toward staff, or eating habits. Each of these is a principle of classification.

- *Make a list of the types represented by your principle of classification.* If you chose "eating habits" as your principle of classification, for example, you might come up

60

with types such as these: the bottomless pit, the doggie-bagger, the gushing gourmet, the constant complainer, the garbage collector, the reluctant sampler.

- *Describe two to four types, depending upon how much you need to say to explain each type.* Use actual examples (the man who made seven trips to the salad bar) or hypothetical examples (the kinds of complaints various customers make, all attributed to the constant complainer).

- *To signal your shift from one subcategory to another, use parallel sentence structure and/or transitions that indicate enumeration* (*first, second, next, finally*).

- *Begin or end your paragraph with the point you want to make.* For example, "As you snicker or groan at the eating habits of others, consider how you appear to those who serve you when you go out to eat."

The following paragraph classifying campers is condensed from a short humorous essay that takes an anthropological approach to human behaviour. Notice that the basis of the classification, modes of shelter, determines which details the writer includes about each group.

Classifying

Sample Classification

Homo Camperus, an abundant and diverse species of nomadic wanderers, can be divided into three sub-species according to their differing modes of shelter: Homo Camperus Motorhomeous, Homo Camperus Fanaticus, and Homo Camperus Miscellaneous. The Motorhomeous sub-species is easily recognizable by the giant, house-like structures its members inhabit, variously known as "motorhomes," "Winnebagos," "camper-trailers," and last but not least, "highway menaces." While members of this sub-species enjoy the campground's version of nature as much as the other Camperus groups, they also need the security of sturdy walls, real beds, and their own porta-potties. Fanaticus, in contrast, does not believe in sleeping under anything but a nylon roof. While Motorhomeous lurks within the relative safety of the forest, Fanaticus braves the windy, treeless beachfront, relishing the challenge of having to extra-stake a tent. For Fanaticus, the tent is the ultimate sign of high status and economic/social well-being, and so the more tents one has, the better. Usually, there are two colossal ones: one tent

61

for sleeping and the other for meals and for planning the daily outings to climb mountains or kayak raging rivers. The third and most abundant sub-species, Miscellaneous, is made up of members of the abnormal and unconventional Camperus who wander into the campground for the first time. Miscellaneous groups never have more than one tent, a small, inferior one that they don't know how to erect. They always forget some key piece of equipment, such as tent pegs, which they end up borrowing from the smug Fanaticus. In windy, rainy, or otherwise inclement weather, they abandon their flimsy shelter and retreat to their cars, to the delight of the cozy Motorhomeous and intrepid Fanaticus.

—James Stevenson

Exercise 6.1

Complete the following diagrams with appropriate categories and examples. Notice that movies can be classified in different ways. Can you figure out two other principles of classification for this subject?

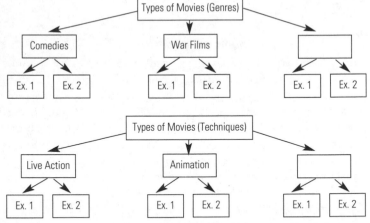

Exercise 6.2

Choose one of the listed subjects and make a four-level diagram showing how you could divide your subject according to two different principles of classification. Use this model:

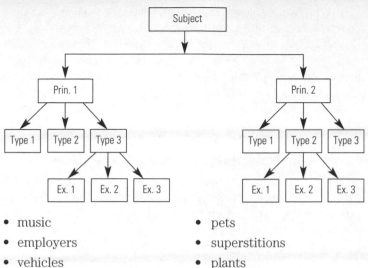

- music
- employers
- vehicles

- pets
- superstitions
- plants

Exercise 6.3

Write a classification paragraph based on one of the principles of classification you developed for the diagram above.

6b Comparing

When you compare, you match similarities and differences in two or more subjects. **Comparison** may be your primary method of development in a piece of writing, as in the sample research paper "*Tom Sawyer* and *Anne of Green Gables:* Two Models of Heroism" (14f). Or you may combine comparison with other methods of development.

To compare subjects effectively, you need a basis of comparison. A basis of comparison tells you which similarities and differences to focus on. For example, if you are asked on a biology exam to compare the fertilization process in mammals and amphibians, you have been given a basis of comparison: the fertilization process. In other writing situations, your purpose and audience will suggest an appropriate basis of comparison. If you are comparing two cars for your company, for instance, your basis of comparison will be determined by the purpose of the report. Is your company thinking of leasing one of the cars? Establishing a dealership? Paying insurance claims? Each of these purposes would lead you to choose a different basis of comparison, such as cost effectiveness, marketability, and amount of damage.

In other writing situations, the basis of your comparison may not be so obvious. Suppose you were writing an essay comparing the roles of the North West Mounted Police and the U.S. Cavalry in the settlement of western North Amercia. You would need to consider many facts and opinions about these forces before deciding on a general similarity or difference to use as a basis of comparison.

When your basis of comparison is not obvious, follow these steps.

List Similarities and Differences

Although making lists may seem time-consuming, you will discover that it is time well spent. Your lists will serve three purposes: they will ensure that you have lots of material, that you compare equivalent aspects of your subjects, and that you provide the same information about both. Let's take an example.

In writing about the differences between First Nations' storytelling and Western storytelling, for instance, one student wanted to reinforce her point by comparing similar folk tales, "The Ghost Owl" and "The Three Bears." She compiled these lists:

"The Ghost Owl"	**"The Three Bears"**
— The main character is a small girl who brings trouble on herself by crying when she doesn't get what she wants.	— The main character is Goldilocks, who brings trouble on herself by following her impulses (sampling the bears' food, chairs, and beds) instead of completing her errand.
— She is put outside the lodge, carried away by an owl, rescued by a hawk, and restored to her home when she has killed the owl and has "grown up" enough to follow grandfather hawk's instructions.	— She is frightened and jumps out of the window when the bears discover her wrongdoing, but her fate is uncertain.
— Animal figures are distinct from humans but equal to humans and part of the same world.	— Animal figures are symbols of human society (the bears live and act like "civilized" humans, not bears).

These lists provide more than enough material for a paragraph, so the student would need to select the most appropriate material for her purpose.

Choose a Basis of Comparison

The next step is to decide on a *basis of comparison,* that is, the general characteristic that will be the focus of your discussion of similarities and/or differences. The lists above suggest two main possibilities: the fate of the main character and the role of animal figures. The student chose the fate of the main character as her basis of comparison because that difference would best support her thesis (see below).

Formulate a Main Idea

The crucial step, too often overlooked, is to decide what point to make about your basis of comparison and put it in a topic sentence. Do not merely say something like *The main characters come to different ends in "The Ghost Owl" and "The Three Bears"* or *Differences between First Nations' storytelling and Western storytelling are evident in folk tales such as "The Ghost Owl" and "The Three Bears."* (For more on topic sentences, see 4a.)

If you are writing a self-contained comparison paragraph, think about the general meaning you can draw from the specific details that led you to your basis of comparison.

Suppose that you were comparing the endings of the two folk tales in response to a short-answer exam question. You know that in "The Ghost Owl," the main character, now a young woman, passes a final test of obedience and returns to her village, where no one recognizes her because grandfather hawk has dressed her as a warrior. Finally she admits she is the girl whose mother put her out for the owls for being naughty. Her mother cries and pleads for forgiveness. The young men ask if they can wear warrior clothes like hers, thus giving her a role in creating the Cheyenne soldier societies. The ending of "The Ghost Owl," you might conclude, emphasizes the reintegration of the girl into the community and the valuable contribution she is able to make as a result of what she has learned from her experience. In "The Three Bears," in contrast, the bears never see Goldilocks again and her fate is uncertain: she might have broken her neck in jumping from the window; she might have become lost in the woods; or she might have found her way home and been whipped for being naughty. The ending thus focuses on Goldilocks' punishment and banishment from the "civilized" society the bears represent. You would combine these ideas about the fates of the two characters in a topic sentence something like this:

> The fate of the main character in "The Ghost Owl" emphasizes the benefits of reintegrating troublesome individuals within the community, whereas the fate of Goldilocks in "The Three Bears" emphasizes the dangers of defying authority.

If you are writing a comparison paragraph as part of an essay, you must figure out a main idea that both explains the specific details relevant to your basis of comparison and shows how those details support your thesis. The student's thesis is that First Nations' storytelling reflects the cultural belief in a universe in which all life is equal and in balance, whereas Western storytelling reflects the cultural belief in a hierarchical order in which humankind is separate from and superior to the natural world. To connect her paragraph on the two stories with this thesis, she might write a topic sentence like this:

> The fate of the main character in the folk tale "The Ghost Owl" reflects Native beliefs about equality and balance in the universe, whereas the fate of Goldilocks in "The Three Bears" reflects Western society's emphasis on hierarchy and separation from nature.

To clarify the connection between her topic sentence and the details about the stories, she would explain that in Native culture, reintegrating troublesome individuals is necessary to restore equality and balance; whereas in Western culture, punishing transgressors or exiling them to a threatening natural world is necessary to maintain hierarchical authority. (For more information on writing comparison essays, see The Comparative Thesis, 8c.)

Organize Your Comparison

Block Method

The simplest way of organizing a brief comparison is the **block method.** In this method, you mention both subjects in your topic sentence, but then say everything about one subject before saying anything more about the other. When you are ready to discuss the second subject, you signal the shift by a transitional word or phrase. Organizing the comparison of the two folk tales by the block method might give you the following paragraph:

Sample Block Method

The fate of the main character in "The Ghost Owl" emphasizes the benefits of reintegrating troublesome individuals within the community, whereas the fate of Goldilocks in "The Three Bears" emphasizes the dangers of defying authority. In "The Ghost Owl," the main character is reunited with her community only when she has "grown up" enough to want to do so and has successfully passed a final test of obedience. Because grandfather hawk has dressed her as a warrior, no one in the village recognizes her until she humbly admits she is the naughty girl whose mother put her out for the owls. The responses of her mother and the young warriors signal her reintegration into the community. Her mother cries and pleads for forgiveness, and the young men ask if they can wear warrior clothes like hers. The warrior clothes represent the strength, courage, and cunning she has learned through following the teachings of grandfather hawk. The ending thus emphasizes not only her reintegration into the community but also the valuable contribution she can make: her instructions to the young men lead to the creation of the Cheyenne soldier societies. In "The Three Bears," in contrast, Goldilocks' fate is uncertain: she might have broken her neck in jumping from the window; she might have become lost in the woods; or she might have found her way home and been whipped for being naughty. The ending thus focuses on Goldilocks' banishment from the "civilized" society the bears represent and her possible punishments for disobeying her mother and flouting social conventions. Unlike the girl of "The Ghost Owl," she is not given the chance to learn valuable lessons from her experience or to contribute to the good of her community.

If the material is too long for one paragraph, you can easily start a new paragraph when you shift to your second subject.

Point-by-Point Method

The **point-by-point method,** in which you shift back and forth between subjects, is sometimes more effective than the block method when you are organizing a longer piece of writing (see Patterns for Comparison Essays, 9c). At the paragraph level, however, shifting between subjects can produce an annoying or confusing ping-pong effect, as you can see in this version of the previous example:

The fate of the main character in "The Ghost Owl" emphasizes the benefits of reintegrating troublesome individuals within the community, whereas the fate of Goldilocks in "The Three Bears" emphasizes the dangers of defying authority. In "The Ghost Owl," the main character is reunited with her community only when she has "grown up" enough to want to do so and has successfully passed a final test of obedience. In "The Three Bears," in contrast, Goldilocks' fate is uncertain: she might have broken her neck in jumping from the window; she might have become lost in the woods; or she might have found her way home and been whipped for being naughty. When the girl in "The Ghost Owl" returns to her village, she is dressed as a warrior, and so no one recognizes her until she humbly admits she is the naughty girl whose mother put her out for the owls. Her mother cries and pleads for forgiveness, and the young men ask if they can wear warrior clothes like hers. In contrast, the bears never see Goldilocks again; if she has made her way back to her home, her mother would have been angry and whipped her. The responses of the mother and the young men in "The Ghost Owl"...

Normally, you would wish to avoid this rapid shifting back and forth between two subjects. Sometimes, however, a paragraph that ping-pongs may be effective for special emphasis or for humour.

Exercise 6.4

Choose two topics from the following and list the similarities and differences between the subjects being compared.

• ice skating and rollerblading (or two other similar sports)

• listening to music and playing music

• love and infatuation

• assertiveness and aggressiveness

• some aspect of two places you have lived

• two ways of celebrating birthdays

Exercise 6.5

Find a basis of comparison for each of the two topics that you chose in Exercise 6.4 above. Then decide what point you would make about each topic.

Exercise 6.6

Select a method of organization (block or point by point) and write a comparison paragraph based on one topic that you selected in Exercise 6.4. Keep in mind that your purpose is to explain, not to persuade or to share personal experience (though of course you may draw on your experience).

6c Defining Terms and Concepts

> "There's glory for you!"
>
> "I don't know what you mean by 'glory,'" Alice said.
>
> Humpty Dumpty smiled contemptuously. "Of course you don't—till I tell you. I meant 'there's a nice knock-down argument for you!'"
>
> "But 'glory' doesn't mean 'a nice knock-down argument,'" Alice objected.
>
> "When I use a word," Humpty Dumpty said in a rather scornful tone, "it means just what I choose it to mean—neither more nor less."
>
> —From *Through the Looking Glass* by Lewis Carroll

Humpty Dumpty may get away with arbitrarily deciding what words mean, but most of us cannot. If we want to communicate, we have to use words in ways that others will understand. Thus when you use words unfamiliar to your readers, or use familiar words in an unfamiliar way, you need to provide **definitions.**

In exams and other kinds of academic writing, you may be asked to define terms to show that you know what they mean. In most writing, however, you provide definitions not to demonstrate your own knowledge but to help your reader understand what you are talking about. Depending on what kind of information your reader needs, you may use a synonym, a class definition, an extended definition, or a restrictive definition.

Synonyms

A **synonym** is a word that means the same, or nearly the same, as another word. Use synonyms, set off by commas or enclosed in parentheses, to define slang expressions, specialized terms of trades and professions, regional and dialect usages, and foreign words and phrases. These examples illustrate how to integrate synonyms smoothly into a sentence:

> At the heart of a microcomputer system is the central processing unit, or microprocessor, as it is also known.
>
> —Bernard Doering

> As we entered the Air India 747, the steward clasped his hands and said, "Namaste" ("Greetings to you").
>
> —Vijaya Rao

Class Definitions

A **class definition** explains a term by saying what kind of thing it is (its class) and how it is different from other members of its class. Cats, for example, are a kind of feline (the class), but so are lions, tigers, cheetahs, leopards, and cougars. To distinguish cats from other felines, you might mention that cats are small and commonly kept as pets.

This is the standard form of the class definition:

> An X is a member of the class Y with the characteristics A, B, C. . . .

> A bailiff [term to be defined] is a person [class] who performs limited functions within a judicial system, such as having custody of prisoners in court, serving warrants, or serving as magistrate for minor offences [distinguishing characteristics].

Extended Definitions

When a synonym or class definition does not offer enough explanation, you will need to use an **extended definition.** Some writers take a paragraph, or even a whole essay, to define a term. In a persuasive essay, for example, you might give an extended definition of the word *violence* to show that it can legitimately be applied to the destruction of the environment.

Here are three ways to expand definitions:

1. Add examples.

2. Give negative examples—that is, words or things that might seem to be included in the class but are not.

3. Use an analogy to compare your term with something more familiar.

For instance, if you wanted to explain random sampling to readers who were not social scientists, you might use the analogy of pulling a handful of assorted candies from a jar. Or, if you wanted to make sure high school students understood the concept of random motion, you might use the following analogy.

Sample Extended Definition

The movement of molecules is referred to as *random motion*. Random motion is defined as "the movement of the smallest possible physical unit of an element or compound, composed of atoms." This definition may seem puzzling. However, if you think of a molecule as a billiard ball, and random motion as the movement of billiard balls, the meaning becomes much clearer. Picture in your mind the green top of a pool table with billiard balls scattered upon it. Each ball represents a molecule. If you close your eyes and push a single ball on the table with a strong degree of force, it will eventually hit another ball and send it into motion. This ball will strike another, and so on, with no set pattern or order. Just as billiard balls move within the boundary formed by the edges of the pool table, so molecules move within the boundaries of the element or compound of which they are a part. This is random motion.

—*Kim Felske*

How often will an extended definition be needed? Don't insult your readers by defining words they know, but never assume your subject is as familiar to them as it is to you. Try to read what you've written with their eyes. Could you clarify what you mean by *oral literacy* by giving an example of storytelling in traditional Inuit families? Could you help to explain what high school students consider "cool" by giving examples of things that are not "cool"? Would an analogy help to explain the principle of indeterminacy to non-scientists?

Restrictive Definitions

Our understanding of words, especially of abstract terms such as *violence, loyalty, pornography,* and *censorship,* is shaped by our own experiences, and we bring these personal connotations to what we read. These preconceptions may lead us to think that we agree (or disagree) with a writer's statements when we don't. You can make sure that you and your readers are talking the same language by using a **restrictive definition.**

A restrictive definition specifies which meaning, from a range of possible meanings, a term will have within a particular context. Restrictive definitions thus allow you to limit your treatment of your subject. You may consider various meanings of the word *censorship,* for example, and then specify that you will use the word to mean the passage of laws designed to prevent the publication of certain material. Accordingly, your readers cannot expect you to discuss other actions that they might consider censorship, such as withdrawing books from libraries. As this example suggests, restrictive definitions are particularly necessary when the meaning of a term is controversial.

Because they establish common ground with readers and mark out the territory you will discuss, restrictive definitions make good introductions. Suppose, for example, you were writing a research paper on the debate over family values. You might well begin your paper by defining the key terms "family" and "values" so that your readers understand your main purpose: to replace the current restrictive definition with a more inclusive definition.

Sample Restrictive Definition

Conservative thinkers often attack social policies they perceive to be harmful to "family values," and yet they seldom define what they mean by "family" or "values." Before the Industrial Revolution, most of the population of Europe lived in extended families consisting of assorted grandparents, parents, children and other adults, related or unrelated, because this was the most efficient economic unit. With the expansion of the middle classes in the early nineteenth century, more couples could afford to establish their own households. These middle-class households made up of parents and children (and perhaps a servant or two) became the ideal that North Americans aspired to. In the ideal nuclear family, the father provided the income, the mother stayed home and looked after the children, and the children obeyed their parents. It is this image of the nuclear family that conservative thinkers generally have in mind when they defend "family values." Yet, as I will show, economic pressures created by divorce, uncertain employment, and the changing role of women are again forcing us to redefine what we mean by family and to recognize the diversity in family values.

Sources of Definitions

When you need to define a word, begin with a standard dictionary such as those published by Gage, Random House, and Oxford. For more detailed information about specialized meanings, changes in meaning over time, and current usage, consult works such as the following, found in the reference section of your library.

- *Unabridged dictionaries.* The *Oxford English Dictionary* provides a history of each word's use and changes in meaning.

- *Specialized dictionaries.* Available for many professions and academic disciplines. Examples: *Dictionary of Business and Economics, Dictionary of Philosophy, A Handbook to Literature.*

Exercise 6.7

Give a synonym or class definition that would explain each of these terms to readers unfamiliar with your subject.

1. trance music (or other term from popular culture)

2. quasar (or other scientific term)

3. the 'hood (or other slang expression)

4. slapshot (or other sports term)

5. *coureur de bois* (or other non-English expression)

Exercise 6.8

Write an extended definition of one of the following terms.
- sweat lodge
- body sculpting
- Rastafarianism
- kung fu (or other martial art)
- pysanka (or other cultural artifact)

• aromatherapy (or other alternative health technique)

Exercise 6.9

Write a paragraph of restrictive definition for one of the following terms.

- patriotism
- intelligence
- euthanasia
- equal opportunity
- justice
- living will

6d Analyzing: Dividing Your Subject into Parts

Analysis is a way of explaining a subject by dividing it into its parts and showing how the parts relate to the whole. We will discuss three types of analysis. **Systems analysis** shows the relation of parts in space; **process analysis** shows the sequence of parts in time; and **causal analysis** shows the relationship between causes and effects.

By dividing up a complex or unfamiliar task, situation, or idea into smaller units, you can often make it easier for readers to grasp what you are saying about your subject. For particular writing assignments, you may use these three types of analysis alone or in combination. In writing a how-to article on making knives, for example, you would use process analysis to develop your material. But in writing an expository essay on knife-making, you might include sections on the process, on the effects of changes in technology, and on the marketing system consisting of suppliers, knife-makers, dealers, and collectors. Or in writing a film review, you might discuss the process of making the film as well as analyze the final product as a system of interconnected parts. For examples of essays and other types of writing developed through analysis, see chapters 11 and 12.

Explaining Systems

We tend to think of a system as a physical object with working parts, such as a car engine or the body's immune system. But more abstract phenomena also operate as systems, such as systems of government and philosophy. When you explain how such abstract systems "work" by showing how the parts are related to the whole, you are also engaged in systems analysis. Aesthetic objects—such as music, dance, drama, film, television shows, comic books, literary works, and visual arts—can be considered as systems in which parts work together to create a whole. For instance, you might find that a certain song creates a mood of angry rebelliousness. To explain how the song creates this mood, you would consider elements such as lyrics, vocal style, instruments, and arrangement. You will find guidelines for analyzing specific kinds of written works in Essays Analyzing Literature (11c), Summaries (12c), Position Papers (13d), and appendix A.

A systems analysis is like a blueprint. You give an objective general description of your subject rather than a subjective particular description. If you were analyzing the functions of the federal Cabinet, for instance, you would discuss the role of the minister of defence, not the personality of the current minister.

Usually you begin by identifying the system and explaining its purpose in a topic sentence. Next you describe the most obvious or most important part of the system, such as the prime minister, and show how other parts function in relation to it. Then you explain the function of each part in relation to the whole. Use appropriate transitions to show how the parts are related.

6d

Sample Systems Analysis: Physical Object

Analyzing: Dividing Your Subject into Parts

In the following example, the writer describes bird feeders in general (not the particular one hanging in her garden) and explains the function of each component.

Bird feeders, which are generally made of wood or plastic, consist of a container for dispensing seeds or nuts, one or more perches, a removable lid, and a means of suspending the container off the ground. The container is generally either a squat receptacle with several openings onto a broader base, which acts as a perch, or a long tube with twig-like perches at various openings. The perches give the birds a stable position for feeding. The removable lid allows the container to be filled and protects the seeds and nuts from getting wet and mouldy. A birdfeeder may be suspended from a tree branch by means of a piece of string or wire passed through a wire loop at the top of the container, nailed to a platform, or attached to a window by suction cups. When filled with an appropriate mixture of seeds and nuts, birdfeeders attract birds for backyard viewing and help them survive summer droughts and winter cold.

Sample Systems Analysis: Abstract System

In this example, the writer shows how the parts of an abstract system—the Hollywood movie studios of the early twentieth century—worked together to create a film industry that continues to dominate world markets.

The Hollywood studio system, which dominated the production of American movies from the 1920s to the 1950s, was essentially a system for mass-producing movies with the same efficiency that cars, guns, and household appliances were produced in factories. At the head of the major studios (such as Columbia, MGM, Paramount, RKO, and Warners) were the movie producers. Like the heads of factories, movie producers controlled the financing of their products and exercised considerable control over how the products were made. The producers hired actors and approved script choices and script writers. They also hired the director for each film, and thus influenced how the action was staged and photographed. Movies were shot under tightly controlled conditions in the huge holdings of land, buildings, and sound stages that comprised the studio lot. The staples of the Hollywood system—westerns, thrillers, science fiction, and horror movies—could thus be shot quickly on ready-made sets. In addition, each studio had all the departments necessary to make a movie, including publicity, costuming, set design, story production, and makeup. Like the personnel of these departments, actors were constantly available on low salary, long-term contract, including such stars as Humphrey Bogart, Joan Crawford, Bette Davis, Clark Gable, and John Wayne. These low-cost production methods enabled the studios to produce hundreds of films a year and thus laid the groundwork for Hollywood's continuing dominance of the world film industry.

6d

*Analyzing:
Dividing
Your Subject
into Parts*

Exercise 6.10

Write a paragraph explaining the parts of a physical object with which you are familiar and showing how these parts function as a whole. Here are some possible subjects.

- weight-training equipment
- a digital camera (or similar equipment)
- a home entertainment system
- a watch
- a cellphone
- a hair dryer

Exercise 6.11

Write a paragraph explaining the parts of an abstract system with which you are familiar and showing how the system functions as a whole. Here are some possible subjects.

- an organization you belong to
- a band, choir, or similar musical group
- a particular ecosystem, such as your backyard
- a role-playing game
- an ad or a commercial
- a family

Explaining Processes

Process analysis has one of two purposes: to explain how something happens ("How Airplanes Fly") or to explain how to do something ("How to Fly an Airplane"). In each case, you emphasize what happens (or should happen) every time the process is repeated ("How to Develop Film"), rather than what happened during one particular instance ("How I Ruined My Sister's Wedding Pictures").

Begin with a topic sentence that identifies the process and its major stages. Then discuss the stages, and the steps within each stage, in the order in which they occur.

The amount of detail you include about each step will depend on your purpose and audience. When you explain how something is done but not how to do it, focus on the major stages so that your readers get a sense of the whole process; avoid giving detailed information about individual steps. On the other hand, when you give directions for readers to follow, discuss each step in detail, drawing your readers' attention to potential problems.

Use transitions indicating time relationships (*next, after, then*) or enumeration (*first, second, third*) to signal when you are moving from one stage or step to the next.

The following paragraph is designed to give readers a general understanding of the process of making Ukrainian-style Easter eggs. For an example of how to give more detailed instructions, see the Sample How-To Article (12e).

Sample Process Analysis

The three major stages in creating an Easter egg are mixing the dyes, waxing, and dyeing. First, the dyes are prepared. Then, a special stylus with a cup-like reservoir is used to cover all the areas of the pencilled-in design that are to remain white in melted wax. The egg is then submerged in the lightest colour dye. After several minutes, the egg is removed with a spoon and wiped to remove any excess dye. All areas that are to remain yellow are then covered in wax, and the egg is placed in the next darker shade of dye. The waxing and dyeing process is repeated until the design is complete and all the desired colours have been used.

—*Laurel Kiehlbauch*

Exercise 6.12

Write a paragraph explaining a process. Choose your own topic or one of the following topics.

- how to operate a piece of equipment
- how to teach a child a particular skill, such as tying shoes
- how to settle disputes with a partner or roommate
- how to make your favourite dish
- how to train a dog to heel

Explaining Causes and Effects

The analysis of causes and effects is basic to much of the writing you are likely to do in school or at work. You may write a research paper for a history course on the causes of the War of 1812; a lab report for botany on the effects of varying the amount of daylight received by tomato plants; or a letter to your insurance agent on the causes of a traffic accident.

Most actions or events worth writing about have multiple causes and effects. Brainstorming, asking discovery questions, and researching will help you avoid oversimplifying your analysis.

For a research paper on the effects of cutbacks in government spending on education, for instance, your first response might be to focus on the financial strain students are under because of higher tuition fees. You would gain a broader perspective, however, by brainstorming about other effects on students and reading about the effects on schools and postsecondary institutions. Your final essay might examine the effects of funding cuts on students, teachers, and institutions. For suggestions about the kinds of causes and effects you might consider, consult Asking Evaluative Questions (7b). For an example of an expository essay developed through causal analysis, see "The Effects of Child Poverty" (11b).

If you are explaining causes or effects that are independent of each other, arrange your material in an order that suits your audience. You might discover, for example, that the three main causes of traffic accidents are poor road conditions, impaired driving, and mechanical failure. There is no causal connection among these three factors (drinking too much doesn't cause the roads to be icy or the car to break down). If you were writing an essay, you would decide which cause to emphasize, and discuss it last. If you were writing a report for the city transportation department, on the other hand, you would discuss the most important factor first.

If you are discussing a chain of causes and effects (A causes B, B causes C, C causes D), make sure that your topic sentence focuses on the most significant cause(s) and effect(s). Arrange your material in chronological order, but to make it clear that you are writing a causal analysis rather than a narrative, choose words and expressions that emphasize causal connections (*a major effect, a second cause, one consequence; caused, resulted, affected; as a result, because, consequently, moreover, therefore, thus*). Suppose you were writing an essay on the effects of the Riel Rebellion on federal politics. Your notes for one paragraph might read as follows:

1. Riel's execution **caused** a renewed demand for rights by French-speaking Québécois.

2. These demands alarmed the federal government; **as a result,** it abolished French language rights in Manitoba.

3. This action **resulted** in loss of support for the Conservative Party in Quebec.

4. This decline in support **caused** the party to lose the next federal election.

5. Quebec's pivotal role in federal politics is a continuing **effect** of its position as the sole defender of the rights of French-speaking Canadians.

In writing your paragraph, you would add a topic sentence emphasizing the most significant effect (the increased power of Quebec). You would also fill in additional details, while keeping the focus on the chain of causes and effects, as in the paragraph below.

Sample Analysis of Causes and Effects

Although the failure of the Riel Rebellion weakened the position of French-speaking Canadians in Manitoba, it had the enormously significant effect of strengthening the power of French-speaking Canadians in Quebec. Before Riel was executed in 1885, Quebec had ignored the struggle of the French-speaking Manitobans to maintain their cultural identity. As a result of his execution, Riel became a martyr to the cause of rights for all French Canadians and the focus for a renewed demand for French rights in Quebec. Alarmed, the federal government abolished French education rights in Manitoba in 1890; Quebec thus became the only province where provincial rights guaranteed the survival of French culture in Canada. The consequence of this action, it soon became obvious, was that no federal government could remain in power if it lacked Quebec's support. The Conservative Party, weakened by MacDonald's death in 1891, lost the election in 1896 mostly because it had offended Quebec by abolishing French rights in Manitoba; the Liberals, led by Wilfrid Laurier, gained power by securing a large majority in Quebec. Since that time, no federal government has been able to ignore the province.

Exercise 6.13

Write two separate lists of causes explaining why you were (or were not) successful in your last job (or job search). Make one a list of independent causes; present the second list as a chain of causes and effects.

CHAPTER 7

METHODS OF PERSUADING

Persuasion takes a wide variety of forms, from the snappy jingles of television commercials to the carefully reasoned arguments of social critics. As these examples suggest, persuasive writing may appeal primarily to our emotions (television commercials) or primarily to our minds (logical arguments). Most persuasive writing—reviews, editorials, opinion pieces, political speeches—appeal to both.

Because the purpose of persuasive writing is to change readers' opinions or behaviour, the nature of your audience greatly influences the extent to which you appeal to your readers' intellect or emotions. Your audience for most writing in college and university will expect you to present carefully considered opinions and to support those opinions with evidence—such as facts, examples, and references to authorities on the subject. We will therefore focus on two strategies for making persuasive arguments: giving reasons and examples, and evaluating strengths and weaknesses. We will also demonstrate how you can give a persuasive edge to methods commonly used for explaining and sharing personal experience.

7a Giving Reasons and Examples

Whenever you state an opinion, your readers' first response is likely to be "Why do you think so?" Giving one or more reasons is the first step toward convincing your readers. The next step is giving examples—specific instances that show your reason(s) to be valid. For the argument to be strong, you must give reasons and examples that readers can verify independently. Consider these examples:

> This street is dangerous at night [opinion] because it is badly lit [verifiable reason]. In one four-block stretch, there is only one street lamp [verifiable example].

> This street is dangerous at night [opinion] because vampires hang out here [reason not verifiable]. Drops of blood on the corner show where there was a vampire attack [example not verifiable].

81

As you can see, both reasons and examples must have some basis in reality. That doesn't mean all readers will agree with you. They may not find your reasons convincing, or they may point to counter-examples. Nevertheless, by using sound reasons and good examples, you can persuade them that your opinion is worth considering. For guidelines on writing essays based on reasons and examples, see Opinion Pieces (13b).

These guidelines will help you use examples effectively.

Guidelines for Effective Use of Examples

- *Include an example to support any important general point.*

Consider these two versions of a paragraph on the Marxist definition of violence. The first is a series of general statements.

> The Marxists maintain that an act of violence is quite different from a violent act. An act of violence is an act that causes harm and suffering whether or not it is done violently. This distinction between an act of violence and a violent act allows the Marxists to point out that acts of violence do not necessarily involve physical force.

In the second version, examples illustrate the main points.

> The Marxists maintain that an act of violence is quite different from a violent act. Stirring a cup of tea, for example, can be done violently and therefore could be described as a violent act. An act of violence, on the other hand, is an act that causes harm and suffering whether or not it is done violently. Such acts do not necessarily involve physical force. To illustrate this point, one need only envision a situation where urban terrorists poisoned the air, with the result that citizens died quietly in their sleep. Although there was no physical contact, there was obviously an act of violence.

Without the **examples**—the specific instances used to explain the general statements—it is difficult to grasp the distinction between an act of violence and a violent act.

- *Make sure your examples are typical.*

Suppose, for instance, you were arguing that mandatory retirement is unfair. You might want to support your position by giving the example of your mother, who was not eligible for a full pension, when she was forced to retire at sixty-five, because she did not begin to work full-time until she was forty. If you used only this example to support your argument, readers might object, saying that your mother's case was not typical and therefore was poor evidence. This example would be effective, however, if you could show that many women are in the same situation. You would also want to use examples of people in different circumstances who also suffer because of mandatory retirement, such as those who change employers or careers.

- **Explain the meaning of your examples.**

An example seems puzzling when its relation to a general statement is unclear.

> Advertisements make life easier in some very basic ways. A good example is the commercials that play a few bars of many songs included on a tape.

How can playing snippets of songs "make life easier"? A sentence or two of explanation would make this connection clear. Explain your point first and then give your example:

> Advertisements make life easier in some very basic ways. One way is by offering the consumer an opportunity to sample products before buying. A good example is the commercials for musical compilation CDs that play a few bars of many songs.

Where there are several steps in the argument, as here, add another sentence after the example to remind your reader of your main point. The paragraph on advertising ends with this sentence showing how the commercial makes life easier:

> These snippets give the consumer a fairly good idea of whether or not the CD suits his or her taste in music and is thus worth buying.

- **Integrate your examples smoothly.**

If you haven't had much practice using examples, you may be tempted to introduce them with awkward phrases such as *An example of this is when* . . . (see Mixed Constructions, 18g). You can integrate your examples more smoothly by using constructions such as these: *for example, a further example, is exemplified by, for instance, an instance is, such as, this point is illustrated in, an illustration of this point is.*

> Another instance of this government's indifference to the needs of ordinary people is the plan to tax basic foods and children's clothing.

> The adolescent's desire to conform is best exemplified by the popularity of a few kinds of designer jeans.

> The half-hour line-ups in the cafeteria are further evidence of the need for more staff.

*Giving
Reasons
and
Examples*

Exercise 7.1

Choose one of the following opinions and give two or three reasons you agree or disagree. List at least two examples to support each of your reasons.

1. *Maclean's* rankings of universities are useful (not useful).

2. Assisted suicide should (should not) be a criminal offence.

3. Young offenders should (should not) be given jail terms.

4. The federal government should (should not) require labelling of all genetically modified foods.

5. High schools should (should not) offer training programs for specific jobs.

7b Evaluating Strengths and Weaknesses

To evaluate means to make judgments about the quality, worth, or importance of something according to specific criteria. Others may arrive at different judgments about the same thing. If you were judging an ice-skating competition, for instance, the scores you gave would likely differ from those of other judges using the same criteria. If you were allowed to discuss the performances, you would likely try to persuade the other judges that your evaluations were more accurate. From this point of view, every evaluation, no matter how seemingly objective, includes an element of persuasion.

When persuasion is your main purpose, your evaluations are likely to have an emotional as well as a logical dimension. To ensure that your judgments are nevertheless fair, you must thoroughly understand the thing you are evaluating. The basis for evaluation is therefore analysis: dividing things into parts to determine how the parts contribute to the whole (see Analyzing, 6d). In evaluating, however, you take analysis one step further: You ask not only "What is the function of this part?" but also "How well does this part fulfill its function?"

Asking Evaluative Questions

There are many perspectives from which to make judgments. Some perspectives depend upon the specialized knowledge of a profession (such as law or medicine) or an academic discipline (such as economics). Others are more broadly applicable. You can make the basis of your own judgments clearer to your readers by identifying your own perspective(s). Are your objections to a film, for instance, aesthetic (the acting is bad) or moral (it glorifies violence), or both?

Here are questions to ask about your subject from four general perspectives.

Aesthetic

Is it aesthetically pleasing? What are its strengths and weaknesses? Do the parts make a satisfying whole? Is the form suited to the content or function? Is it well-made? Is it appealing to its intended audience or users? For an example of evaluation from the aesthetic perspective, see the Sample Review (13i).

Moral

Is it morally right or wrong? Why? Who does it help or harm? Is it ethical? Does it promote values I accept or reject? What are they? Why do I accept or reject them? For an example, see the sample opinion piece "Why I Won't Buy a New Car" (13c).

Logical

Is it true? What are the arguments for and against it? Is the reasoning logical? Is the information accurate and complete? Does the evidence justify the conclusions or recommendations? For a detailed example of how to evaluate the logic of an argument, see Evaluating Logical and Emotional Appeals (13d).

7b

Evaluating Strengths and Weaknesses

Practical

Is it practical? What are its advantages and disadvantages? Will it work? Is it cost-effective? Is it useful?

You can clarify your thinking about your subject by considering each set of evaluative questions. You might use brainstorming diagrams or make parallel lists of good and bad points.

Suppose, for example, that you were writing a persuasive essay on whether pornography should be banned. You might begin with these points.

	Against Banning	For Banning
Aesthetic	Some "porno-graphic" works have literary and artistic merit	Most pornography is crude and boring
Moral	Right to freedom of expression	Contributes to violence against women and children
Logical	Difficulty of defining "pornography"	Research studies suggest social harm
Practical	Difficult to enforce	Protect children from sexual exploitation

Deciding Which Questions to Answer

Often your subject or your form will limit the range of evaluative questions you answer. If you are writing a short essay, it is better to consider one set of questions thoroughly than to skim through them all. For a longer essay, you may appeal to more readers and do more justice to your subject by considering two or three aspects—the aesthetic and moral dimensions of a book, for example, or the moral and practical issues facing the health professions.

Whether you consider both sides of a question or only one depends on your purpose and audience. You may emphasize either the good or the bad, but if your judgments are too one-sided, you are likely to bore or alienate your readers. Suppose, for instance, you were writing about hiking in the Laurentians. You could emphasize either the pleasures or the pains of hiking. But if the picture you paint is too rosy or too gloomy, readers may reject it as unrealistic.

Writing Evaluative Paragraphs

When you evaluate, you support your opinion by giving reasons, examples, and other kinds of evidence. This paragraph, taken from a beginner's guide to opera, focuses on the reasons for starting opera-going with *Madama Butterfly*.

Sample Evaluative Paragraph

The best piece for opera novices is that perennial favourite, Puccini's *Madama Butterfly*. Why has this suicidal geisha made such an impact? The answer is found in the stylistic term that describes this genre of opera—*verismo,* or truth. Operas in this tradition deal with real people handling their real situations with real emotion. The heroines are typically vulnerable, abused, forgotten. Puccini capitalized on this idea more or less successfully in *Manon Lescaut, Suor Angelica, Turandot, Tosca,* and *La Bohème.* But the most sorrowful, most charming, most naïve, is Cio-Cio-San, the teenage heroine of *Madama Butterfly,* who falls in love with the philandering Captain Pinkerton of the U.S. Navy and commits hara-kiri when he deserts her. The music is exquisite, beautiful yet coloured with sadness, and the drama disturbingly realistic. If nothing else, it's worth the price of admission to see an opera that is set in Japan, involves American characters, and is sung in Italian.

—Peter Phoa

7b

Exercise 7.2

On what grounds (aesthetic, moral, logical, practical) would you evaluate each of the following? Several of the topics can be approached from various perspectives.

Evaluating Strengths and Weaknesses

1. A city council decision to expand a major residential street.

2. A community theatre production of *The Vagina Monologues.*

3. A school board decision to reduce services for special needs children (such as the hearing impaired).

4. The exercise classes at a local health club.

5. A proposal to designate a building as an historic site.

6. A rapper's latest recording.

7. A proposal to raise the age for obtaining a driver's licence to 18.

8. An educational institution's decision to raise admission standards.

Exercise 7.3

State your position on one of the subjects in Exercise 7.2. List the arguments you would use to support your position.

Exercise 7.4

Write a paragraph based on your list of arguments in Exercise 7.3.

7c Using Other Methods to Persuade

As the three paragraphs on shoplifting in chapter 1 demonstrate, you signal your purpose in a piece of writing partly through the language you use. You can give a persuasive edge to any of the strategies discussed in chapters 5 and 6 by using evaluative language in your topic sentences and throughout your paragraphs. Methods of explaining (classifying, comparing, defining terms and concepts, and analyzing) allow you to present a more logical, more carefully reasoned argument. Telling stories, describing people, places, and things, and using analogies—all these heighten the emotional appeal of your writing.

The following analogy between the behaviour of a rich family and the behaviour of rich nations, for example, makes a strong appeal to readers' emotions.

Sample Analogy: Persuasive Writing

Picture a rich family living on a hill in splendid luxury. Look down on the plains around the hill and see the people in shacks, starving; hear the children cry. The rich family sends down a bit of food and clothing once a year, but otherwise they live as always. "We have the right to enjoy our wealth," they say. "We cannot feed and clothe and care for all those people," they explain as they add another foot of barbed wire to the fence around their property. Meanwhile the anger and frustration of the poor grow against them. The rich Western nations are very much like this family. A recent estimate numbered over 1.2 billion people living in poverty on the plains of the world spread at our feet. Like the rich family, we send bits of food and clothing. Like the rich family, we make it harder and harder for the poor to get in. Meanwhile the anger and frustration of the poor grow against us.

—Ken Ainsworth

Here are two cautions about using analogies in persuasive writing:

1. Do not use analogies to make unfair emotional appeals—ones that arouse prejudice. For example, smearing an opponent's reputation by charging that "Voting for X would be like voting for the Devil" might appeal to some voters, but would likely alienate many more.

2. Analogies do not provide strong logical support for an argument. Because you are comparing things that are basically different, your analogy may break down if it is pushed too far. Readers who spot weaknesses in your analogy may reject your argument. See Position Papers (13d).

Exercise 7.5

Write a persuasive analogy to illustrate one of the following subjects.

- the plight of refugees
- the disadvantages of a particular occupation
- the advantages (disadvantages) of decriminalizing marijuana
- the problems of not being able to read
- a subject of your choice

- Resources for Writers and Writing Instructors—a directory; also material on style and usage.

  andromeda.rutgers.edu/~jlynch/Writing/links.html

- The University of Victoria Writer's Guide.

  web.uvic.ca/wguide

- Indiana University Writing Resources—short entries on a number of topics, including paragraphs and topic sentences.

  www.indiana.edu/~wts/wts/resources.html

PART 3

WRITING ESSAYS

CHECKLIST | *Essays*

	OK	NEEDS WORK

Purpose and Audience

1. Does the essay have a clearly defined purpose (to explain, to persuade, to share your personal experience)? ☐ ☐

2. Does the essay meet the needs of your intended reader? ☐ ☐

Thesis

3. Does your thesis state a specific idea that the rest of the essay develops? ☐ ☐

Development

4. Is all the material in the essay relevant to your thesis? ☐ ☐

5. Are you satisfied that you have adequately supported your thesis? ☐ ☐

6. Are the connections among your ideas as clear as possible? ☐ ☐

Essays that Begin with the Thesis

7. Does the introduction identify your subject and the range of material you will cover? ☐ ☐

8. Does the introduction end with your thesis? ☐ ☐

9. Do your paragraph divisions indicate the major sections of your essay? ☐ ☐

10. Does each topic sentence clearly state the main point of the paragraph and show how the paragraph relates to the thesis? ☐ ☐

11. Do transitions help your reader to follow the connections among your ideas? ☐ ☐

12. Does the conclusion restate the thesis, sum up the main points, and suggest a broader context or the implications of your subject? ☐ ☐

Essays that Lead Up to the Thesis

13. Does the introduction identify your subject, arouse the reader's interest, and suggest the structure of your essay? ☐ ☐

14. Are your paragraphs arranged in order of increasing importance? ☐ ☐

15. Do transitions help your reader to follow the sequence of ideas, events, or details? ☐ ☐

16. Does the conclusion sum up the ideas, events, or details by stating or clearly implying your thesis? ☐ ☐

Comparison Essays

17. Have you effectively used either the block or the point-by-point method of organization? ☐ ☐

Research Essays

18. In a research essay, have you included appropriate and correctly documented secondary sources? ☐ ☐

19. Is this material relevant to your thesis? ☐ ☐

20. Have you explained why you agree or disagree with this material? ☐ ☐

CHAPTER 8

THE KEY TO WRITING ESSAYS: THE THESIS

8a What Is an Essay?

"Write an essay," your instructor says. But what, exactly, is an essay? The term essay can be applied to a wide variety of non-fiction writing: light newspaper columns and impassioned letters to the editor; thoughtful magazine articles and scathing movie reviews; academic articles and the research papers you write in many of your courses. The common factor in all these types of writing is that they have a thesis, a main point to make about their subject.

8b What Is a Thesis?

A thesis states an opinion about a subject and presents one or more reasons to support it. In an **expository essay,** this opinion is the overall point you want to explain: "What this means is . . . " In a **persuasive essay,** this opinion is the argument you want to convince your readers to accept: "What you should think (or do) is . . . " In a **personal essay,** this opinion is a generalization based on your personal experience: "What this means to me is . . . "

A good thesis does more than state an opinion. It also gives one or more reasons to support the opinion: "You should do this for these three reasons . . . " As this example suggests, setting out your reasons allows you to control the content of the essay. Of all possible reasons for holding a particular opinion, you will discuss only those you have mentioned. Your thesis thus tells both you and your reader what you intend to cover.

You can formulate a better thesis if you follow these guidelines:

- ***State an opinion rather than merely restating your subject or essay topic.***

Suppose, for example, that your subject is *group homes for the mentally disabled* and you have narrowed this subject to the topic of *licensing regulations.* You will not have a thesis if you merely restate your subject: *This essay is about group homes for the mentally disabled.* Merely repeating your topic is no more useful: *This essay will discuss the licensing of group homes for the mentally disabled.* A thesis that states an opinion will give you a much clearer focus for your essay: *To prevent the exploitation of clients, social services should tighten regulations governing the licensing of group homes for the mentally disabled.*

- **State an opinion rather than a fact.**

Factual statements provide little focus or control over the content of the essay. You could turn a fact such as *Satellite dishes give Canadians access to hundreds of foreign television channels* into a thesis by stating your opinion of the effects of this situation: *By giving Canadian viewers access to hundreds of foreign channels, satellite dishes threaten the Canadian television industry.*

- **Make sure your thesis states your opinion, not the writer's.**

When you are analyzing a piece of writing, you will include the writer's main point about his or her subject somewhere in your analysis, but it will not be your thesis. Your thesis will explain *your* interpretation of the piece or evaluate its strengths and weaknesses. For example, the thesis of a newspaper editorial might be that Canadian judges should allow trials to be televised. After analyzing the editorial, you might arrive at a thesis stating that the writer's reliance on American examples weakens the argument.

- **Make the thesis as precise and specific as possible.**

If you state a well-defined opinion with one or more reasons to support it, you will know exactly what points to develop in the body of your essay. Avoid generalizations: *These stories have a lot in common* or *The Second World War had a big impact on Canada.* Instead, state the most important similarities in the stories or the most important social, political, or economic effect(s) of the war: *The diversification of manufacturing brought about by the Second World War transformed the Canadian economy.*

There is no one right thesis on a subject. Your thesis will reflect your unique way of looking at your material. It will be shaped by your purpose, your audience, your chosen essay form, and your methods of development.

Exercise 8.1

Consider the following sentences as thesis statements for an essay. If you think the sentence makes a clear point that would control the content of the essay, write **C**. If it doesn't, explain how it could be improved.

1. There is at least one television set in 97 percent of Canadian homes.

2. Science fiction is popular because it gives readers the opportunity to explore new ideas.

3. This essay will analyze Canadian foreign policy during the 1950s.

4. Between 1950 and 1990 the depiction of women in films changed enormously.

5. In the essay "My Wood," E. M. Forster argues that owning property damages a person's moral and spiritual health.

8c Discovering Your Thesis

Normally you will need to gather some material or even write a first draft before you can figure out your thesis. In fact, if you formulate a thesis first and then look for information to support it, you are likely to distort your subject.

To figure out your thesis, follow these steps:

Discovering Your Thesis

1. ***Gather information about your subject. Use one or more of these methods—brainstorming, freewriting, asking discovery questions, keeping a journal, conducting interviews, or doing research.*** See Part 1: The Writing Process: An Overview for more information on the first four of these. See chapter 12 for information on interviews and chapter 14 for information on how to use research materials.

2. ***Group this material into three or four categories.*** For ideas on how to divide your material, see the sections in chapters 5, 6, and 7 on specific methods of development, such as classification, analysis, comparison, and evaluation.

3. ***Formulate a thesis that focuses on the meaning of these broader categories.*** Suppose, for example, that you have been asked to write an essay on your first job. If you

have come back to school after a career as a nurse, you might write a personal essay on the satisfactions and frustrations of nursing when you began work twenty years ago; an expository essay explaining working conditions then; or a persuasive essay arguing that working conditions for nurses have not improved much over the twenty years. Whatever your focus, you would begin by jotting down information about various aspects of your job.

Nursing Twenty Years Ago

1. Earned $275/month with reasonable rates for room, board, and laundry in nurses' residence.

2. Advancement by seniority.

3. Good job security.

4. Not many chances to develop new skills.

5. Performed menial and routine tasks, no clinical specialization.

6. Worked 40-hour/five day week; split shifts and short changes (e.g., work 3:30 p.m.–midnight, then 7:30 a.m.–4 p.m.); understaffed.

7. Nurses supervised or administered; did little nurturing or ministering to patient.

8. Nurses expected to follow doctor's orders, not to make independent decisions.

9. Basic level of technology.

10. Doctors viewed nurses as subordinate.

11. Little interaction with management.

12. Education required: basic three-year diploma; training based on practice.

You would then group these aspects of nursing into more general categories, such as these:

• financial dimensions of employment (1,2,3,6)

• professional responsibilities (4,5,8,9,12)

• possibilities for emotional satisfaction (7,10,11)

8c

Discovering Your Thesis

To work out an overall statement about nursing twenty years ago, you would first need to decide what point you could make about each of these dimensions of the job. You might choose the following points:

- Twenty years ago, nurses worked long hours with strenuous shift changes for low wages, but their jobs were relatively secure.

- Opportunities for nurses to show initiative and develop new skills were quite limited.

- The emotional satisfactions of nursing were also limited by lack of direct contact with patients and their subordinate position to doctors and hospital administration.

The main idea that seems to emerge is that twenty years ago nursing was a secure job but one with limited opportunities for intellectual growth and emotional satisfaction.

The way you formulate your thesis depends on the kind of essay you are writing and the emphasis you want to give to each of your points.

The Personal Thesis

Whether a personal essay is narrative, descriptive, or reflective, your thesis should make a point about what your experience *meant* to you. Often this is a point about what this experience taught you about yourself, about others, or about life itself.

> As a young woman seeking independence, I saw only the job security that nursing promised, not its limited opportunities for intellectual growth and personal satisfaction.

The Expository Thesis

The thesis for an expository essay is the generalization that emerges from your analysis of your material. The thesis explains the significance of your subject by telling your readers *what* its parts are, *how* it got that way, *why* it has the nature it has, or all three. This thesis explains *why* nursing twenty years ago was as it was.

> The relative abundance of health-care dollars meant that nursing jobs were secure; however, the hierarchical nature of the system meant that nursing provided limited opportunities for intellectual growth and emotional satisfaction.

The Persuasive Thesis

The thesis for a persuasive essay tells readers *what* they should think or do and *why*. You reach your thesis by evaluating the strengths and weaknesses of your subject (see Evaluating Strengths and Weaknesses, 7b). Your thesis may focus on strengths (*Nursing was a good career choice twenty years ago because of the job security it offered*) or weaknesses (*Nursing was a bad career choice because of the limited opportunities for intellectual growth and emotional satisfaction*). On most issues, however, readers are more likely to be convinced by a thesis that gives a balanced perspective.

> Nursing twenty years ago bore little relation to the idealized notions invoked by critics of today's practitioners. Although jobs were secure, the profession offered few opportunities for intellectual growth or emotional satisfaction.

The Comparative Thesis

When you are comparing, whether in a personal, expository, or persuasive essay, your thesis should do more than state the most important similarities or differences in your subjects. It should also explain how or why they are similar or different. If you were comparing working conditions in nursing twenty years ago and today, for instance, you might discover that opportunities for intellectual growth and personal satisfaction have increased, but job security has decreased. Your thesis might explain the reasons for these differences in this way:

> Changes in medical technology and in the structure of the health-care system make nursing more intellectually and emotionally satisfying than it was twenty years ago, but cuts in health-care spending make jobs less secure.

Exercise 8.2

Choose two of the following subjects. For each subject, gather material and develop a thesis for a personal, expository, persuasive, and comparative essay. Use the nursing example above as a guide.

- street racing
- working part-time
- violence in sports
- your favourite book, film, or television program
- being a teenager

CHAPTER 9

ESSAY STRUCTURE

Essays, like houses, come in a variety of shapes, but they all have a structure—a principle of organization that binds the parts together. The structure serves two purposes: to show your readers how parts of your essay relate to each other and to create interest. Your choice of structure for a particular piece of writing will depend upon which of these purposes is more important.

The overall structure of your essay is determined by where you put your thesis—near the beginning or near the end. Since most essays for academic courses begin with the thesis, we will discuss this method in detail. Ending with the thesis is most effective for some kinds of personal and persuasive essays. In this chapter, you will find two patterns to follow when you choose this method.

Comparison essays present special problems of organization. We offer two possibilities, the block method and the point-by-point method. For suggestions about how to organize specific kinds of essays, see the appropriate section.

9a Beginning with Your Thesis

When you put your thesis in the introduction, it provides a framework for the rest of the essay. This pattern emphasizes the results of your thinking.

Advantages and Disadvantages

The main advantage of this method is its immediate clarity. By stating your main point first and then providing the evidence to support it, you never leave your reader wondering about the relevance or significance of your material. This method is particularly effective when you are discussing a complex or technical subject at some length, for most readers will have trouble following several pages of specific detail if they don't see how your evidence connects with your main point. For this reason, you will probably organize most of the essays you write for academic courses with the thesis first.

Beginning with your thesis may not be the best strategy, however, if you are writing on a controversial subject or on a topic that is unfamiliar to your readers. You may alienate readers who feel forced to agree or disagree with your conclusions before they have had time to consider the issue.

The Basic Components

Thesis and Topic Sentences

Your thesis, you will recall, gives your opinion about your subject and your reason(s) for holding that opinion. By giving your reasons in the order you plan to discuss them, you create a map to guide your readers through your essay. To show them where they are along the way, you use topic sentences that restate your reasons as points you will develop in your middle paragraphs.

In the following example, you can see how the thesis and topic sentences create a structure that focuses the reader's attention and controls the content of the essay.

Essay Topic   Are fairy tales suitable for children? Write a 1,000-word essay in which you defend your position.

Thesis   By providing models of hope, courage, and determination, fairy tale heroes help children to see the value of developing these virtues in their own lives.

Topic Sentences

— From the story of Jack and the magic bean seeds, children learn that even seemingly foolish hopes can lead to success.

— Children who have felt abandoned like Hansel and Gretel can learn the value of courage in adversity from Gretel's brave rescue of her brother.

— Cinderella has been criticized recently for waiting passively for Prince Charming to rescue her, but a closer reading of this tale shows that she, too, uses hope, courage, and determination to solve her own problems.

Giving an essay such a clearly defined structure is not easy; you won't achieve a perfectly worded thesis and matching topic sentences on your first try. In the process of gathering material, you may discover a tentative thesis and major categories (such as courageous characters and hopeful characters). These

Beginning with Your Thesis

categories—or the thesis—may change when you write an outline or a draft, since your ideas will usually become clearer, and so will your understanding of how they relate to each other. Then, when you revise, you can rewrite your thesis and topic sentences so that they provide a clear, logical framework.

The Introduction

In this type of essay structure, the opening sentences define the range of material you will cover and provide a context for the thesis, which ends the introduction. The opening sentences thus act like the framing shots of a movie, setting the scene and introducing the characters before the action begins.

Your introduction can be based on any of the methods of developing ideas discussed in chapters 5, 6, and 7. In academic essays, for example, you may classify the material you plan to discuss (such as types of fairy tales), define a key term from your thesis (such as autism), or sketch the development of a current situation (such as previous attempts to decriminalize marijuana). For a more general audience, you may want to create interest by giving a vivid example, telling a relevant anecdote, or describing a scene.

Whatever method you use, be sure to give your readers all the background information they need, including authors and titles of works, and dates and places of events.

Remember the following points when you are writing your introduction:

- ***Avoid making large claims that the rest of your essay does not support.*** Do not, for example, begin by saying *Children are not really frightened by fairy tales* unless you can (and will) provide hard evidence to support the generalization.

- ***State your thesis, not your topic.*** You do not need to include a sentence that merely repeats the assigned topic, such as *In this essay I will discuss the suitability of fairy tales for children.* The title of your essay should make the topic clear.

- ***Focus on the big picture, not the details.*** While you may choose to open with an example or incident that captures the essence of your argument, be wary of including detailed information that belongs in the body of the essay.

Sample Introduction

In the past, fairy tales were criticized as too unrealistic to provide suitable models for children. Recent critics are more likely to condemn fairy tales as too violent and/or too sexist. A closer examination of three popular fairy tales, *Jack and the Beanstalk, Hansel and Gretel,* and *Cinderella,* shows that this criticism is unjust, for these tales provide vivid examples of hopeful, courageous, determined characters who solve their own problems. Fairy tale heroes thus help children to see the value of developing these virtues in their own lives.

Middle Paragraphs

Sometimes, such as when you are tracing the development of a concept or analyzing a chain of causes and effects, your material will determine the order of your middle paragraphs. Usually, however, you will have to decide how to arrange your points. Consider how you can best keep your audience interested. You might begin with the point that your readers will find easiest to understand and end with the most difficult. Or you might build interest by beginning with your least important point and ending with the most important.

To see how you would decide which point is most important, consider the structure of the essay on fairy tales. The thesis and topic sentences suggest three blocks of material: Jack as a model of hope, Gretel as a model of courage, and Cinderella as a model of hope, courage, and determination. Because *Cinderella* has been most criticized (in *The Cinderella Complex,* for example) and there are more points to make in its favour, it makes sense to put this tale at the end.

You can't always cover a block of material in a single paragraph. To support the point about *Cinderella* with adequate examples, for instance, you would need several paragraphs. Whenever your discussion of a point takes up more than half a page (typed, double spaced), divide your material into subpoints, each with its own topic sentence. Use an umbrella topic sentence to tie the block of material together and show how it relates to the thesis.

9a

Beginning with Your Thesis

Sample Umbrella Topic Sentence

Cinderella has been criticized recently for waiting passively for Prince Charming to rescue her, but a closer reading of this tale shows that she, too, uses hope, courage, and determination to solve her own problems.

Topic Sentence [Subpoint 1]	Because Cinderella never stops hoping that she can go to the ball, she makes every effort to accomplish the difficult tasks her stepmother sets. [Examples]
Topic Sentence [Subpoint 2]	When she is returned to her rags and cinders, Cinderella is still brave enough to demand to see the Prince. [Examples]
Topic Sentence [Subpoint 3]	Far from waiting passively to be rescued, Cinderella makes a determined effort throughout the tale to solve her own problems. [Examples]

Conclusion

Your conclusion should draw together the evidence you have presented to reinforce the main idea of the essay as a whole. Instead of merely summarizing your main points, you emphasize their implications. While you don't want to raise new issues that should have been discussed earlier, you do want to show how your essay fits into a wider context. Your conclusion should have three basic components: a restatement of your thesis, a brief explanation of the significance of the major points, and a suggestion of the broader implications of the subject. You can present this last element in one of three ways:

- Move from the specific to the general to suggest that the material you have covered is part of a larger issue.

  Thus in a world too often disrupted by dislocation, divorce, and death, fairy tales offer children a hope of happiness.

- Compare your subject with another subject with which your reader is likely to be familiar.

  And, whatever the critics say, fairy tales are much less violent and sexist than the television programs most children watch every day.

- Stress the significance of your subject by emphasizing its causes or effects.

  Children may learn these moral values elsewhere, but nowhere else will they experience so satisfying an entry into the magic of reading.

Sample Conclusion

Children, like adults, learn who they are and what they can be through the examples of others. The hope, courage, and determination modelled by Jack, Gretel, and Cinderella show children that these virtues can help them to create happier lives for themselves. In doing so, these tales add an ethical dimension to children's education, a dimension that is too often missing in modern life.

For examples of essays beginning with the thesis, see Sample Essay Analyzing Literature (11d) and Sample Literary Research Paper (14f).

9b Leading Up to the Thesis

If you choose this method, your thesis may appear in the middle of your essay or at the end, or it may be implied rather than stated directly. This pattern emphasizes the process of your thinking rather than your conclusions.

Advantages and Disadvantages

By delaying the presentation of your thesis, you can create suspense and interest. This approach is particularly effective in personal essays, in which you invite readers to share the process of coming to understand an experience. Leading up to your thesis is also useful in a persuasive essay when you want to convince your readers to consider a potentially controversial point of view or to think in new ways about an old problem.

The danger with this method is that you may end up with many details but no main point. You can prevent this problem by structuring your essay according to one of the patterns discussed below.

Questions and Answers

In this pattern, you ask a question in your introduction that the rest of the essay will answer. You may consider and reject possible answers until you conclude with one that seems satisfactory; or you may give a series of partial answers that add up to a comprehensive one.

Introduction The introduction sets out the problem or issue and asks the question to be answered.

Middle Paragraphs In the body of your essay, you examine possible answers in detail. Each answer forms a major section of the essay, composed of one or more paragraphs. You can help your readers follow the structure of your essay by repeating key terms and using parallel sentence structure in each answer. Arrange your paragraphs in a sequence such as simplest to most complex, or weakest answer to strongest answer.

Conclusion In the conclusion, you present the best or most comprehensive answer as your thesis. You can signal that you've reached your thesis by repeating the question from the introduction or by summarizing previous answers.

The following example demonstrates how the question and partial answers pattern can work.

Introduction [Question]	How can teachers help reduce violence in school?
Middle Paragraphs [Topic Sentences]	We can watch for signs . . . We can discuss the issue with students . . .
	We can also teach students ways of resolving arguments . . .
	Most important, we must model good problem-solving behaviour in our conflicts with students . . .
Conclusion [Thesis]	To reduce violence in schools, we must educate both ourselves and our students about the uses and misuses of power.

The sample opinion piece "Why I Won't Buy a New Car" (13c) displays elements of this pattern. Note that the question to be answered is raised in the title.

9b

*Leading Up
to the
Thesis*

Specific Details to General Meaning

In this pattern, you begin with particular details and end with a thesis, either stated or implied, about the meaning of the experience as a whole.

Introduction The introduction plunges your reader into the subject of your essay and arouses interest through narrative or descriptive detail. It gives a sense of structure by suggesting the final event of the narrative (*We wouldn't rest until we found the*

106

lost treasure of the Incas) or the scope of the description (*The old neighbourhood was unrecognizable*).

Middle Paragraphs In the body of the essay, fill in the specific details. As units of thought, your paragraphs will correspond to units of your narrative (*first week, next day, that afternoon, the moment had come*) or description (*the streets, the houses, our house*). Arrange your paragraphs in a chronological or spatial sequence that will lead naturally to the generalization in your conclusion. Foreshadow this generalization by references to thoughts and feelings (*I wondered whether we were on a fool's errand*), or by choice of diction (*narrow streets, cracked side-walks, shabby houses, our house shrunken and decayed*).

Conclusion In the conclusion, you sum up the meaning of the experience, either through explicit commentary (*The real treasures were those we had left behind: family, friends, and country*), or through an image that makes the point (*Staring back at me was the image of a white-haired old man, his face deeply creased by sorrow and worry. Several moments passed before I recognized my own reflection in the glass*).

For an example of this pattern, see the sample descriptive essay "Smokey Mountain" (10d).

9c Patterns for Comparison Essays

You can use either the block or the point-by-point method to develop a comparison essay. We discussed both of these methods in detail in chapter 6, when we described how to arrange material in paragraphs developed through comparison. Both methods have advantages and disadvantages.

Block Method

When you use the block method, you cover all the aspects of one subject before you discuss the other.

Advantages: Clarity and Simplicity

The block method gives you a chance to develop all your ideas on one subject before you turn to the other. It is therefore simple to work with when you don't have much time to organize an essay—in an exam, for instance. The block method can work well for short essays on familiar subjects, as in comparisons of places you have lived or people you have known. It is also effective when you are using a brief treatment of one subject as a basis for a more lengthy treatment of another. Finally, if you are comparing more than two subjects, you will probably need to use the block method to avoid fragmenting your material.

An important advantage of the block method is that you are less likely to distort your material by trying too hard to find similarities or by exaggerating the importance of one aspect of a subject. The sound patterns in one poem, for example, may contribute much less to the meaning than do the sound patterns in another.

Disadvantages: Repetition and Loss of Focus

One disadvantage of the block method is that readers may forget what you have said about your first subject by the time you make similar points about your second subject. For this reason, you may have to repeat points. Another danger is that you may lose your focus on the basis of your comparison: the common element you are discussing (such as the setting of the two stories or the economic effects of two policies). As a result, your reader may decide that you have discussed both subjects but never actually compared them. To avoid this problem, make sure your analysis focuses on the same element(s) of both subjects.

Sample Outline: Block Method

If you were using the block method to organize an essay comparing the advantages of working with the advantages of going to school, your outline might look like this.

I. The advantages of working
    A. Friendships with co-workers
    B. Money
    C. Free time

II. The advantages of going to school
    A. Friendships with other students
    B. Learning new ideas and skills
    C. Achieving goals

III. Working compared with going to school
    A. Friendships at work and school
    B. The immediate rewards of money and free time compared with the long-term rewards of learning and a sense of achievement

Notice that this structure leads naturally to putting your thesis at the end, where you draw together your comparisons.

Point-by-Point Method

When you use the point-by-point method, you deal with one aspect of both subjects before moving on to another aspect of both subjects.

Advantages: Focus and Conciseness

An important advantage of the point-by-point method is that it helps your reader to grasp the most important similarities and differences by bringing specific points about your subjects closer together. It thus avoids one of the main disadvantages of the block method: repetition. This emphasis on points of similarity and difference also keeps you focused on the task of comparing. For these reasons, this method is often better for organizing a lengthy and complex comparison.

Disadvantages: Complexity and Fragmentation

With this method, you have to identify all the points of similarity and difference you plan to discuss before you begin writing. For this reason, it is difficult to use for in-class essays. Another disadvantage is that if you don't have much to say about each point, your essay may ping-pong rapidly from one subject to the other. You can correct this problem by gathering more material or by combining subpoints so that you can write separate paragraphs on each aspect of each subject, as illustrated in the outline below.

Sample Outline: Point-by-Point Method

Thesis Both myths and fairy tales can give us insights into cultural values, but fairy tales provide more useful role models for children because they portray more realistic characters who manage to solve their problems.

> I. Cultural values in myths and fairy tales
>   A. Cultural values in myths
>   B. Cultural values in fairy tales
> II. Characters as role models in myths and fairy tales
>   A. Nature of characters
>   1. Superhuman characters in myths
>   2. Realistic characters in fairy tales
>   B. Ability of characters to meet demands
>   1. Failure of characters in myths
>   2. Success of characters in fairy tales

C. Fate of characters
   1. Unhappy endings of myths
   2. Happy endings of fairy tales

You will find an example of the point-by-point method of organizing a comparison in the Sample Literary Research Paper (14f).

CHAPTER 10

PERSONAL ESSAYS

When you write personal essays, you share your thoughts, feelings, and experiences with your readers. But since you are writing an essay, your readers will also expect you to explain what your experience means. As we consider three kinds of personal essays (narrative, descriptive, and reflective), we will discuss how to fulfill your readers' expectations. Since most of your personal essays are likely to be based on events in your life, we will examine narrative essays most closely.

10a Narrative Essays

Like other essays, **narrative essays** must have a point, a main idea. To see why a main idea is important, let's consider an example.

Suppose you decide to write about "My Kayak Trip." The title, as you can see, doesn't suggest any point about the trip. It offers no principle to help you select which events to include and which to leave out, or how to arrange them effectively. So you might begin at the beginning, go on to the end, and stop. But would all the events of your trip, presented in that manner, interest anyone except your best friend?

Imagine, then, that you decide to focus on one incident and write about "A Frightening Kayak Trip." You would now have a way of deciding what to include in your essay, and you might even think about how to present your material—such as describing your nervousness as you approached a patch of white water and then flashing back to the events that led up to that moment. Readers interested in kayaking might find your experience thrilling to read about. But what about readers who will never find themselves in a similar situation?

Think about your harrowing experience. What did you learn from it? There are many possible lessons that you might have learned—the dangers of overconfidence, for instance, or the power of nature, or the joy of unexpected courage. Most of us learn these lessons at some time or another. A main point about

111

what you learned, if it is true to your experience, will give your readers a second level of interest. They will not only find out what happened, but will also discover the meaning of the experience, both for you and for similar experiences in their own lives. This meaning will be the thesis that you state or imply through the telling of your story. It will give readers a new perspective on themselves or the world they live in.

What you have learned should not be a moral tacked on to the end—*From this incident I learned never to kill frogs.* It should emerge from the way you present the concrete details of the experience as well as the specific points you make. Writing *I was frightened* depicts your state of mind much less vividly than writing *Whenever I see little ripples in the river I think of the powerful currents beneath the surface, and my mouth goes dry with fear.* When you convey the unique quality of your experience through details such as these, your readers will understand more readily the meaning of the experience for you.

Writing Narrative Essays: The Process

Follow these guidelines when writing a narrative essay:

1. Focus on a single experience; you will then have room for the wealth of detail you need to make your essay interesting.

2. Make a central point about the meaning of this experience. You may discover this point in the process of writing.

3. Include only events and details relevant to the central point.

4. Provide enough specific details about *who, what, when, where, why,* and *how* for a reader to understand how events and actions relate to the central point.

5. Create interest through vivid, concrete diction (4f), varied sentence patterns (4g), and other devices (4g).

6. Put your thesis at the beginning, at the end, or at the point in the narrative where the meaning of events becomes clear to you.

7. Within this overall structure, arrange your material to create a specific effect, such as suspense, humour, or pathos.

8. Make the sequence of events clear to readers by using transitional words and phrases to indicate time relationships (*the next morning, now that I look back*).

10b Sample Narrative Essay

Unwelcome Guest: The Case of the Snake
by Sydney Singh

In the backwater village in Guyana where I grew up, snakes were not uncommon. But they were rarely seen. They hid from humans, and for a very good reason: we killed them as routinely as we killed rats, mice, and other rodents. In my childhood, I may have killed a dozen snakes or so, but I do not recall the circumstances and details of any of the killings, except the last one. So fresh and vivid is my memory of this particular death that it would appear as if the event occurred only yesterday, and not forty years ago.

It was a very hot day in July, and I was home alone. I came out into the front yard, and there it was: a snake of unusual size, at the edge of the vegetable patch. For a moment I stood still, petrified with fear. The snake was unlike any I had seen before. It was brown as the earth, and larger than the common garden variety: about five feet long and two inches thick. Its head was held erect, a foot from the ground. There was dignity in its posture. Yet, my first impulse was to kill it. And I did.

Armed with a long, heavy piece of firewood, I struck. A sudden blow: a broken back. The snake immediately doubled up in a paroxysm of pain. As it writhed and thrashed in agony, I struck again and again, savagely and unerringly. With each blow, its convulsive struggle grew less and less. Eventually it lay still. I poked its limp body with the end of the stick; it made no movement. The intruder was dead.

Gradually, the thumping of my heart subsided, and my initial fear vanished. I felt quite elated at my daring feat, and could hardly wait for my father to come home so I could proudly show him the victim of my fearless courage. In the interim, I went inside to do some chores. A few minutes later, I came outside to glory in my act of bravery. Much to my horror, I saw another snake near the body of the dead one. I froze in my tracks. The newcomer was identical to the snake I had killed earlier, only slightly smaller. Even in my limited understanding, I recognized it was the female of the species, the mate of the dead snake.

My first thought was to kill her too. But I was arrested by her strange behaviour. She sniffed at the dead snake. Then she nudged him indifferently. When there was no response, she became more aggressive. She nudged him fiercely and frantically, urging him to move. Then realization seemed to dawn on her: her mate was dead. What followed was as incredible as it was fascinating. She threw herself on her mate; then she

113

jumped high in the air and fell upon the body of her lifeless husband. She did this several times, wild with grief. Finally, wearied of her exertions, she gently rested her head on the dead body. After a little while, she slowly slithered into the thick grass and disappeared.

The spectacle of grief was not new to me. I had seen it in the exaggerated wailing of our women at funerals, and in the mournful cries of animals which had lost their young to sickness or starvation. But I had never seen such a display of genuine grief as that shown by the dead snake's companion. Child though I was, I was not without a moral sensibility. I realized, even then, what I had done, and my heart grew sick. It grew even sicker when my father musingly observed that the snakes were merely passing through our yard, on their way to some unknown destination. Later in life, I would refer to them as sojourners.

My father neither commended nor scolded me for my action. But in my guilty conscience I interpreted his words, "Dey was just passin' through," as a tacit expression of disapproval. That night I hardly slept at all. The dead snake and his disconsolate companion tormented my consciousness. I wondered where they came from, where they were going, and what would become of the widow. And then, for the first time, the enormity of my crime sank home: through my wanton act of cruelty, I had killed the husband, leaving the wife to continue, alone and lonely, on a journey they had begun together. There was no thrill in my victory, only a remorse sharper than a serpent's fang.

Many years passed before I realized that my aversion to snakes was associated with a myth that was part of my education. Snakes, we were taught both in school and in church, were our mortal enemies; it was the snake that was responsible for humanity's loss of paradise. According to the Bible, Satan, disguised as a snake, successfully tempted Eve to eat the forbidden fruit, and for his role in her disobedience God pronounced a curse upon the serpent: "And I will put enmity between thee and the woman, and between thy seed and her seed; it shall bruise thy head, and thou shalt bruise his heel" (Genesis 3:15).

This curse has informed our relationship with the snake. Through the ages humans have systematically hunted the snake, and in many parts of the world decimated snake populations, to the detriment of our own survival. Yet there is no record that snakes have hunted men; few people in the world have died from snake bites. But perhaps more important, ever since that episode in the Garden of Eden, the snake has been the archetypal symbol of evil. We associate it with deceit, cunning, and treachery. A person who betrays us, for example, is referred to as "a snake in the grass." A sly person has "beady snake's eyes." It is no exaggeration to say that the snake is perhaps the most maligned creature in the animal kingdom.

Sample
Narrative
Essay

114

Many years ago, in an introductory literature course, I read a poem by D.H. Lawrence entitled "Snake." This poem did not lessen my loathing for snakes, but it gave me a whole new perspective and respect for these creatures, which inhabited the earth eighty million years before the appearance of humans. In the poem, the speaker tells of his encounter with a snake that has come to drink from his water-trough. His first instinct, like mine, is to kill the snake: "The voice of my education said to me, 'He must be killed'." But the speaker, much to his credit, resists the temptation; instead, he feels "honoured" that the snake should seek his hospitality. However, after the snake has drunk its fill and is about to return to the "horrid black hole" from whence it came, the speaker, overcome by "a sort of horror," picks up a log and throws it at the water-trough. He misses the snake, but is still racked with guilt:

I thought how paltry, how vulgar, what a mean act!
I despised myself and the voices of my accursed human education.

The poem concludes with the speaker's regret at the departure of the snake; a wish for its return; and a realization that he has missed a rare opportunity:

And so, I missed my chance with one of the lords
Of life.
And I have something to expiate;
A pettiness.

So do I.

10c Descriptive Essays

If the unifying principle of narrative essays is *what happened to me,* the unifying principle of **descriptive essays** is *what I saw.* Keep this distinction in mind because narrative essays may include descriptions of people, places, and objects, and descriptive essays may include accounts of things happening. In a descriptive essay, however, the focus is on rendering your impressions of some part of the physical world and its meaning for you.

Subjects

You can write descriptive essays about places, people, or other animate and inanimate things. You might write, for example, about the town or neighbourhood in which you grew up to show

115

that the community was either close-knit and friendly, or alien and frightening. You might write a character sketch of a coach who taught you the importance of dedication, or you might focus on a family heirloom to explain its meaning in your life.

Image and Meaning

As in narrative essays, concrete images create meaning more effectively than do direct statements. Specific images of people, places, and objects allow your reader to see through your eyes and thus to understand the basis of your thoughts, feelings, and judgments. In the paragraph that follows, taken from the sample descriptive essay "Smokey Mountain" (10d), the writer uses repeated images of water, culminating in the reference to the hurricane, to convey his complex attitude toward the scene.

> These were the fringe dwellers of Manila, people who survive in an industry brutally isolated from the rest of the population. As I looked down from the safety of my perch high above the swarming crowd, the garbage appeared as faint streams spread across the valley. Bits of tin foil and splintered glass sparkled like breaking waves in the sunlight. The smear of black smoke rising out of spontaneous combustion appeared like thick steam from the water's surface. From where I stood, the whole scene had a certain beauty about it . . . but then, from the right distance, so does a raging hurricane.

This passage emphasizes the way a Canadian observer might feel safely distant from this scene of poverty and squalor. But it also conveys, in the image of the hurricane, the writer's recognition of the potential for violence and upheaval. Because we are encouraged to "see" this meaning for ourselves, the images are more effective than a direct statement of the author's reactions would be.

Organization

For short descriptive essays, such as "Smokey Mountain" (10d), it often works well to allow the meaning of the whole to emerge gradually from the accumulation of details. But to maintain readers' interest in longer descriptive essays, you may need to state your main point near the beginning and bring in other methods of development—such as a comparison of one person with another, or an analysis of the effects of a shifting population on a town.

Whatever overall structure you choose, you should arrange the parts of the essay by an appropriate principle of organization, usually spatial. This spatial organization may be literal (you could move from one part of the town to the next) or figurative (you could move from what is "easy to see" about a person to what is "hard to see"). Most important, your method of organization should culminate in an image that conveys the dominant impression you want to create.

10d Sample Descriptive Essay

Smokey Mountain
by Bill Howe

The young boy struggled up the side of the hill. His legs were straining under the weight of the sack he had slung over his shoulders, and his one arm was flailing to catch his balance as he teetered over the narrow path. His shirt and trousers were soiled with sweat and dirt, and his legs were buried deep inside his oversized rubber boots. A floppy cap sagged over the side of his blackened face, hiding the scowl of dignified scorn he directed at the intruders. He quickly turned away and made off towards a sculpture of bed springs, tires, and scrap metal.

The hill I was standing on is known to the Filipinos as Smokey Mountain. It has been built up over many years from garbage deposits delivered from the streets of Metro Manila. Over eight million people contribute every day to this towering masterpiece, but its dismal appearance has not discouraged the poor who find their home within its refuge of waste. A population of some 15 000 squatters has developed into a thriving community, complete with a division of labour natural to such territory. There are people who sort through the garbage for cherished bits of plastic and metal, people who work in the distribution centres selling salvaged goods to local recycling plants, and people who go out into the streets at night to collect the garbage from the richer districts before it is diluted by the rest of the collection.

Most of the people migrated here to escape the hopeless life in the remote provinces, only to find the economic depression of their new surroundings worse than what they had left behind. The putrid smell of rotting debris wafting through the air continually reminds them of their own decay. The villagers are plagued with diseases contracted in their own backyard. On a good day, their labour might earn them only two or three dollars, but still they consider themselves fortunate to be able to

117

earn money at all. The people appear proud and content with their life, and the children play in the garbage pile as if it were a giant sandbox filled with buried toys.

From where I stood, I had a panoramic view of the flow of garbage below. The convoy of tawny yellow dump trucks formed a brilliant streak which faded into the distant skyline of Manila. As the trucks dropped off their loads, people eagerly surrounded the untouched deposits, in hopes of discovering some carelessly discarded treasure to take home to their families. Tin cans, tires, wooden crates, plastic bottles, discarded clothing—nothing was overlooked for its value on the salvage market.

Attacking the hill from below was a huge bulldozer burrowing into the debris like a mechanical mole. As it lurched forward, it uncovered a trail of pristine spoil, its rutted tracks quickly filling with pools of mud freshly squeezed from the rubble below. The people followed the beast as though it was their master. As their bent frames waded slowly through the soggy mess, they seemed enslaved to the garbage beneath their feet, imprisoned by their own poverty.

These were the fringe dwellers of Manila, people who survive in an industry brutally isolated from the rest of the population. As I looked down from the safety of my perch high above the swarming crowd, the garbage appeared as faint streams spread across the valley. Bits of tin foil and splintered glass sparkled like breaking waves in the sunlight. The smear of black smoke rising out of spontaneous combustion ap-peared like thick steam from the water's surface. From where I stood, the whole scene had a certain beauty about it . . . but then, from the right distance, so does a raging hurricane.

One of the dump trucks passed me as I was leaving the smouldering mountain. I grinned to myself as I read the words inscribed across its side boards—"Manila on the Go!"

10e Reflective Essays

If narrative essays present a person acting, and descriptive essays present a person perceiving, **reflective essays** present a mind thinking and feeling about a particular subject. The emphasis shifts from the outer world to the inner world.

Subjects

Reflective essays allow you to explore the meaning of your experiences through methods other than narration and description. You might define what friendship means to you, for instance, by discussing the qualities and behaviour that characterize relations between friends. Or you might explore the meaning of friendship by classifying your friends, by comparing friends and acquaintances, or by developing an analogy such as "a friend is like a favourite pair of shoes." Or you might evaluate your own behaviour as a friend.

Another way of reflecting upon your experience is to focus upon causes and/or effects: what causes you to be a good or poor student or employee? what causes you to act outrageously or timidly? what are the effects in your life of being Native, White, Sikh, Asian, Black, French-Canadian? of being Catholic, atheist, Jewish, Muslim? of being an immigrant or Canadian-born? of growing up in a certain time, place, family, social class? of having your particular body, mind, temperament?

Organization

Because the emphasis in reflective essays is on thinking and feeling, you may find yourself shifting back and forth between making generalizations and giving specific details. To give the sense of a person thinking and feeling, you may allow the structure of your essay to mirror the sometimes unexpected movements of your mind. The trick is to find a balance between too loose a structure that lets the essay fall apart and too tight a structure that stifles your personal voice. Try using one of the patterns for leading up to your thesis (9b), the block or the point-by-point method of organizing comparisons (9c), or the weighing of alternatives characteristic of evaluation (7b).

10f Sample Reflective Essay

In this essay (a shortened version), the writer reflects upon the effects of living with—and without—a diagnosis of a disability. As she searches for a language for her experience, she moves back and forth between past and present. Transitions guide readers through these shifts in time.

A Language of My Own
by Camille Collett

I remember the day that I was diagnosed. Labelled. Legitimized. Before anyone had a name for my inability to function in normative situations

119

(whatever those are), I was just different. *Extremely shy and withdrawn*. I was different and completely outside of the world that everyone else appeared implicitly to understand. *A good little girl—quiet and reserved*. These words described what others saw, but they did not describe the chaos of my inner world.

By the time I was old enough to understand that thinking was a process, I really believed that everyone else in the world thought the same way that I did. This meant that everyone had thousands of thoughts occurring simultaneously—like a wall of televisions all tuned to different channels blasting images and noise. The fixed volume on all the units made it difficult to differentiate one unit from another. Thinking, for me, was a process of focusing on one noise for a brief moment of absorption, without any retention, before, distracted, my thought pattern clicked onto a different television unit. As material became more detailed, my attention span diminished even further. As a consequence, I became a wealth of information that I could not organize or communicate except by impulsively blurting out facts which were unconnected and irrelevant to the events around me.

Eventually, life became too complicated to compensate for what was going on inside my head. At four, I could play piano sonatas by ear. But when I tried to learn to read music and consciously pay attention to what both hands were doing, I became frustrated and angry. No one would understand that the notes dancing off the page were art in and of themselves, engaging my curiosity. I became absorbed in a process of meaning that I didn't understand. Overwhelmed, I retreated and lived inside of myself. Inside I could make it calm and quiet.

After seventeen years of the qualified professionals asserting that I merely typified the shy, quiet young woman, someone heard me. Someone listened to my voice. The diagnosis validated the experiences that went unseen. Attention Deficit Disorder (ADD). Three small words became an identification number, indelible marks on my body: a woman with a behavioural and learning disability.

ADD, or ADHD (Attention Deficit Hyperactivity Disorder), as it is also called, results from developmental deficiencies that make it hard to inhibit, initiate, or sustain responses to tasks or stimuli, especially when there are few consequences. In other words, having weak internal mechanisms for regulating behaviour, children with ADD often act impulsively and have trouble concentrating on tasks unless their environment is highly structured. Although the medical community cannot agree on the actual cause of ADHD, recent research reported in the *Globe and Mail* suggests that ADHD may be linked to a deficit in a gene that regulates the body's use of thyroid hormone. According to the *Globe and*

Mail, this is the first time that a "specific inborn flaw has been linked to a common behavioural problem." Inborn flaw. Flawed merchandise. Quality control down. The words "common behavioural problem" are inadequate. The words imply that all ill-mannered and rude children are the result of a bad gene pool. Simultaneously, words mean too much and not enough.

The signs had been there since I was born, but the medical community was blinded by expectation. I was a textbook case. My failure to thrive became a "milk allergy" and my refusal to eat was "normal." My nature came to be described as quiet and reserved (like a good little girl) rather than as withdrawn and removed. Except when people, uninvited, tried to invade my interior space, and then I would rage like a wild beast until I was left alone. Ambidextrous until I was eight, I was tested for brain dominance—not because I used both hands, but because it took me so long to decide which hand to use that I never did anything in school. The testing successfully determined that my right hand was dominant by 1%. Of course testing can only do so much, and deciding which hand to use was replaced by which color crayon to use and later, in junior high school, by whether to use pen or pencil. I wanted to think, but it hurt my head, so I absorbed myself in books. Books became my reality and I lived inside them.

When I ventured outside the world of books and tried to talk about my frustration, I was invisible. I was white. I was blonde. I was the child of two highly educated individuals. According to the experts, I was merely the typically rebellious child of pushy parents. When I disagreed, I was told that girls don't have to do math and science. When I said I wanted to, I was told I couldn't know what I wanted because I was the child of pushy parents. When I said that the only person I was disappointing was myself, I was told that at fifteen I couldn't possibly have that kind of self-awareness.

Disability is one of those silent words that no one speaks. At least not around me. Feeling invisible, I wait for someone to speak in a language that recognizes, even if it doesn't always understand, difference. A language that I can speak as a woman with a disability. Without that language, my head is filled with speaking silence. Awkward silence. The kind of silence that follows the disclosure of difference, eyes shifting away from the body that spoke. Yet, I feel uncomfortable asserting my identification with disabled women because it reduces all of us to a common denominator. I am also afraid that the community I identify with the most will refuse to recognize the disability that cannot be seen. Medication is my only visible link to that community. I am afraid of being invisible.

121

Some people believe that I should rejoice in my invisibility, that I should consider it a luxury that I don't have to deal with the challenges of being visually or physically disabled in an abled world. They don't understand that access to the world is something I fight for every day, because unlike the stairs that exclude the crippled, the barriers that exclude a woman with learning disabilities are unseen.

Searching for a language true to my experience, I turn to writers who challenge this kind of unquestioned cultural authority. Women writers like Audre Lorde, Toni Morrison, and Adrienne Rich have found a language for their self-awareness. Donna Williams' *Nobody Nowhere*, which describes her experience growing up with autism, was a special gift, a validation from someone who understands unseen difference on her own individual terms.

The language that I await, the language that will allow me to bridge the gap between my inner world and the world outside, is beginning to come. Being disabled is a different life experience. It is a unique perspective in a world where perception is often taken for granted.

10f

Sample
Reflective
Essay

CHAPTER 11

EXPOSITORY ESSAYS

When you write an expository essay, your purpose is to explain something to a particular audience. Your subject might be a short story, an historical event, a current situation, a theory. To move beyond saying what your subject is to saying what it means, you need to use methods of development such as analysis, comparison, and definition. (For a reminder of these methods, see chapter 6, Methods of Explaining.) The meaning you see in your subject—your interpretation of it—serves as the thesis for your essay.

11a Writing Expository Essays: The Process

Regardless of the subject of your expository essay, the steps in the process of formulating your thesis and organizing your material are the same.

Choosing a Primary Method of Development and a Focus

Some essay assignments state or imply a primary method of development and a focus (*Compare legislation governing impaired driving in Ontario and Quebec*). Others simply give a list of possible subjects (*Native land claims*), leaving you to choose your focus. If a primary method of development is not given or implied, make notes on what each method of explaining could contribute to your essay.

You might begin work on an expository essay on child poverty, for example, by making the following list:

Method of Development	Possible Material
Process Analysis	Not applicable?
Systems Analysis	How agencies dealing with the needs of poor children fit into the system of social services

Writing Expository Essays: The Process

123

Method of Development	Possible Material
Causal Analysis	What causes poverty among children
	How poverty affects children's short-term and long-term development
	How poverty among children affects society as a whole
Classification	Child poverty by region
	Child poverty by types of households
Comparison	Differences in the development of impoverished children and middle-class children
	Child poverty in Mexico and Canada
Definition	Meaning of poverty

From a list of possibilities, such as that given above, you need to choose a focus for your essay. If you are writing for a newspaper or a magazine, you can let your own interests and your assumptions about the interests of your readers guide your choice. Suppose you were writing on child poverty for *Chatelaine*. Your reader profile might suggest that most of its readers were middle-class women with children. To appeal to their interests, you might decide to focus on differences in the development of middle-class children and impoverished children. Your primary method of development would therefore be comparison.

When you are writing an essay for a course, on the other hand, you are likely to choose a focus that reflects the concerns, objectives, or methodology of that field of study. Sociologists, for example, study the relationships between groups and society as a whole. For a sociology course, you might focus on what causes child poverty or how child welfare agencies fit into the system of social services. For these topics, analysis would be your primary method of development.

Gathering Material

There are many sources of material for expository essays. For subjects you are familiar with, brainstorming will often give you enough information. From working in restaurants, for example, you could write an essay explaining why staff turnovers are rapid or why some restaurants fail and others succeed. For course-related subjects, you may find material by asking systematic discovery questions (see Essays Analyzing Literature, 11c, and Position Papers, 13d).

But sometimes you may have to gather information from other sources. You can conduct interviews (12a) and other types of field research for material on subjects of local interest. And of course there's a wealth of print material on most subjects (see Compiling a Working Bibliography, 14b).

However you gather material, keep your focus and method of development in mind. They will help you decide what information is relevant to your essay.

Formulating a Thesis

Once you have gathered various bits of information, you need to ask yourself what they add up to. This process of synthesizing your material will lead you to a main idea, a thesis. A good thesis for an expository essay should **explain** some aspect of your subject: why one definition of a controversial term is better than another; how the setting in a short story contributes to the theme; what causes abusive relationships among family members. It should state an opinion about your subject and give reasons that set the limits of your discussion. A statement such as *Child poverty has many causes* does neither. In contrast, this thesis states an opinion and clearly defines the scope of the essay: *Child poverty has many causes: among them are parental lack of responsibility; scarcity of convenient, subsidized child-care facilities; inadequate social assistance programs; and an economy increasingly reliant on low-paying, part-time jobs in the service sector.*

Including Other Methods of Development

You can often write your first draft using only your primary method of development. When you revise, however, you may discover that to explain the meaning of your subject clearly and fully, you need to add definitions of terms (*poverty, adequate nutrition*), comparisons (*rates of language development in middle-class children and poor children*), or other material. To create interest, you may use the methods for sharing personal experience we discussed in chapter 5. In writing about child poverty, for instance, you could tell a story about a child's visit to a food bank, describe the child's living conditions, or use an analogy such as "For a child, being poor is like living with a chronic and debilitating disease." The sample expository essay shows how you can bring a human dimension to an abstract concept such as child poverty. Readers—even most instructors!—will appreciate the human touch. If you are unsure whether this approach would be appropriate for a course-related essay, ask your instructor.

Organizing Your Essay

Expository essays written for college and university courses are usually organized with the thesis up front in the introduction, topic sentences showing how each middle paragraph relates to the thesis, and a restatement and extension of the thesis in the conclusion. This method of organization offers your instructor a well-defined framework and emphasizes what he or she is most interested in—your interpretation.

If you are writing in a different situation or for a different type of reader, you may want to consider leading readers through your explanation before you state your thesis in the conclusion. (For more information on both these methods of organization, see chapter 9, Essay Structure.)

Let's consider the choices facing the writer of the sample expository essay "The Effects of Child Poverty." This piece, based on interviews and first-hand observation, was intended for readers of a local newspaper. Since many readers would not have any direct experience of poverty and thus might not understand its grim realities, the writer begins with facts and details that lead gradually to the thesis.

11b Sample Expository Essay

The Effects of Child Poverty

Jimmy is a two-year-old living with his mother and baby sister in government-subsidized housing. The complex is reasonably well maintained if you ignore the rusting shopping carts abandoned here and there, and the mattresses soaking up rain in the disposal bins. Today is a good day at Jimmy's place because there is food in the fridge. A week from now the fridge will be empty and it will be ten days before the child tax credit comes through. It is now about two o'clock and Jimmy has been staring at the soaps for three hours. His mother feels she should turn off the television and take him to the playground, but he outgrew his rain boots a couple of months ago. Not that the playground offers much for him to do: two of the three swings are broken, the slide is gritty, and the sand around it is pebbled with shards of broken beer bottles. The local library has plenty of books for children, but it's five kilometres away and his mother has no money for bus fare. The relief day care centre is closer and it has other children for him to play with, but his mother is reluctant to take his sister there because she has run out of baby food and does not want anyone to know.

Jimmy's situation helps to define child poverty in Canada. The problem is not just that Jimmy is missing out on the extras. His family fits the federal government's definition of poverty: more than half his mother's monthly income is spent on food, shelter, and clothing. Even so, the children are poorly clothed and fed. Because most poor children in Canada live in single-parent families headed by women, Jimmy's situation is fairly typical. In 1989, the International Year of the Child, the House of Commons unanimously passed a resolution to end child poverty in Canada by the year 2000. Ten years later, according to a report on the progress of Campaign 2000, the number of poor children in Canada had increased by 60 percent (Deanna Shorten, "Children and Poverty," *Our Voice,* May 1999, p. 7). The year 2000 has passed; child poverty remains.

How does poverty affect Jimmy? How does poverty affect all children? How does poverty affect our society?

Let's begin with the basic physical needs for shelter, clothing, and food. Jimmy's need for shelter has been met by the subsidized housing his mother was lucky to get. The reduction in rent does not, however, give her more money to spend on food and clothing. The amount of the subsidy is just subtracted from her welfare cheque. At two, Jimmy doesn't worry about designer labels, but his mother worries about replacing the rain boots and snowsuit he's outgrown. Without appropriate clothing, Jimmy won't be able to attend a play group when he turns three. Jimmy's opportunities are thus limited by a scarcity of clothing.

Meanwhile, what happens if Jimmy doesn't get enough to eat? Children between one and three, according to nutritionists, need 4-5 servings of grain products, 4-5 servings of vegetables and fruits,

127

2 servings of meat or meat alternatives, and 3 servings of milk products every day. Of course, these servings are quite small (half an apple, one third of a cup of dry cereal), but a child needs food from all the food groups every day. Unlike adults, who can cope reasonably well with periodic food shortages, a child deprived of food will be stunted both physically and intellectually. After a week of crackers and bargain macaroni dinners, Jimmy is lethargic, uninterested in his toys, and only too willing to park himself in front of the television. He falls asleep when his mother tries to read to him. He is among the one in three children in Edmonton who, according to the Edmonton Social Planning Council, are malnourished (Shorten, p. 7). At two, going on three, most children can understand complex sentences and repeat simple ones. If they've been read to, they can identify a picture of an elephant or a farm. The effects of Jimmy's nutritional deficiencies show up in his inability to talk in sentences and the limitations in his vocabulary. He can't identify a picture of a horse or pick out a red crayon.

The widening gap between what Jimmy knows and what other children his age know means that he's likely to do poorly in grade one. Children who are tired, cold, and hungry can't learn much. Schools are increasingly called upon to provide children with a place to sleep, warm clothing, and food. In some schools, teachers spend much of their time trying to meet children's physical needs. Moreover, many children like Jimmy succeed in school only if they get extra instruction. But as schools try to do more with less money, helping some children often means depriving others. In Jimmy's neighbourhood school, funding for a teacher's aide was taken from money originally earmarked for library materials. As a result of the poverty of some children, educational opportunities for all children decline.

The broader effects of poverty are also visible in the current strains on the health care system. For example, inadequate nutrition for expectant mothers often results in low birth-weight babies. Research studies indicate that such babies not only need more hospital care at birth, but may also need more hospital care as adults. In a low birth-weight baby, organs such as the liver may not be fully functioning. The baby with the underdeveloped liver is more likely to need a coronary bypass as a middle-aged adult. Expensive, high-tech procedures that drive up health care costs are thus, in part, the effect of a diet of crackers and macaroni.

The costs of poverty extend far beyond welfare cheques and rent subsidies. Poverty creates a cycle of deprivation, failure, and despair. Children raised in poverty are more likely to become part of a permanent underclass of people who no longer believe they can break out of the poverty cycle. The effects of poverty, however, are not confined to the poor. Limitations in education and health care decrease the quality of life available to all citizens.

Purpose and Audience

When you write an essay on a piece of literature, your purpose is not to describe its content but to explain some part of its meaning. By reading the piece carefully, you develop a general sense of its major themes, such as the theme "character is fate" that runs through Thomas Hardy's novels. Then you analyze the work, or a portion of it, such as a scene of a play or the setting of a novel, by asking questions like those below. As a result of this analysis, you can refine your sense of theme and show how you arrived at your interpretation.

Since you are writing primarily for an instructor familiar with the work, you may be unsure of how much to say. You don't need to provide all the details you would for someone who had never read it, but you do need to use quotations and examples to show how you arrived at your interpretation.

Writing about Literature: The Process

When you analyze imaginative works of literature, you concentrate on their aesthetic qualities and moral implications. When you analyze works of nonfiction, such as essays, research articles, and proposals, you may focus more on the validity of the arguments they present. You will find suggestions about how to analyze and evaluate nonfiction in Summaries (12c) and Position Papers (13d).

You can write a more effective essay on imaginative works by following these steps:

1. *Decide on a focus and a method of development.*
Most assignments in introductory literature courses give you a focus. You may be asked to explain how one or more elements, such as the setting, characterization, or title, relate to the theme of the work as a whole. The method of development for this type of literary criticism is **analysis,** the division of something into its parts in order to explain the whole more clearly. For example, you might analyze the structure and imagery of a poem to explain how they contribute to the theme.

In addition to analysis, some topics require **comparison:** *Compare the theme of initiation in stories X and Y.* Other topics will ask you to assess the strengths and weaknesses of a

11c

Essays Analyzing Literature

work: *Which film version of* Macbeth *presents a better interpretation of the thematic implications of Lady Macbeth's madness?* For this topic, in addition to analysis and comparison, you would use **evaluation** as a method to develop your ideas.

Topics such as these provide specific directions about what to focus on and how to develop your ideas. If your topic is more general, such as *Discuss three poems by Margaret Atwood,* use the discovery questions on pp. 131–132 to help you find a focus.

2. *Analyze the relevant element(s) or section(s) of the work.*

Use as a guide the discovery questions for imaginative literature given in the next section.

3. *Formulate a thesis.*

The thesis should make a point about the theme of the work and about how each element you have analyzed conveys that theme. Be sure that you have not merely restated the essay topic (for example, *This essay will analyze the use of landscape in a poem by Margaret Atwood*) or made a vague generalization (*Many poets use landscape to express a theme and mood in their poetry*). To direct your reader's attention to a specific use of landscape and thus to limit the content of the essay, you would need a thesis such as this one: *In Margaret Atwood's poem "Journey to the Interior," landscape mirrors the struggle against depression.*

4. *Organize your essay.*

In your introduction, give the authors and titles of all the works you plan to discuss and establish the **focus** of your essay. Put your thesis at the end of your introduction.

In the body of your essay, keep your reader's attention focused on your subject by beginning each paragraph with a topic sentence that identifies one aspect of your subject. If you were writing an essay on colour symbolism in *The Great Gatsby,* for instance, each middle paragraph might begin with a topic sentence that stated the significance of a particular colour in the novel.

> White symbolizes Daisy's empty life and the dream Gatsby associates with her.

> Throughout the novel, gold symbolizes money.

> Red suggests both the glittering wealth of rubies and the blood of harsh reality.

Good topic sentences focus your reader's attention on the function of an element.

NOT   This poem has five stanzas. [descriptive summary]
NOT   In the first stanza, the speaker talks about . . . [narrative summary]
BUT   Each stanza of the poem represents a different stage of life. [analysis]

Give reasons, details, examples, and quotations to support each interpretative point that you make in your middle paragraphs. Be sure to clearly link the point and the supporting evidence.

In your conclusion, restate your thesis and summarize your most important points. If appropriate, suggest a broader context into which your interpretation fits (*The distrust of conventional values that we have seen is typical of the postwar period*).

Discovery Questions: Imaginative Literature

Subject What is this work about?

Genre What kind of work is this (descriptive essay, revenge tragedy, dramatic monologue)? What are the characteristics of this genre?

Setting What is the time, place, and social environment in which the work is set? (Alice Munro's *Lives of Girls and Women* is set among the working poor in rural Ontario in the late 1940s and 1950s.) What effect does the setting have on characters' lives? What values are associated with different times, places, or social environments? In drama and film, what do costumes, lighting, sets, and music contribute to the setting?

Structure How is the work put together?

Narrative/Dramatic Structure: What sets the plot in motion? What are the main events? Does the plot reach a crisis? How are the events arranged (chronologically, shifting from present to past, shifting from main plot to subplots)? What is the underlying issue or purpose that connects the events (a spiritual quest, a critique of society, a revelation of the main character's true nature)?

Poetic Structure: How are the thoughts and feelings organized? Why does the poem begin and end as it does? Does the structure follow the conventions of a particular kind of poem (an Italian sonnet, for example)?

11c

Essays Analyzing Literature

Characterization What are the characters like? Is there a broad range of characters? How would you classify them? Are the characters given depth and complexity or are they stereotypes? What techniques are used to portray them (appearance, characteristic actions, speech, opinions of others, self-revelation)? Do characters change? What do we learn about the workings of race, class, gender, or other factors from the way characters live their lives?

Point of View Whose eyes do we see through? Whose voice do we hear? In stories and novels, this voice is referred to as the narrator. Because you cannot be sure that the voice you hear in a poem is the poet's, it is customary to use the term *speaker* when you refer to the point of view in a poem.

Is the narrator (stories, novels) or the speaker (poetry) a participant, referring to himself or herself as "I"? How reliable is this narrator or speaker?

Is the narrator or speaker a non-participant, referring to the characters as *he, she,* or *they*? Is the narrator/speaker omniscient, seeing into the minds of all the characters? Does the narrator/speaker comment directly on the characters or the action?

Style (Diction and Sentence Structure) What are the effects of language level (formal, standard, informal) and word choice? Are there any unusual or especially effective words? In poetry, what effects are achieved through the sounds of words? How does word choice contribute to the characterization, setting, and theme? What are the effects of sentence patterns? Does the writer favour long, complex sentences or short, simple ones? Are sentence fragments used to create emphasis, excitement, informality? Is parallelism used distinctively? (For more information on the effects of variations in sentence pattern, see Improving Your Sentence Structure, 4g). In poetry, how are lines and stanzas used? In films and plays, what are the effects of the pacing of dialogue and action? How do these elements of language contribute to characterization, setting, and theme?

Style (Imagery and Symbolism) Does the writer use any significant figures of speech (similes, metaphors, personification)? (For more information on figurative language, see Adding Interest, 4g). Do images and symbols create patterns of meaning? How do imagery and symbolism contribute to the characterization, setting, and theme?

Theme What is the central idea of the work?

Integrating Secondary Sources

If you wish to integrate other critics' interpretations into your essay, you will find help in Integrating Research Material (14e) and in the sample literary research paper "*Tom Sawyer* and *Anne of Green Gables:* Two Models of Heroism" (14f). For information on how to cite your sources, see appendices B and C.

11d Sample Essay Analyzing Literature

The following sample essay demonstrates how you can analyze a piece of writing to show how the author develops a theme. Here is the poem the essay analyzes:

Warren Pryor

When every pencil meant a sacrifice
his parents boarded him in town
slaving to free him from the stony fields
the meager acreage that bore them down.

They blushed with pride when, at his graduation,
they watched him picking up the slender scroll,
his passport from the years of brutal toil
and lonely patience in a barren hole.

When he went in the Bank their cups ran over.
They marvelled how he wore a milk-white shirt
work days and jeans on Sundays. He was saved
from their thistle-strewn farm and its red dirt.

And he said nothing. Hard and serious
like a young bear inside his teller's cage,
his axe-hewn hands upon the paper bills
aching with empty strength and throttled rage.

—*Alden Nowlan*

Wasted Sacrifices in "Warren Pryor"

In his poem "Warren Pryor," Alden Nowlan explores the sad consequences of good intentions. Like most parents, Warren's parents want the best for him. Their vision of a good life for their son, however, is

133

based on what they imagine he wants, not what he really wants. For this reason, their sacrifices create a trap of duty from which Warren cannot escape. Every element in this poem—structure, sound patterns, rhythm, diction, and imagery—reinforces the central irony: children who are forced to fulfill their parents' dreams end up with lives as imprisoning as those their parents dreamed of escaping.

Nowlan develops the contrast between what Warren wants and what his parents want for him through the sequence of events and shift in point of view that create the structure of the poem. The poem begins with Warren's parents painfully scraping together the money for their son to live in town and complete high school. The second stanza is devoted to their enormous pleasure and pride when he graduates and gains "his passport from the years of brutal toil" (l. 7). In the third stanza, when Warren gets a job in a bank, his parents "marvel" that he now wears his good clothes every day but Sunday. The final lines of this stanza, which describe the parents' triumph at rescuing their son from "their thistle-strewn farm," mark the turning point of the poem.

In the fourth stanza, Nowlan abruptly shifts the point of view and at last we see Warren himself: caged, miserable, strangled by his parents' sacrifices. The rigid structure of the poem emphasizes the imprisonment Warren feels as he paces in his teller's cage. Most of the lines have ten syllables. Every stanza has four lines and the same rhyme scheme: abcb. The rhythm of the lines, especially in the first two stanzas, is mostly regular iambic pentameter:

> ˘   / ˘   /   ˘   /   ˘   / ˘ /
> When every pencil meant a sacrifice
> ˘   /   ˘   /   ˘   / ˘ /
> his parents boarded him in town

When the point of view shifts in the fourth stanza, so does the rhythm: "And he said nothing." The extra stressed syllables and the dramatic pause within the line give us a vivid sense of Warren's agony.

Both the diction and imagery of "Warren Pryor" emphasize the theme of wasted sacrifices. The words describing the farm—"stony fields," "meager acreage," "barren hole," "thistle-strewn"—make it easy for us to see the hardships his parents have endured. Surely his assistance would have made their lives easier; instead, they "slaved" in "lonely patience" to "free" their son. The allusion to the Twenty-Third Psalm in the comment "their cups ran over" suggests their complete happiness when Warren secures a job in a bank. Indeed, the cup of their contentment spills over the "milk-white shirt" he wears to work.

By comparing Warren to a "young bear," Nowlan suggests that the son is by nature unsuited for the job his parents delight in. The simile stresses his youth, power, wildness. He is both literally in a cage—the barred cubicle bank tellers used to work in—and figuratively imprisoned by his parents' expectations. The idea that Warren is trapped in a bank seems especially apt, for he will spend his life paying for the sacrifices his parents have made for him. The metaphors describing Warren's hands emphasize his sacrifices. His hands are "axe-hewn" (strong and roughly made), suggesting that he is better suited to wielding an axe than handling paper bills. His hands are "aching with empty strength" because, in the irony that concludes the poem, he longs to do exactly the work his parents' sacrifices have kept him from. As he strangles his frustration, he sacrifices his own desires so that his parents can keep their illusions.

Nowlan develops the real sadness of wasted sacrifices through every element of "Warren Pryor." Through the first three stanzas, we share the parents' pleasure in their own accomplishments. The central irony of the poem, of course, is that they have gained their happiness at the expense of their son's. Throughout the poem, Nowlan's skillful diction and imagery emphasize the sad reality of what their sacrifices have actually accomplished. While they congratulate themselves on rescuing him, Warren paces within the cage his parents' sacrifices have created for him. In a few short lines, Nowlan vividly captures the all-too-common conflict between parents' expectations and their child's fulfillment.

11d

*Sample
Essay
Analyzing
Literature*

CHAPTER 12

OTHER TYPES OF EXPOSITORY WRITING

12a Interviews

When you are writing an expository essay, interviews can provide additional information and create interest. Conducting an interview, or a series of interviews, is often the best way to obtain information about local people, issues, and events. If you were writing an essay on the Cree Circle Dance for an anthropology class, for instance, you might supplement your reading by arranging to interview participants, spectators, and Cree elders about its significance. Interviews are also interesting as self-contained pieces of writing, because they allow readers to enter into another person's world.

Conducting a good interview takes planning. Here are some guidelines.

Preparing for the Interview

1. *Choose your informant carefully.* The most obvious choice is not always the best one. The drummer in a band, for instance, may have shrewder insights into the band's strengths and weaknesses than the lead singer. If possible, ask someone knowledgeable about your subject for names of people who would make good informants.

2. *Make a list of questions that will give you the information you need.* To help you both relax, start the interview with straightforward questions you already know the answer to. Limit your list to a small number of topics that will allow you to shape your material to suit your purpose. Alternate key questions with less relevant ones, so that you can finish your notes on important points while your informant answers the next question. Finally, avoid asking questions that can be answered yes or no. Instead, ask open-ended questions that

12a

Interviews

invite full responses: "How do you see the band developing over the next few years?"

3. **Decide whether to take notes or to tape record the interview.** Your choice will depend on how comfortable you and your informant feel with each method and how you plan to use the material. Transcribing an interview is quite time-consuming, so if you plan to use only a few direct quotes and paraphrase the rest of the material, taking notes should be sufficient. Tape the session if you want a lengthy first-hand account of the informant's experiences, or if you plan to present your material in a question-and-answer format. Taping is also wise if misquoting your informant could cause trouble. Test the equipment ahead of time so that you and your informant won't be distracted by technical problems.

4. **When you request an interview, identify yourself and your project.** Explain why the interview is important and how you will use the information. Give the person a sense of what you already know about the subject so that he or she will know how technical to be in response to your questions.

5. **Arrange a convenient time and place for the interview and suggest how long you think the interview will take.**

Conducting the Interview

1. Express appreciation for the interview.

2. Tell the person again how you will use the information, and assure him or her that confidential information will remain confidential.

3. Refer to your list of questions as necessary, but don't stick to it so rigidly that the interview becomes boring.

4. Ask your informant to clarify, expand upon, or give examples of points. Specific details bring interviews to life.

5. If you are taking notes, don't try to write down everything your informant says. Jot down facts and opinions as you would in taking notes for a course, using key words and ideas to

help you remember the context (and write up your notes before you forget!). Take down a few direct quotations to capture the informant's personality and point of view. Before you end the interview, review your notes with your informant to make sure they are accurate and complete.

6. If appropriate, jot down details of the person's appearance, actions, manner of speaking, and the place so that you can include them in your piece.

Writing Up the Interview

You can present interview material in a variety of ways: in a question-and-answer format; as an edited transcript; or as an essay combining quotations, paraphrased material, background information, and a character description. You are probably most familiar with the question-and-answer format. This form, which works like a dialogue between you and your informant, is effective when you want to ask probing questions about a series of topics. The edited transcript, in contrast, allows your informant to tell a story without interruption, with you providing an introduction. Using the third method, you can select and arrange your descriptions and interview material to emphasize points you want to make.

Here are some guidelines for writing up your interview:

1. Use only the material that best suits the purpose of the piece you are writing.

2. Combine material from different parts of the interview if doing so allows you to explain a point more fully.

3. You may edit direct quotations to eliminate repetition, correct obvious mistakes, and so forth, as long as you do not distort the meaning or lose the flavour of the original.

4. If you discover that you need to check facts or fill in missing information, make a list of questions and call your informant. Try to call only once.

After the interview, write a brief letter to the person you interviewed, expressing your thanks. If possible, send the person a courtesy copy of the piece in which you used the information.

Interviews

138

12b Sample Interview

The following piece illustrates an interview written in essay form. It gives a vivid sense of its subject, a young immigrant from India. See if you can figure out what questions the interviewer asked.

Conveniently Canadian
by Todd Babiak

"I guess the first thing I did was look at girls. Right off the plane."

Bobby Mehra squints his eyes and smiles, head bobbing to the Pearl Jam song. As he thinks of something to say, he spies on the skater kids who are crowded around the slushie machine.

"In India we didn't have that freedom. They say you're too young for that. Man, back there when you're fourteen, you don't even think about them, let alone look at them, you know, sexually. You deny a lot there. They say it's improper. Unless you're a poverty kid. Not to brag or anything, but my dad had a high job, eh. We were well off in India. We gave up a lot to come here, but I prefer the freedom. Not only to look at girls when you're fourteen, but other freedoms too. You know."

Bobby is seventeen. Since arriving in Canada four years ago, he has perfected his English, lost his Hindi accent, and forgotten how to write his native language. Every Saturday he works in the Mac's store his parents operate. Along with his convenience store shirt, he wears baggy green pants and Doc Martens with a two-inch sole. Carefully constructed sideburns highlight his amply gelled short hair.

"Here there is so much style. Back in India, the only magazines we ever read were comic books. What you look like is so important here. Another difference is the studies. Studies were way harder there. When you're young, and you're good middle class, you don't have parties, you don't drink, you don't smoke. You have to be twenty-one there to buy a pack of smokes, eh. I guess I still have a bit of that in me. Peer pressure doesn't do anything to me; I've never taken a drink in my life. I've been everywhere, all the bars, but I don't drink. Basically, it's just so different to be young there. You don't get depressed about girls or working or money. You just work on your studies like crazy. Now I'm used to the Canadian way. I'm lazier."

Bobby turns up the radio when a U2 song comes on, his favourite group. As customers present him with bread, sour cream, super size Cokes and French Onion Sun Chips, he comments on the heat, the melting snow. *I can't believe how nice it is. Hope it stays this way.*

"My parents are the coolest people I know. I had my first girlfriend a year after I came here. They were like, *This is Canada*. My dad said, *You are completely independent, whatever you do you are still my son*. It's not like that with all brown kids. I mean I can't date a my-own-race girl. Once I tried. Basically, she was Muslim and we had to keep it a total secret. Not just because I'm Hindu but if you're from India, young girls don't date. She was pretty cool but we got nailed—her dad found out. It was awful. One thing about her I didn't like is that she was mad, disgusted, when she found out I'd had white girlfriends. She only dated brown guys. I hate that shit."

He replaces the coffee filters, checks prices on sour candies and wipes counters as he talks. He likes working. After he graduates from high school this summer, he plans to study Business Administration. He wants to work for a large corporation. Or a small bank. Two of his friends come in and they discuss tonight's plans. *A movie? This girl's party?*

"There's been a little bit of racial discrimination with my parents. I mean, my dad had a really high job in India. He comes here knowing English, with so much education, and he can't get an office job. Not even a file clerk. Everywhere he went, *You don't have any Canadian experience*. My dad would never call it discrimination, but . . . . All I know is it makes no sense.

"There is racism. This one guy in grade 8 said something racist, he called me a racist name. Basically I beat the shit out of him right in front of the teacher and got suspended for three days. In grade 10 I felt it a bit with a teacher. I'd never been late, I had good grades and I wasn't a shit in class. I'm late one day, by around eight minutes, and she kicked me out. My white friends were late all the time and she always let it go. I told her I felt like she was being racist and she got really mad. The principal got mad at me too. Oh well, I felt it, you know."

He tends to a bevy of customers.

"This is a good one. I just remembered it. Don't tell my father this one, don't tell him any of it. He just doesn't like to hear it. One night me and my buddies were in the McDonald's drive-through. And the girl at the speaker said they were closing. She asked us to tell the car behind us that they were closed. So I lean my head out the window and tell the guy behind us—a white guy in a taxi. About 25. The guy got out of the cab and called me a Paki. Said something like, *You should respect me more than that, Paki*. So we didn't order, we backed up and chased him. But we didn't get him. Don't tell my dad this, right. We saw him again a few weeks later, parked at the side of the street. Basically I asked him, eh, you know, why did you say that? So he starts to get out of the car, and he's putting on gloves. So some of my friends, big guys, showed up and

140

he took off. I still hold anger against that, against him, against racist people. I'm young, I just want to go out there and finish it.

"Don't get me wrong. Most of my friends are white. Everyone is equal. When that guy said those things to me, it was my white friends who said, *Let's get him*. If I have a friend, I don't care what colour he is. I'm Canadian.

"I love learning about other cultures too. In the last few months I've been trying to get this Greek girl, eh. So I'm learning about her culture. It's great, you know. In India, there was so much religious tension. I was young but I remember the car bombings, the little wars. So much fighting. Even at school, with some kids whose parents taught them to fight Muslims or whatever. It's much better here for that. It's the exact reason my parents came here. For my future. I understand now, too, that even if I beat up that racist guy, it wouldn't fix anything. He'd just hate me more, he'd hate brown people more. He'd tell his family, his parents and eventually his kids about hating Indians. I guess that doesn't solve anything. I'm getting older. I'm not so young and stupid anymore, you know."

12c Summaries

A summary is a brief statement of the main points or events of a longer work, with enough detail to explain those points or events for a particular purpose and audience. A government committee, for instance, might publish a twenty-page summary of its two-hundred–page report on the fishing industry, whereas television listings give two-sentence plot summaries of the week's movies. Summaries (also called abstracts, précis, synopses, briefs) abound in school- and work-related writing.

Although writing a summary may seem easy, it isn't. In order to summarize something briefly and accurately, you have to understand it thoroughly. Before you can summarize, then, you must analyze the work—determine the meaning of the whole and how the parts contribute to that meaning.

Plot Summaries

Plot summaries tell your reader, in condensed form, what happens in novels, films, and similar narratives. You will find plot summaries useful when you write reviews (13h) or essays and research papers analyzing narrative works (11c). Most plot summaries are a paragraph or two in length, depending on the amount of detail appropriate for your purpose and audience. Follow these steps:

1. Analyze the work (see Essays Analyzing Literature, 11c) to determine the issue that lies at its heart: Is it the conflict between good and evil? Or the misfortunes of "star-crossed lovers"? Or humans' inability to control the forces of nature? State this issue in your topic sentence, along with the author or director and title of the work.

2. In the body of the paragraph, describe the main events of the plot that illustrate this issue. Make the causal connections among these events clear to your reader by emphasizing why an event occurred and by explaining its effects. If you are summarizing a long or complex work, you might want to set up a classification of events, such as the events in the main plot and events in the subplot. Present events in the same order as in the original unless you need to modify this order to fit your classification. Include other elements, such as characterization and setting, as necessary to explain the plot.

3. End your summary with the last major event in the original. Your concluding sentence should remind your reader of the main point about the work stated in your topic sentence.

Sample Plot Summary

We will illustrate these principles with a plot summary of L. M. Montgomery's *Anne of Green Gables*, one of the novels discussed in the sample literary research paper (14f).

In *Anne of Green Gables*, L. M. Montgomery creates the story of a young orphan girl whose task is to win a secure place in the community. Anne has been sent, by mistake, to the farm of an elderly brother and sister who had wanted a boy to help with the chores. Although an imaginative, talkative, hot-tempered girl was not at all what he had in mind, Matthew Cuthbert is quickly won over. His sister's acceptance of Anne is more conditional, and since Marilla has charge of the child's upbringing, Anne must continually prove her willingness to change behaviour that Marilla and other adults find unacceptable. Anne loses her temper when insulted by Marilla's friend and neighbour Mrs. Rachel Lynde; scandalizes churchgoers by appearing in Sunday School with wildflowers on her bonnet; is accused of losing Marilla's brooch; refuses to attend school after being insulted by the teacher; makes her best friend, Diana, drunk on Marilla's homemade wine; unintentionally leaps into bed with Diana's imperious great-aunt; accidentally dyes her hair green; and almost brings disaster upon herself and her friends by her fanciful imagination. Gradually, however, Anne learns to curb her excesses. By the end of the novel she has made a place for herself in this small Prince Edward Island community and truly becomes Anne of Green Gables.

Summaries of Nonfiction Books and Articles

When you summarize a nonfiction book or an article from a newspaper, magazine, or scholarly journal, your purpose is to explain briefly what the work says, not to argue with it. Self-contained summaries appear in annotated bibliographies or as abstracts accompanying research papers, formal reports, and proposals. More often, you are likely to integrate your summary into a review (13h), position paper (13d), or research paper (14). Follow these guidelines for analyzing the work and writing the summary.

Analyzing Nonfiction

1. Write down complete bibliographical information for the article, chapter, or book. Use the format (MLA, APA, or other) appropriate to your audience (see appendices B and C).

2. Identify the writer's thesis. It is most likely to appear in the introduction or conclusion. To make sure you understand the thesis, restate it in your own words. If there is no explicitly stated thesis, formulate the main idea in your own words.

3. Identify the main sections. Look for guideposts: Does the thesis outline the structure of the piece? Do topic sentences or transitions indicate stages in development (*the first point, the second argument*)? Do headings or other typographical devices suggest the main divisions?

4. State the main idea of each section in your own words.

5. Locate and record subpoints and examples for the main idea of each section. Using point form will remind you not to merely paraphrase every sentence. Include brief quotations when the author's own words seem particularly important. Put quotation marks around any three or more consecutive words, and include the page reference.

12c

Summaries

6. Define all the key terms in your own words and include them in your summary. Pay special attention to words in italics or boldface. Look up any unfamiliar words.

7. Sum up by linking the writer's purpose and audience (if applicable) to the work's structure and focus (see Finding a Focus, 2e). Example: "This article explains [purpose] three methods [structure] consumers [audience] can use to protect themselves against fraud [focus]."

Writing the Summary

1. Give complete bibliographical information (author, title, place of publication, publisher, date), either as a heading or in the first sentence of your summary.

2. State your summing up and the writer's thesis in a sentence or two.

3. Explain the main idea of each section, with enough subpoints and examples to make the main idea clear. Show how these points connect with each other by using terms that emphasize the writer's purpose or methods of development, such as causal analysis, comparison, or classification: *This article explores two contrasting theories about the causes of breast cancer. The genetic theory holds that . . . The environmental theory holds that . . .*

4. Keep the material in the same order and proportion as in the original. Do not exaggerate the importance of a point you find especially interesting, or leave out a point that you find difficult to understand.

5. Use denotative (emotionally neutral) language, and focus on the article or chapter itself rather than your responses to it. Mention the writer frequently to make it clear that you are presenting his or her opinions on the subject, not your own. Remember to use quotation marks and to give page references for all quotations.

6. Do not mix your own ideas with the material you are summarizing; you may not be able to distinguish them a few days or weeks later. If you have been asked (or want) to include an evaluation of either the content or the style, put your evaluation, clearly indicated as such, in a separate paragraph.

Article to Summarize

As you read the following article, notice how Kerry Bowman links concerns about deadly infectious diseases in Western countries with broader concerns about poverty and environmental destruction in developing countries.

Please Don't Eat the Animals
by Kerry Bowman

Canada may finally be getting some relief from its latest worrisome diseases. SARS is declining in Toronto and, in Alberta, there have been no new cases of Creutzfeldt-Jakob—mad-cow disease. It's time now to ask where these diseases are coming from and what can be done to prevent them.

SARS and mad-cow represent what's known as zoonotic infections—diseases transmitted from animals to humans. Researchers believe SARS was spread to humans from a cat-like animal, the masked palm civet, regarded as a delicacy in southern China where the illness festered for months before going global. Mad-cow is transmitted by eating infected cattle.

From SARS, to West Nile virus, to Ebola fever, humans are catching our animal cousins' diseases. In the medical world, we are frequently told that the cross-species jump of infections is wildly improbable—until it occurs. Currently, we have had no idea what is coming in the future until we get an epidemiological retrospective of what has occurred in the past.

Evidence indicates chimpanzees from central Africa are the original source of the HIV/AIDS epidemic, and that transmission was through a simian immunodeficiency virus (SIV). The source of human contact is thought to be exposure to blood from chimpanzees killed for "bush meat."

The bush-meat crisis—the slaughter of animals such as chimpanzees, gorillas, and bonobos for meat—has increased as logging companies build roads deep into formerly unreachable forests, allowing hunters easier access to prey. Almost more worrisome than HIV/AIDS is that new research has identified other SIVs in other African primate species, raising the possibility of more catastrophic epidemics with increased consumption of bush meat.

Ebola, one of the world's deadliest diseases, has killed 114 out of the 128 humans who contracted it in the latest outbreak in the Congo. Although not the primary carrier of Ebola, gorillas are the likely link in the most recent outbreak. They succumb to Ebola, and in turn, the virus is

145

passed on through the consumption of their meat. In the November, 2002, outbreak alone, the disease is estimated to have killed between 600 and 800 Western Lowland gorillas. The decimation of the world's great apes and other primates can be seen not only in ethical terms and scientific loss, but also represents a clear and present danger to global health.

Humans have a long history of catching animal-borne viruses. Of the more than 1,700 known viruses, bacteria and other pathogens that infect humans, about half come from animals. When our ancestors descended from the trees, they picked up parasitic worms from animals on the savannah. When humans migrated from the savannah to Europe and Asia, new infections emerged such as bubonic plague from rats; gangrene, tetanus and brucellosis, largely from eating wild game. When humans began to settle into farming societies, more zoonotic illness emerged. Not so long ago, we caught measles from dogs and tuberculosis from cows.

So are animal-borne diseases not inevitable? Growing evidence suggests the process may be accelerating due to massive demographic changes and environmental degradation. In central Africa, the forced relocation of huge populations under colonial rule, rapid urbanization and the logging that opened the forest to bush-meat hunters has set the stage for even more spread of disease. Add to this mix a very poor public-heath infrastructure and civil unrest. In Asia, it is not surprising the SARS epidemic came from southern China, where the proximity of wild animals—many shipped in from tropical zones— and domestic animals with human settlements has supplied the perfect breeding ground for a new genetically recombined virus. The risk is compounded because consumers and animals are often not from similar ecosystems and have not coexisted for long periods of time.

Consumption of bush-meat in Asia and Africa has gone from occasional domestic use to a rapidly growing commercial enterprise. In middle Africa, this is largely due to western logging initiatives; in Asia, to growing economic power and increased trade with neighboring countries—allowing many more people to indulge a tradition of eating wildlife dishes called *ye wei*—literally, "wild taste."

Biodiversity is richest closest to the equator, the very area where burgeoning human populations exist—many living in poverty and extreme heat without access to running water, the perfect conditions for viruses to fester and emerge as new zoonotic disease. Contemporary global travel guarantees that virtually any place on Earth can be reached within 36 hours, in many cases, time enough to allow for incubation before symptoms emerge.

The belief has been that developing nations have more urgent priorities than conservation of animal species. The false dichotomy is: people or the environment. The reality is the two are inseparable; destructive environmental practice produces high costs at all levels of development.

How can we prevent a new animal-borne disease from becoming the next pandemic? The answers will be found in a weave of environmental protection, poverty alleviation and global health initiatives. The often-ignored growing inequality in access to basic standards of human health and well-being is staggering. We now know that this comes at a high price.

Somehow, ethical considerations have not been enough to act. Let us hope that threat to global health will be.

—*The Globe and Mail*,
July 7, 2003, A11

Sample Article Summary

In "Please Don't Eat the Animals" (*The Globe and Mail*, July 7, 2003, A11), Kerry Bowman argues that we should stop eating exotic and endangered species of animals so that we can maintain the biodiversity of our planet and avoid the health risk created by deadly new diseases transmitted from animals to humans. After identifying a number of deadly diseases—SARS, West Nile virus, Ebola fever, and AIDS/HIV—Bowman explains how people get sick by eating animals. AIDS/HIV, for example, originated with chimpanzees infected with a simian immunodeficiency virus (SIV). People who ate these chimpanzees contracted AIDS, which then spread rapidly to other people. Similarly, those who consume gorilla flesh as yet another exotic "bush meat" risk infection from the deadly Ebola virus.

Bowman argues that the risk to human health from zoonotic infections (diseases caught from animals) is intensifying for three reasons: first, the destruction of animal habitats in Africa and Asia makes it easier to create and satisfy the market for "wild taste"; second, poverty, social upheaval, and poor health services mean that people in these regions get sicker and infect others more rapidly; and third, travel brings people from all over the world closer together, allowing a disease to be communicated before the carrier even knows he or she is sick.

Bowman concludes by pointing out that we can preserve the diversity of species on our planet and also protect ourselves from

12c

Summaries

zoonotic diseases by improving the standard of living and pro-
tecting the environment in developing countries. [246 words]

12d How-To Articles

Books and articles telling how to do something fill the shelves of
bookstores and the pages of newspapers and magazines. You
can find advice on how to manage your money or your children,
choose a doctor or a spouse, deal with anger or the plumbing.
Since you probably have skills that other people would like to
learn, you too can write how-to articles.

Although how-to articles cover a wide range of subjects, the
method of development is basically the same: **process analysis.**
In each piece of writing, you are explaining the steps in a process
or procedure (see Explaining Processes, 6d).

Writing How-To Articles: The Process

Follow these steps:

1. Choose a process or procedure that you can explain in five
   to ten steps. Sharpening a pencil is too simple; building a
   spacecraft is too long and complex.

2. Decide how much explanation and what level of language is
   appropriate for your intended audience. If you were telling
   children how to make cookies, for instance, you might say,
   "Put the mixing bowl in the refrigerator for an hour. Then
   take small pieces of dough and form them into balls about
   half the size of your fist." For experienced cooks, you would
   say, "Chill the dough and form into balls."

3. Write a short introduction pointing out the benefits of learning the procedure. Include a list of tools or materials required
   and where to obtain them, if appropriate.

4. Describe the steps for your procedure in the order in which
   your reader will follow them. Number the steps or use transitional phrases that clearly identify them (*the first step, the
   next step, the third step*). Explain the purpose or reason for
   each step, and give enough detail for the reader to carry it out.

5. Mention any problems that your reader may have in carrying
   out the steps and suggest how to solve them.

6. Write a short conclusion emphasizing the desirable qualities of the finished product or the benefits of learning the procedure.

12e Sample How-To Article

Most how-to instructions are meant to be followed, but the form also lends itself to satire or humour, as in the example below.

How to Experience Treeplanting in the Comfort of Your Own Home
by Teresa Willman

Have you ever wanted to experience treeplanting but you did not know where to start? Well, here is how to experience a day in the life of a treeplanter without leaving your home. All you will need is a shower, some old clothes, a stairmaster or treadmill, peanut butter, and a lot of patience.

You will need to make a few preparations the night before. First you should place the clothes you will wear the next day in a bucket of muddy water. Next you should turn the heat off and open all the doors and windows. Then you should put the stairmaster or treadmill in the shower and put a backpack of rocks beside the shower. Finally you should set your alarm for five in the morning.

When your alarm goes off, press the snooze button. Keep doing this until 5:45 a.m. Then jump out of bed, quickly put on the wet clothes from the bucket and run to the kitchen. Grab a loaf of bread and the peanut butter and make five sandwiches. Eat one of the sandwiches now and put the rest in a plastic bag. If you know someone who has a pickup truck, have the person drive along a gravel road at high speed while you sit in the box. If not, sit on a washing machine during the spin cycle and hug a bag of ice.

After one hour go to the shower and turn on the cold water. Put the backpack of rocks on your back and get on the stairmaster or treadmill, setting it at the most difficult level. Stay on the stairmaster for two hours. Then you can eat one of your sandwiches but remain in the shower as you eat it (do not take longer than five minutes). Repeat this exercise for eight hours. It is helpful to sing mind-numbing songs such as the theme song to *The Brady Bunch* or *Flintstones*.

After eight hours you can turn off the shower, get back on the washing machine or truck and remain there for another hour. Turn the radio very loud and try to have a nap during this time.

Next, go to the kitchen, grab any food you can find and eat it as fast as you can. Make sure you eat until you are completely full. Next get yourself a warm beer, find some clean clothes and take a shower. Use dish soap to wash yourself and an old T-shirt to dry yourself. If you have enough energy, you can play an instrument or read a book before you go to bed.

There you have it: a day in the life of a treeplanter. This exercise is just a brief example of the physical endurance a treeplanter needs to survive an average day. If you want to experience the real thing, phone a local reforestation company. The manager will gladly sign you up.

Sample
How-To
Article

CHAPTER 13

PERSUASIVE ESSAYS

13a Persuading Your Audience

In any form of persuasive writing, your purpose is to change or reinforce your readers' opinions and, in some cases, to encourage those readers to act. How can you make your writing persuasive? Persuasion, as we discussed in chapter 7, rests on two principal kinds of appeals to readers: logical appeals and emotional appeals. **Logical appeals** are the reasons and evidence you present to support your position. Through logical appeals, you demonstrate your ability to think critically about an issue, to evaluate other points of view, to see connections between general principles and particular facts. **Emotional appeals** are the direct and indirect ways you engage readers' feelings: by referring to shared values, for instance, or by using emotionally charged language.

To choose an effective combination of appeals for a particular piece, you need to decide whether you are writing for a friendly audience, a hostile audience, or a neutral audience.

A friendly audience is one that shares your basic concerns but needs to be roused to action or renewed commitment. A parent speaking to community league members about building a new playground would be addressing a friendly audience, receptive to the idea but perhaps needing to be convinced that it was practical. For reviews, letters to the editor, or opinion pieces on noncontroversial topics, you can usually assume you are writing for a friendly audience.

At the other extreme is the hostile audience, actively opposed to your position. An employer trying to persuade workers to accept cutbacks in wages would face a hostile audience. For a hostile audience, you need to consider emotional appeals as well as logical appeals. Hostile workers, for example, might be more willing to accept lower wages from an employer who argued that "we're all in this together" than from one who seemed unconcerned about their welfare. When you write essays on controversial subjects, such as abortion and euthanasia, you will need to take special care not to alienate readers hostile to your position.

Most of the essays you write for courses are directed to a neutral audience—readers who expect a carefully reasoned argument and are skeptical of emotional appeals. These readers will pay more attention to persuasive pieces that do not take extreme positions, that consider the merits of different points of view, and that present extensive evidence to support their position. In Position Papers (13d), you will find a chart for evaluating logical and emotional appeals in works by other writers. You can use the same questions to test your own persuasive writing.

Organizing Persuasive Essays

How you arrange the parts of your essay will be determined by what your readers need to know and what you think they will find most convincing.

If you expect strong opposition, either because you are writing for an audience that you know is hostile or because you are taking an unpopular stand on a controversial issue, you may want to anticipate your readers' objections by discussing the merits and drawbacks of the counter-arguments first, before presenting your thesis and the arguments that support it. By the time you reach your conclusion, your opponents may be more willing to acknowledge the validity of your position than they would have been if your thesis had appeared in your introduction.

This type of organization also works well if you are writing for a friendly but perhaps complacent audience. To encourage readers to think more carefully about a position they may take for granted, you might begin with arguments upon which there is widespread agreement, and then raise the question of whether the situation is really as satisfactory as it appears.

When you are writing for a neutral audience, it is usually best to state your position up front. Your readers will appreciate a clearly defined thesis in your introduction, topic sentences that indicate the stages of your argument, substantial paragraphs that show clear reasoning and a careful use of evidence to support your points, and a conclusion that summarizes and extends your argument.

Here you will find guidelines for four types of persuasive writing: opinion pieces, position papers, letters to the editor, and reviews.

13b Opinion Pieces

Opinion pieces are short persuasive essays, based on your own knowledge and experience, about an issue of interest to general readers. Columnists such as Heather Mallick, Allan Fotheringham, and Margaret Wente write opinion pieces for newspapers and magazines.

Many opinion pieces employ the strategy of giving reasons with examples as supporting evidence (see Giving Reasons and Examples, 7a). To create interest, they often begin with a personal anecdote. You will see this pattern in the sample opinion piece that follows. Notice that the writer gives partial reasons for not buying a new car, leading up to a complete statement of his thesis in the final paragraph.

13c Sample Opinion Piece

Why I Won't Buy a New Car
by Peter Banks

The third time my car broke down within a year, my friend Rebecca teased me, "Why don't you just buy a new one?" This advice was coming from someone whose parents gave her a Miata convertible for her sixteenth birthday. The carefree way she suggested I "just buy a new one" echoed through my mind for quite some time. I began to realize that in our throwaway society, many people are all too willing to "just buy a new one" regardless of any future consequences. However, an object that is more technologically advanced is not necessarily superior.

Many North Americans are deceived by the notion that acquiring the latest inventions will somehow bring them happiness. Although many new objects can bring enjoyment, they do not make the consumer any better as a person. The media prey on society's search for material happiness. Automobiles are often portrayed as the means to achieve power, success, inner peace, and popularity. They are often shown as the instant ticket to becoming a sex symbol. The one thing that advertisements seem to neglect is that these fancy machines are just that—fancy machines. The driver of a red Lamborghini would still be the same person if he or she were behind the wheel of a rusty brown station wagon. However, the media continue to portray the acquisition of material possessions as the avenue through which goals such as peace, good work, family stability, and personal happiness can be achieved. Mini-van commercials are loaded with images of loving families enjoying quality time together. Sports car advertisements attempt to associate driving that particular car with popularity and sexual attractiveness.

While consumers are racing to keep up with the latest in technology, many valuable resources are needlessly wasted. Thousands of auto wrecking yards across North America are filled with vehicles left to rust into an ecological nightmare. Although some are eventually crushed and recycled for future use, these instances do not occur as often as they could. Many of the mechanical components left in these automobiles are still in perfect working order. However, because the majority of modern engines are composed of a tangled web of hoses and computer chips, any working parts from the older cars are completely incompatible. This makes re-using any of the older parts impossible, thereby putting to waste an entirely functional mechanism.

The needlessly complex mechanical designs of new vehicles make it impossible for individuals to take responsibility for even the most basic car maintenance. With consumers wholly dependent upon the dealership's mechanical services, the dealership is free to list exorbitant prices, to which customers must agree. When the alternator of my 1981 Honda Accord wore out, my dad and I simply rebuilt a part from an auto wrecker and replaced it ourselves. The design of the engine compartment left every component easily identifiable and accessible. The entire job took just over an hour and we spent less than eighty dollars on it. The alternator on Rebecca's Miata, however, is buried far beneath the engine block. This particular part, which is prone to wear out with accumulated mileage, is positioned so that when it does have to be replaced, the entire engine must be removed. However, a regular garage will probably not have the necessary equipment to work on this particular vehicle. When her alternator does go, Rebecca will thus have to take her car to the Mazda dealership and pay whatever price is asked.

If I did buy a new car, it probably would not break down as often as the one that I am currently driving. But it might destroy my relationship with my dad. The easiest, most enjoyable times my dad and I spend together are while we work as a team, desperately trying to repair my car. I know that "I love you" has always been a hard thing for him to come out and say. But as I think back, nothing says it louder than the time we spent working in the garage last summer. I was shocked to find him using the old, crooked tool box that I made for him in grade 5. I almost broke into tears when I saw that crooked, unsymmetrical Father's Day present loaded up with tools, while Dad's numerous other boxes, which are much sturdier and more convenient, sat in the basement unused. Buying a new car would end the wonderful times my father and I spend together doing repairs, times that I have grown to cherish.

No, I won't buy a new car. It would cost too much—in the destruction of the environment, the waste of precious resources, the loss of self-reliance, and the loss of human contact.

13d Position Papers

In a **position paper,** your purpose is to present arguments showing why you agree or disagree with something you have read. Writing this kind of essay will help you develop your critical thinking skills, for it requires you to analyze, evaluate, and formulate your own opinion.

Writing Position Papers: The Process

Here are the main steps:

1. ***Summarize the piece you are responding to (see Summaries, 12c).*** Be sure to state the subject of the article and the author's thesis, describe the organization of ideas, and state the most important points in each section.

   Summarizing the article is a useful first step because it helps you to understand the author's ideas. Including a brief version of your summary in your position paper will help your readers understand your response.

2. ***Analyze and evaluate the author's logical and emotional appeals (see the chart, below).*** If you agree with the author, make a list of additional points and evidence to support the position; make a second list of opposing arguments, so that you can refute them. If you disagree or partially disagree, make a list of counter-arguments and evidence.

3. ***Identify the writer's basis of evaluation (see Evaluating Strengths and Weaknesses, 7b).*** Is the writer's position based on moral, practical, logical, or aesthetic criteria, or a combination of these perspectives?

4. ***Clarify your own basis of evaluation.*** Do the points you agree with reflect your moral position on the subject? Do you doubt the practical advantages of the author's position?

5. ***Formulate your thesis.*** It should present both your evaluation of the writer's point of view and your own opinion.

155

6. *Organize your response to include opposing arguments.*
One way to do this is to briefly summarize other views about your subject and indicate why you agree or disagree before you develop your thesis in more detail. You might use this method if, for example, you wanted to argue that positions X, Y, and Z were all based on self-interest rather than on the common good.

Another possible approach is to take up an opposing argument point by point, examining its strengths and weaknesses and pointing out alternatives. You might adopt this method if, for instance, you wanted to argue against a series of proposals contained in a speech or document. These two methods are examples of an evaluative or "pro-con" structure, that is, an organization based on arguments for (*pro*) and arguments against (*con*) your position.

Evaluating Logical and Emotional Appeals

Logical Appeals These questions test the validity of the author's reasoning and evidence.

- Does the author assume the truth of a point that needs to be argued?

- Does the author trivialize or distort opposing points of view?

- Does the author oversimplify an issue by reducing it to two extreme alternatives?

- Are causes and effects actual or hypothetical? Do predicted effects seem exaggerated or unlikely?

- Are faulty causal connections made? Watch for these problems with causal reasoning: (1) claiming that what is true in some instances is true in all instances; (2) claiming that something happening after an event was caused by it; (3) claiming a single cause or effect of something that may have multiple causes or effects.

- Does the author make sweeping generalizations that are difficult to prove or disprove?

- Do all the points support the thesis? Have important points not been taken into consideration?

- Are key terms defined (6c)?

- Do comparisons proceed from a common basis (6b)?

- Are examples used appropriately (7a)?

- Are facts and figures accurate, up to date, and taken from reliable and identified sources? Are they used appropriately (14a)?

- Are authorities cited within their field of expertise?

- Is the evidence sufficient to support the points made?

Emotional Appeals These questions help you define the author's values and attitudes.

- Does the author appeal to values he or she assumes readers share (such as patriotism, family values, concern for the environment)?

- Does the writer make personal attacks on those who hold different opinions or appeal to readers' prejudices against certain groups?

- What attitude toward the subject (such as anger, concern, sadness) does the writer convey through choices in diction, sentence structure, and other stylistic devices? What uses, if any, does the writer make of humour, wit, irony? (For suggestions about analyzing and evaluating style, see Improving Your Style, 4g.)

- What relationship with the reader (friendly, hostile, expert) does the author establish through direct comments, choice of personal pronouns, or emotional appeals (10a)?

- Are emotional appeals appropriate to the purpose and the audience?

- How does the author's personality, as reflected in the piece, affect your response?

13d

Position Papers

Sample Evaluation of an Article

Let's work through these steps for a position paper that responds to Paul Sullivan's article below.

A $55-Million Ride—Worth Every Cent

by Paul Sullivan

The leaders in my city are about to spend $55 million on a bobsled run.

My city, of course, is Vancouver, as of last week, host of the 2010 Winter Olympics. And by the time the last national anthem has been played, some time in February, 2010, we'll have spent $4.5 billion—never mind $55 million—to make the whole thing happen.

But, in the bewildering swirl of words and emotions stirred up in the wake of the news that the Olympics are really coming to Vancouver, I can't stop thinking about the bobsled run.

Actually, it's called the Whistler Sliding Centre and when it's finished in 2007, it will accommodate not only bobsled races, but luge and skeleton races as well. What are luge and skeleton races, you ask? As far as I can tell, in skeleton, you go downhill really fast on a sled. In luge, you go downhill really fast on a sled, on your back. It's not the sort of thing that appeals to most rational people, so it doesn't get a lot of coverage in the sports pages. You may not know, for instance, that the current world bobsled champion is a Canadian, Pierre Lueders, of Edmonton.

Canada already has one world-class sliding facility in Calgary, a legacy of the 1988 Winter Olympics. So, you ask again, we need another one for $55 million?

Right now, there's a tent city in Victory Square, in the heart of the city's Downtown Eastside, where people are asking themselves that question.

The protesters aren't exactly sure why they're protesting or who their targets are, but they're poor and inarticulate, unlike the Vancouver Olympic bid committee members, who are rich and smooth and much better at getting what they want. The tenters want more social housing, welfare, free jobs, that sort of thing, and they're going to stay there, at least until the city's leaders have slept off their Olympic champagne hangover, and figure out what to do about it. At some point, perhaps Councillor Jim Green, who was a high-profile advocate of social housing and jobs for the poor before he went to city hall, may even explain to these folks why it's a good idea to spend $55 million on a sliding centre. That money could buy a lot of social housing. I'd like to be there for that one.

So what if we're already in the red? The provincial deficit is forecast to be $3.2 billion at the end of the fiscal year in March, but that's less than the original $4.4 billion estimate. And if these guys figure spending $55 million to bring the skeleton races to Vancouver is a good idea, who are we to argue?

Of course, I suspect you could divide $4.5 billion in Olympic funds evenly among the city's drug addicts and wipe out the problem overnight. (Let's see. Divide $4.5 billion by an estimated 10,000 addicts and you get $4.5 million each. They could spend a couple of months getting clean at the Betty Ford Center and still have enough left over to buy a condo in Whistler to take in the 2010 sliding events.)

Such a thing will never happen, should never happen. We already have enough drug wealth in this town and, apart from the luxury car dealers and the luxury condo developers, who benefits? Whereas, if you build a $55-million track for the skeleton races, "they" will come.

"They" are the television networks, who will beam tantalizing images of Vancouver to the tourists and conventioneers of the world. "They" are the people who will bring dollars to invest in the B.C. economy and keep the 2010 benefit alive long after the Games have moved on. "They" are us, the people of Vancouver and Whistler, who will have to work together to stage the biggest sports event on earth. For the first time since Expo 86, we have a common purpose. Even if right now we don't know skeleton from slalom, by 2010, we're going to be experts.

That, after all, is the point of laying out $55 million for the Whistler Sliding Centre. Today, despite the natural splendour that sold the International Olympic Committee, Vancouver is a mess, a chaotic patchwork of two dozen municipalities and as many nationalities and cultures. We all seem to want different things. Now, we have an opportunity to come together.

Granted, that opportunity means saying yes to the skeleton races and keeping a straight face long enough to sell this marvellous nonsense to the world.

But if we can do that together, we can do anything. Even, one day, do something really marvellous and solve the intractable poverty and misery of the Downtown Eastside.

—*The Globe and Mail*,
July 7, 2003, A13

13d

*Position
Papers*

Steps in Preparing Your Position Paper

1. *Summarize the article you are responding to.*

   For a summary of Sullivan's article, see the Sample Position Paper (13e).

2. *Analyze and evaluate the author's logical and emotional appeals.*

   Strengths

   - Sullivan indicates his awareness of logical arguments against his position.
   - Sullivan's emotional appeals to civic pride and community spirit remind us of the benefits of cooperation.
   - Sullivan's humour and irony support his "we're all in this together" attitude.

159

Weaknesses

- Sullivan trivializes the basic moral question about the use of government resources.
- He also oversimplifies the position of protesters by reducing the issue to two alternatives: *either* "we" spend $4.5 billion to host the Olympics *or* we divide the money among Vancouver's drug addicts.
- Sullivan predicts economic and moral benefits for the Greater Vancouver region from the Olympics, but gives no evidence to support his points.
- Sullivan does not consider practical and moral objections to the Olympics raised by First Nations, environmentalists, and other groups.
- He appeals to readers' prejudice against disadvantaged groups by characterizing the tent city protesters as ignorant, inarticulate people who want "free jobs, that sort of thing" and by identifying them with drug addicts.

3. *Identify the writer's basis of evaluation (see Evaluating Strengths and Weaknesses, 7b).*

Sullivan's argument is based on both practical and moral grounds. He argues that television coverage of the Olympics will have the practical benefits of attracting tourists, conventioneers, and investors. He also argues that working together to host the event will have the moral benefit of encouraging cooperation among the "chaotic patchwork" of municipalities, nationalities, and cultures that make up the Greater Vancouver region.

4. *Clarify the basis of your evaluation.*

I disagree with Sullivan's position on logical, practical, and moral grounds.

5. *Formulate your thesis statement.*

The strengths of Sullivan's piece derive from his skillful use of emotional appeals. These strengths do not outweigh the logical, practical, and moral weaknesses of his argument.

6. *Organize your essay to include opposing arguments.*

You could begin by writing a paragraph or two taking up all the arguments against your position or you can address these arguments one by one throughout your essay. You can make the main points in the body of your essay much more obvious with strong topic sentences. In each topic sentence, make a point about some aspect of the writer's logic, evidence, or use of emotional appeals.

13e Sample Position Paper

*Sample
Position
Paper*

The 2010 Olympics: Taken for a Ride?

In "A $55-Million Ride—Worth Every Cent," columnist Paul Sullivan justifies, on practical and moral grounds, the $4.5 billion that will be spent to stage the 2010 Vancouver/Whistler Winter Olympics. Television coverage, he argues, will attract tourists, conventioneers, and investors long past the games themselves. More important, hosting the games will bring a unity of purpose to the "chaotic patchwork" of municipalities, nationalities, and cultures that make up Greater Vancouver. Learning to work together, Sullivan maintains, will ultimately allow the region to solve other common problems, including "the intractable poverty and misery of the Downtown Eastside." The strengths of Sullivan's piece derive from his skillful use of emotional appeals. Those strengths, however, do not outweigh the logical, practical, and moral weaknesses of Sullivan's argument.

One of Sullivan's strengths is his ability to create a friendly relationship with the reader, a sense that "we're all in this slightly crazy thing together." He creates a strong emotional bond by carrying on a dialogue over the need for the Whistler Sliding Centre, a facility for sports with which readers, like the writer himself, may be unfamiliar: "What are luge and skeleton races, you ask? As far as I can tell…." This tactic allows Sullivan to distance himself both from the "leaders" responsible for this decision and from the protesters in the Downtown Eastside: "The tenters want more social housing, welfare, free jobs, that sort of thing, and they're going to stay there, at least until the city's leaders have slept off their Olympic champagne hangover, and figure out what to do about it." Having joined the writer in poking fun at both sides, the reader then becomes part of "us, the people of Vancouver and Whistler," with an opportunity to share a "common purpose": "Granted, that opportunity means saying yes to the skeleton races and keeping a straight face long enough to sell this marvellous nonsense to the world."

By drawing readers into this relationship, Sullivan creates a strong emotional appeal. This appeal is heightened by other stylistic devices that reinforce community spirit, such as references to "my city," the

161

playing of "the last national anthem," and "the current world bobsled champion" from Edmonton. Most tantalizing of all is Sullivan's assurance that if we learn to cooperate, "we can do anything"—even "solve the intractable poverty and misery of the Downtown Eastside." What this piece offers, then, is freedom from hard choices: we can have the Olympics *and* eradicate social problems.

Such a vision is attractive, but Sullivan offers no evidence to support his claims for either practical or moral benefits. According to a news release by the Canadian Centre for Policy Alternatives, the Winter Olympics are likely to result in a "substantial net cost to British Columbians in the order of $1.2 billion" (par. 2). Figures compiled by the No Games Coalition suggest that this is a reasonable projected loss, given the debts resulting from previous Olympics in Canada: Montreal, 1976—$1 billion over budget; Calgary, 1988—$539 million over budget. The results from Australia are even more sobering. Politicians assured taxpayers that the Games would be self-financing. According to the official report of the Auditor General of New South Wales, however, the Games incurred a $2.3 billion loss (par. 10).

Furthermore, Sullivan weakens his position by trivializing and oversimplifying opposing views. His explanation of what the protesters want is dismissive: they "want more social housing, welfare, free jobs, that sort of thing." He does not mention provincial budget cuts that have severely curtailed programs for the disadvantaged. His suggestion that "you could divide $4.5 billion in Olympic funds evenly among the city's drug addicts and wipe out the problem overnight"—a suggestion he of course rejects—sets up a false dichotomy: *either* we stage the Olympics *or* we turn the money over to drug addicts. This suggestion also makes an unfair emotional appeal, since readers may associate the protesters with the city's "10,000 addicts." In this instance as in others, Sullivan attacks not the arguments against the Olympics but the people who make them. He characterizes the tent city protesters as not only "poor and inarticulate" but also ignorant: they "aren't exactly sure why they're protesting or who their targets are."

If the tent city protesters are "poor and inarticulate," this is not the case with other groups that objected to Vancouver's Olympic bid. Sullivan does not address the concerns raised by First Nations, environmentalists, local businesses, provincial taxpayers. Nor does he address the basic moral question about the allocation of resources. In the face of a provincial deficit of over $3 billion, it is not enough to shrug one's shoulders and say, "… if these guys figure spending $55 million to bring the skeleton races to Vancouver is a good idea, who are we to argue?"

The final cost of the Olympics, as Sullivan says elsewhere, is expected to be $4.5 billion. Some of that cost will be recouped. But if the experience of other host cities is any guide—and what else do we have?—taxpayers will be left with a hefty bill. No amount of cooperation learned through hosting the games will alleviate the misery of the Downtown Eastside and similar areas without a massive infusion of government funds and government will. It should not be the place of governments to provide circuses while people are hungry.

Works Cited

Canadian Centre for Policy Alternatives. "Olympics Cannot Be Justified on Economic Grounds." *Creative Resistance.* 14 Feb. 2003. 18P. Retrieved 10 Nov. 2003 from <http://www.creativeresistance.ca/awareness01/2003-feb14-olympics-cannot-be-justified-on-economic-groupds-ccpa.htm>.

No Games 2010 Coalition. "Do the Olympics Generate Money for the Economy?" *Creative Resistance.* 14 February 2002. 50P. Retrieved 10 Nov. 2003 from <http://www.creativeresistance.ca/awareness01/2002-dec02-do-the-olympics-generate-money-for-the-economy-no-games-coalition.htm>.

Sullivan, Paul. "A $55-Million Ride—Worth Every Cent." *The Globe and Mail* 7 July 2003. A13.

13f Letters to the Editor

Most letters to the editor are intended to persuade readers that something is good or bad: the premier is doing a good job or a lousy job, park trails should or should not be paved, nurses should or should not have the right to strike. They are generally short, about 250–500 words. Paragraphs within the letter are also short because letters are usually printed in narrow columns. The following guidelines will help you make your point quickly and effectively:

1. ***Focus on a particular issue of interest to a number of readers, and, if possible, link that issue to a current situation.*** A general plea for world peace, for example, is less likely to hold your readers' attention than an argument against selling arms to warring countries. Identify the issue in your first paragraph.

2. ***Explain why the issue concerns you.*** Are you writing as a spokesperson for a relief organization? As a pacifist? As a citizen upholding the ideal of Canada as a peacekeeping nation?

3. ***Instead of condemning people who hold other views, try to establish common ground with them.*** Summarize their positions accurately and acknowledge the extent to which their point of view may be true or understandable. You might acknowledge a country's need to defend itself, for example, but point out that access to more powerful weapons increases the likelihood of bloodshed.

4. ***State your own position and your reasons for holding it. Be brief but specific.***

5. ***If possible, suggest a practical action that readers can take.*** They can't ensure world peace; they can write a letter to an MP.

13g Sample Letter to the Editor

In this letter, the writer focuses on a local issue to raise public awareness and encourage appropriate action.

As a person who works downtown, I understand merchants' concerns about panhandlers blocking access to their businesses, and sometimes, like other readers, I feel uncomfortable when I'm asked for change. Nevertheless, I am angered and saddened by City Council's proposed bylaw against panhandling.

Banning panhandlers may improve the image of the downtown, but it won't relieve us of our individual and collective social responsibilities. Canadians give generously to relieve poverty and suffering in distant places; we should be equally eager to address poverty and suffering in our own communities. When communities were smaller, everyone knew who needed outgrown clothing or vegetables from the garden. But with growing populations we have become strangers to each other, and so we find it easier to write a cheque for disaster relief than to drop a loonie in an outstretched hand.

Perhaps what we need most in our cities is to reestablish this personal relationship in giving. There are many ways this can be done. With a little thought, each of us could find one or more ways that suit our age, gender, and resources. Here are some possibilities:

- Volunteer at a soup kitchen or food bank.
- Take an extra lunchbag with you for the panhandler you pass every day.
- Carry $5 gift certificates from a supermarket or fast-food chain.
- Carry bus tickets, even if you don't ride the bus.

- Get involved with local anti-poverty groups.

- Give generously to vendors of *Our Voice* and similar publications.

If you have a framework for personal giving, you can say no to requests that fall outside that framework without feeling angry and resentful at being asked. Then dealing with panhandlers will become just another part of living in a vibrant, diverse city.

—*Deirdre Summers*

Burnaby

13h Reviews

You are probably most familiar with the brief reviews of books, films, television programs, and eating places printed in newspapers and general-interest magazines, such as *Maclean's* and *Time.* These reviews are intended to give casual readers some sense of whether a new movie is worth seeing or a new restaurant worth trying.

Longer reviews—often called **review articles** or **review essays**—are designed for readers with some knowledge of the subject. Car enthusiasts, for example, might read the reviews of all the new models in *Car and Driver,* even if they are not planning to buy a car. Academic journals often carry review articles on research in specific areas, such as intelligence testing. Because these reviews provide substantial background information and extensive commentary, they are useful sources of information for research papers.

We will focus on guidelines for writing brief reviews for a general audience. If you wish to expand your treatment of your subject into a review essay, you can do so by consulting appropriate sources of information: other reviews, other works by the same person or group, articles relevant to your subject, biographical dictionaries, newspaper files, and so forth.

Follow these guidelines when writing a brief review:

1. *Include identifying information somewhere in your review.* The most essential information (determined by your intended audience and type of publication) usually appears in a separate heading before your review or in your introduction. Here is what you should include:

Book review author, title, publisher, price, type, length, hardcover or paper. As applicable: name of editor, translator, or other contributors; supplementary material provided (such as maps, illustrations, appendix, index); date of publication; edition.

CD-ROM review title, publisher, price, system requirements.

Computer software review product, manufacturer, price, system requirements. As applicable: other products in category, ordering information.

Film review title, director, distributor, type, principal actors. As applicable: date of release; length; suitability rating; other contributors (music, special effects, etc.).

Live performance review as applicable: title, name of person or group, place, date(s), type, price.

Product review manufacturer, model, price. As applicable: availability, warranty, service record.

Recorded music review title, person or group, type, label, price.

Restaurant review name, address, type of food, business hours, price range, credit cards accepted, availability of alcoholic beverages, decor, service. As applicable: reservation requirement, dress code.

2. *Try for a lively introduction, one that will catch your readers' interest and convey your general opinion of what you are reviewing.*

3. *Give readers a sense of the whole through a brief summary or description.* Don't include so many details that you leave readers nothing to discover. Never give away surprise effects or the endings of films, plays, or novels.

4. *Discuss what you liked and disliked about what you are reviewing, with specific examples.* Try for a balanced view: even the aspects you like the most may appeal only to certain people. For suggestions about what to consider, see Evaluating Strengths and Weaknesses (7b).

5. *End with a snappy summary of your overall judgment.*

13i Sample Review

Here is a sample restaurant review, written for an alternative newspaper.

Sublime Subs, Rapturous Wraps

In a hurry but tired of McMeals? For a fast, tasty, and reasonably healthy alternative, try Badass Jack's Subs and Wraps.

Specializing in home-cooked meats and buns (no processed meats or frozen buns for these guys), Badass Jack's offers seven different subs on sourdough or multigrain buns with an array of fresh vegetables. Or let your friendly server create a wrap: a flavourful tortilla piled high with chicken, beef, or seafood; your choice of vegetables; the whole thing topped with a zesty sauce (try Kathmandu Curry or Caribbean Jerk, or for the less adventurous, Tennessee BBQ and Texas Ranch). You can also ask for these sauces on chicken and beef subs. Beware: one of our party found the BBQ sauce overpowering.

Vegetarians take note: in addition to a vegetarian sub and wrap, BAJ's serves falafel and several salads.

An assortment of beverages, including Stewart's sodas, and modest desserts round out the menu.

BAJ's is a fast-growing local chain, and it's easy to see why. Good food, fast, friendly service, and a warm Southwestern decor that's a definite step up from pink molded plastic. And speaking of steps up— except for two chairs, seating is bar-table style, a drawback for people with disabilities or short legs. But you can fax ahead and eat at home in comfort.

Badass Jack's Subs and Wraps, with ten locations in the Edmonton area; also in Calgary, Red Deer, Grande Prairie, Saskatoon, Winnipeg, Kingston, and Brandon. Hours 11 a.m.–11 p.m. weekdays, 11 a.m.– midnight Saturday, 11 a.m.–10 p.m. Sunday. Under $10.

13i

Sample Review

CHAPTER 14

RESEARCH PAPERS

14a

*Purpose
and
Audience*

A **research paper** is an expository or persuasive essay in which you include facts and opinions from other sources to support your analysis or point of view. As you will see in the sample research papers "*Tom Sawyer* and *Anne of Green Gables:* Two Models of Heroism" (14f) and "Male Involvement in Social Services and Healthcare Volunteer Programs" (14g), those sources are usually published books and articles on the subject. But research material can also include interviews and other data that you gather yourself.

14a Purpose and Audience

The purpose of a research essay is to examine a subject in greater depth than would be possible on the basis of your own knowledge. In many cases, you may not have any prior knowledge to draw upon. How many of us, without using research material, could write an essay on the introduction of Buddhism into China, for example? Writing research essays is one of the best ways to extend your knowledge of a subject.

A research paper should not be merely a compilation of other people's ideas, however. To make sure it isn't, you need to have some idea of where you are going before you do research. You can use brainstorming or discovery questions (2a and 2c) to figure out the questions you will need to answer in your paper. Or, if you know something about your subject, you can write a draft first and then find research material to broaden or clarify your thinking.

Many research paper topics ask you to respond to a work of literature or to other readings. In these assignments, you need to understand the **primary** source(s) as well as you can before you choose your research or **secondary** sources for the essay.

As you carry out your research, you are likely to find unanswered questions and areas of disagreement among your sources. Writing a research paper will allow you to take part in the ongoing debate about your subject.

In the world of work, research papers are written by specialists for other specialists. Citations and references allow specialist readers to evaluate the sources of facts and opinions and to follow up possible lines of investigation. As a student writing a research paper, you are learning to act like a specialist in a particular field. You will therefore present your material differently than you would for a general audience. You will use a more specialized vocabulary, maintain a slightly more formal tone, and assume your readers' general familiarity with the subject. (For example, a biologist would explain what DNA is for a general audience but not for other biologists.) Nevertheless, a research paper should not sound as though it has been compiled by a committee. The best research papers are those in which the style and tone reflect something of the writer: flashes of wit, clear thinking, depth of knowledge, sudden insights, and a feeling for language.

14b Compiling a Working Bibliography

In research, your first step is to compile a **working bibliography:** a list of ten to twenty books, articles, and other material on your topic. A working bibliography of this size should give you six to eight usable references, an adequate number for a research paper in an introductory course (students in advanced courses are generally expected to have a more thorough knowledge of what has been written about a topic). Beginning with a longer list of references will allow you to eliminate material that turns out to be unavailable or irrelevant, without having to do another search. It will also ensure that you do not depend too heavily on one or two sources. If your material is too limited, you may get an inaccurate idea of the central issues of your subject or find it hard to develop your own perspective.

• Using your library's online catalogue, search for **books** by author, title, or subject. Subject searches are often the most useful, allowing you to locate dozens of potentially valuable items in seconds. They can also be frustrating if you have not chosen appropriate search terms or if you fail to limit your search sufficiently. If you need help, consult a reference librarian.

• Search for **articles and other material** through electronic databases. Two of the most valuable databases are *Expanded Academic ASAP* (book reviews and journal articles in humanities, education, science, and social science, as well as general topics) and *MasterFILE Premier* (articles and pamphlets on a number of topics, including business, multiculturalism, and consumer health). Both of these databases contain the full text of more than a thousand journals and magazines published since January 1990. You can access these databases from library computers or, if you have the Internet, from a home computer.

- Other sources you may find in your library's reference section include hard copy and CD-ROM versions of **bibliographies and indexes.** These research aids list books and print-based articles arranged by subject and author. While you will normally be interested in the more recent books and electronic articles, you may also wish to look up older sources: books no longer in print, or articles prior to 1980 that have not been transferred to electronic databases. Be sure to consult a reference librarian for help with using these resources.

- You may also find material on your topic on the **World Wide Web.** Be cautious, however, about the authenticity and credibility of information from general websites, listservs, and newsgroups. If you are unsure about the reliability of your sources, check with your instructor. For useful websites created by academics and librarians, see the Web Links at the end of this chapter (and at the end of each part of this book).

- Use the most up-to-date material available, especially for topics related to science, technology, and current issues and events.

- For topics in most fields, try for a balance between books and articles. Books generally provide a broader scope and a fuller treatment of a topic, but they may be harder to obtain. Articles are more specialized, more current, and easier to find if you have Internet access. (In the sciences, research proceeds so rapidly that you may need to rely primarily on articles.)

- For each entry in your list of possible sources, include the call number or electronic address so you can easily retrieve the book or article.

- Preparing your working bibliography in a computer file will enable you to cut and paste once you are ready to do the works cited or references page of your essay.

14c Taking Notes

Skim each item in your working bibliography and select the six to eight most relevant to your topic. You are now ready to gather material from these sources. Making careful notes as you read will help you understand the material and figure out how it fits with your own ideas on the topic. You may find it most efficient to make these notes on the same computer file as your working bibliography.

Taking notes will also help you to avoid **plagiarism,** a serious academic offence that many students commit unintentionally. Plagiarism is the use of others' words *or ideas* without acknowledging the source. While there is a clear moral difference between intentional and unintentional plagiarism, the consequences are the same: penalties may range from a mark of zero on your paper to expulsion from your college or university.

Intentional plagiarism usually involves

- handing in a paper done wholly or in part by another person

- pasting together passages from one or more sources and using them without quotation marks and without acknowledging the source(s).

Unintentional plagiarism may include

- occasionally failing to use quotation marks to indicate quotations

- paraphrasing or summarizing in language too close to the original source

- omitting in-text references and/or a works cited or references page.

Whether you are **quoting, summarizing,** or **paraphrasing,** you must acknowledge the source of information and ideas *in the text* of your essay AND *in the list of sources* at the end of your essay.

Quoting

Quote sparingly in your preliminary notes so that you won't be tempted to copy long passages into your essay. Be sure to put quotation marks around any passage of three or more consecutive words you take directly from the source, and record the page (for printed texts) or paragraph number (for unpaginated electronic texts) where the passage can be found in the original, along with the author's name and a short form of the title. This information will allow you to keep track of your sources so that you can identify them appropriately in in-text citations and in your list of sources. For more information about quoting, see appendix B (for MLA style) or appendix C (for APA style).

Summarizing

You will need to condense most of the material in your research sources. Read the passage(s) until you can summarize the essence of the material using mostly your own words. To review, see Summaries of Nonfiction Books and Articles (12c). Again, record the author's name, short title, and page(s) or paragraph number(s).

Paraphrasing

To paraphrase means to write in your own words a passage that is more complex or technical than your own writing style. Sometimes a paraphrase includes a brief explanation or definition. A paraphrased passage will be about the same length or a little longer than the original. Be sure to record the page(s) or paragraph number(s) as well as the author's name and short title.

Once you have a working bibliography and a full set of notes on the most relevant sources, you are ready to begin the first draft of your research paper. As you write, include author, title, and page or paragraph number for each quotation, summary, and paraphrase. When you revise, make sure these references are in the appropriate format. For more information on documentation, see the explanations and examples below (14d) and appendices B and C.

14d Documenting Sources

Acknowledging or **documenting** your research sources means that you state, within the body of your essay, at least the author and the exact location of all quoted, summarized, and paraphrased passages AND that you include a list of those sources at the end of your paper. Failing to include BOTH of these methods of referring to your sources constitutes **plagiarism.** As explained in Taking Notes (14c) above, plagiarism is a form of stealing: stealing someone else's words, facts, or ideas. And like other forms of stealing, it is illegal.

You need not fear plagiarism if you do your own work and document the material you use from research sources completely and accurately. Do not attempt to mislead instructors as they are trained to recognize academic dishonesty. Intentional plagiarism of essays available on the Internet is easily detected; your instructor knows your writing style and will immediately suspect dishonesty if you try to pass off someone else's words as your own.

You can prevent the panic that may lead to deliberate or unintentional plagiarism by allowing at least three weeks to gather material, draft, and revise your research paper. Providing documentation of your sources at each stage of the process will give you the confidence to hand in a satisfactory paper.

In North America, two main styles of documentation are used. The MLA style, developed by the Modern Language Association, is used primarily in the humanities, and the APA (American Psychological Association) style is used in the social sciences. Both styles require **in-text citations,** basic information identifying the source of your research material at the place you use it in your essay. Both styles also require a list of sources at the end of the paper to cross-reference the information given in the in-text citations.

Determine which style you should use for your research essay; then read through the explanations and samples in appendix B (MLA) or appendix C (APA).

Documenting Quoted Material

You are most likely already familiar with acknowledging quoted material. When you **quote** three or more words directly from a source, you must enclose these words in quotation marks. An exception occurs when you quote passages of more than forty words or four lines of typing: such long quotations are indented but not enclosed in quotation marks. For more information on quoting, see Quotation Marks (22e) and Quoting Effectively, appendix A3.

Whenever you quote, you must acknowledge the source. In the sentence where a quotation appears, you must state the author (and, in APA style, the date of publication), and the page or paragraph number locating the quoted passage in your source.

Imagine, for example, that you were writing the sample literary research paper "*Tom Sawyer* and *Anne of Green Gables:* Two Models of Heroism" (14f). In your research you might have come across the following paragraph in James L. Johnson's book *Mark*

173

Twain and the Limits of Power (Knoxville: U of Tennessee, 1982). In this paragraph, Johnson argues that because Tom's village is not portrayed realistically, Tom is not changed by his seemingly serious experiences:

> Simply put, St. Petersburg is not a world in which children are easily turned into adults, for such a change requires that the child meet a real world and adjust himself, painfully but with more or less success, to its undesirable circumstances. Much of the idyllic quality of Petersburg is attributable to the fact that Twain has excluded from the novel a world in which experience produces consequent changes in character. Tom's world is one in which "adventure" replaces "experience"; his encounters with the alcoholic Muff Potter, the grave-robbing Dr. Robinson, the vengeful Injun Joe—encounters which should ordinarily produce some difference in his perception of the world—leave his character essentially untouched. (51)

14d

Documenting Sources

If you were not careful to indicate quoted material and its source in your notes, your essay might contain a sentence like the one following.

Undocumented Quotation—Plagiarism

Tom Sawyer's adventures leave his character essentially untouched.

Documented Quotation

Tom Sawyer's adventures, as James L. Johnson argues, "leave his character essentially untouched" (51).

The revised sentence demonstrates one way to show the necessary information. For other examples, see the sample research papers at the end of this chapter.

Documenting Summarized or Paraphrased Material

Because integrating summarized and paraphrased ideas from your research sources is, in some regards, more complex than quoting directly, you may be tempted to ignore the requirement to document. Let's suppose, for example, that you transferred your paraphrase of Johnson's passage from your notes to your essay without acknowledging the source.

Undocumented Ideas—Plagiarism

Tom's village, St. Petersburg, is not presented as a real world. A real world turns children into adults by forcing them to adjust to aspects of life they find undesirable. Twain presents St. Petersburg as idyllic (simple and charming) partly by excluding the kinds of experiences that would produce changes in character. In this idyllic world, Tom has adventures, such as his encounters with Muff Potter, Dr. Robinson, and Injun Joe, rather than experiences that would change his character or his way of looking at the world.

How would you show that these ideas came from Johnson? If you merely added a citation at the end (Johnson 51), you would avoid plagiarism, but your reader would still not be sure whether all the ideas in the paragraph were Johnson's, or merely the last point. You can clearly distinguish your own thinking from the work of others by introducing the author's name at the beginning and putting the appropriate citation at the end, as in the following example.

Documented Paraphrase

James L. Johnson argues that Tom's village, St. Petersburg, is not presented as a real world. A real world turns children into adults by forcing them to adjust to aspects of life they find undesirable. Twain presents St. Petersburg as idyllic (simple and charming) partly by excluding the kinds of experiences that would produce changes in character. In this idyllic world, Tom has adventures, such as his encounters with Muff Potter, Dr. Robinson, and Injun Joe, rather than experiences that would change his character or his way of looking at the world. (51)

In most cases, you should not rely so heavily on a single critic; you should also use your own interpretation and examples from your primary source(s). Even so, this paragraph is an improvement because the reader knows whose ideas are being presented. If you are careful to identify others' facts and opinions, your reader has more confidence that what remains is your own.

For other ways of acknowledging your sources, see appendices B and C, as well as the examples in the research papers at the end of this chapter.

Creating a List of Sources

For each source you have cited—given an in-text citation for passages quoted, summarized, or paraphrased in your essay—you must provide further information so that a reader can locate the source. This information is compiled in a list of bibliographical entries on a separate page following the end of your paper. (Even though this bibliography is separate, it is still a numbered page of your essay.)

Check the requirements for the **works cited** (MLA) or **references** (APA) page in appendices B and C, respectively. Be sure also to look closely at these items in the sample research papers that follow below.

14e Integrating Research Material

At earlier stages of your education, you may have written research papers in which you merely collected information on a subject and presented it in an orderly fashion. In postsecondary courses, however, research papers, like other kinds of essays, must have a thesis, a main point that the research material addresses.

In drafting your paper, you may be so intent on organizing your material that you lose track of your thesis. You may find it helpful to review the requirements of a thesis statement (see chapter 8) and the benefits of an outline (see Making an Outline, 3b). You may also need to revise your middle paragraphs to show more clearly how your research material relates to your thesis and to the specific points you make. We will illustrate this process with two examples, one non-literary and one literary.

Non-Literary Example
Sample First Draft

Marleen C. Pugach of the University of Illinois has recommended these selection criteria for prospective Education students: 1) basic skills testing, consisting of entry-level tests in reading, mathematics, and written and oral communication; 2) a minimum grade point average; and 3) a structured interview to assess the applicant's personal qualities (161-63). At universities such as Oregon State and Northern Kentucky, students must successfully complete a two- to five-day full-responsibility teaching experience prior to being accepted into a teacher training program. The number of drop-outs increased from approximately 5% to 25% (Edgar 96).

This draft paragraph serves the writer's need to gather together information from a variety of sources. However, it does not serve the reader's need to understand the significance of this information because the point of the paragraph gets lost among the examples.

Here is the material as it appeared in the student's final draft. With the added topic sentence, sentences explaining the relevance of each example, and a summarizing sentence to connect this material to the thesis, the original paragraph has become two.

Sample Final Draft

If teaching is to be regarded as the important job that it is, pride must first be generated within the profession itself. One way to do this would be to have a more rigorous and effective set of criteria that applicants must meet before they are allowed entrance into the profession. Marleen C. Pugach of the University of Illinois has recommended a set of criteria that would function together to provide "entry-level hurdles to encourage self-selection, to serve as initial points in the process of continuous judgment of student progress, and to assist faculty members in making discriminations between applicants based on multifaceted data" (161). Pugach recommends these selection criteria: 1) basic skills testing, consisting of entry-level tests in reading, mathematics, and written and oral communication; 2) a minimum grade point average; and 3) a structured interview to assess the applicant's personal qualities (161-63).

Another criterion used in universities such as Oregon State and Northern Kentucky is also helpful in selecting suitable candidates. Students must successfully complete a two- to five-day full-responsibility teaching experience prior to being accepted into a teacher training program. The number of drop-outs increased from approximately 5% to 25% (Edgar 96). Clearly, such intensive selection policies would be a strong force in attracting applicants who seriously wish to pursue teaching. At the same time, these policies would deter students who now casually drift into teacher education, such as those I overhear in the undergraduate lounge. The sense of personal achievement that would come from gaining entrance to a faculty with such high entrance standards would contribute to a feeling of professionalism among candidates.

—Carol Murray

Literary Example

Showing how your own interpretation of a literary text relates to other critics' opinions takes practice.

We will look first at a draft paragraph on *The Adventures of Tom Sawyer* written before consulting the critics. Then we will discuss two ways of integrating other interpretations.

Sample Draft Paragraph: Student's Analysis

In *The Adventures of Tom Sawyer,* the adults are not presented as models of behaviour. In fact, they are often shown to be acting like children. When Tom tricks Aunt Polly at the beginning of the book, for instance, Aunt Polly has been attempting to trick him. Similarly, Tom shows off at Sunday School when Judge Thatcher visits, but the superintendent and the teachers are also described as "showing off." Even serious events in the adult world seem to parallel Tom's actions. The fight that ends with Injun Joe murdering Dr. Robinson has many of the same elements as Tom's fight with the new boy in town. It is no wonder then that even after his harrowing escape from the cave and his recovery of the treasure, Tom returns to playing at robbers. The adult world is not portrayed as different from the world of childhood, and so there is no reason for Tom to grow up.

Sample Draft Paragraph: Adding Support from Research Material

In this revised paragraph, the material from Johnson that we noted earlier is added to summarize and expand the point that the writer made in the topic sentence.

The adults in *The Adventures of Tom Sawyer* are not presented as models of behaviour, but simply as older versions of Tom himself . . . [continue with examples from the original draft]. It is no wonder then that even after his harrowing escape from the cave and his recovery of the treasure, Tom returns to the boyhood world of playing at robbers, for the adult world offers no incentives for growing up. James L. Johnson argues that Tom's adventures "leave his character essentially untouched" because "such a change requires that the child meet a real world and adjust himself, painfully but with more or less success, to its undesirable circumstances" (51). But St. Petersburg, as Johnson points out, is an idyllic world, not a real world that would bring about change.

Sample Draft Paragraph: Synthesis of Student's Analysis and Research

In outstanding research papers, the writer does more than cite authorities to support points: he or she synthesizes material from various sources by showing basic similarities and differences. This synthesis then provides a context for the writer's own interpretation. Note how the writer of the sample research paper demonstrates her grasp of the debate about Tom Sawyer's relationship to the adult world in the following paragraph.

What, then, is the relation between Tom and his world? Robert Regan supports the view, originally put forward by Walter Blair, that the narrative strands of the novel "trace Tom's progress from childishness to maturity" (Regan 116). Several critics disagree. They argue that because the adults of St. Petersburg are essentially childish, there is no impetus for Tom to change (Fetterley 300; Johnson 51; Miller 73; Whitley 60).

Numerous incidents in the book support this contention . . . [continue with examples from the original draft].

As you can see, crediting your sources, integrating research material, and synthesizing different points of view are never easy tasks. We have used a literary topic to demonstrate these techniques because essays on literature are the first type of research paper that many students have to write. As you continue in college or university, however, you will find that these skills are increasingly important in all your courses.

14f Sample Literary Research Paper

You will notice that this research paper presents a comparative analysis of two novels. Pay close attention to the thesis and to the way each major point announced in the thesis is worked out in the middle paragraphs.

Tom Sawyer and *Anne of Green Gables*: Two Models of Heroism

by Lanette Thornton

When we think of heroic quests, we usually envision a pattern very much like that of Mark Twain's *The Adventures of Tom Sawyer:* the hero engages in a series of adventures through which he proves his worth and is rewarded with riches and the love of a beautiful maiden. In this version of the heroic quest, as is obvious from the way I've described it, the hero is male. L. M. Montgomery's *Anne of Green Gables*, I will argue, presents a female version of the making of the hero. In the mythic pattern of separation, initiation, and reintegration into the society, Tom's tests of courage and his rewards are largely external, and neither he nor his world is transformed by them. Anne's tests, on the other hand, are largely internal, and her rewards depend upon her ability to transform both herself and her world.

Tom's separation from his community lies in his flouting of convention. Although one critic has argued that finally "Tom sacrifices freedom to gain community" (Towers 520), the first episode of the book seems to bear out John Whitley's contention that Tom "is never in any danger of expulsion from the community" (64). In this episode, which sets up our expectations for the rest of the novel, Tom escapes punishment for sneaking jam by outwitting his Aunt Polly. Her response—"a gentle laugh" (8)—immediately establishes her as an indulgent parental figure who likes Tom's mischievousness:

> He 'pears to know just how long he can torment me before I get my dander up, and he knows if he can make out to put me off for a minute, or make me laugh, it's all down again, and I can't hit him a lick. I ain't doing my duty by that boy, and that's the Lord's truth, goodness knows . . . . Every time I let him off my conscience does hurt me so; and every time I hit him my old heart 'most breaks. (8)

Furthermore, the "model boy" of the village—Tom's half brother Sid—is presented as dull and self-righteous, always willing to get Tom into trouble by tattling. Whenever we as readers, like Aunt Polly, are ready to condemn Tom's lying, his thoughtlessness, his prankish behaviour, Twain reminds us, usually through Aunt Polly, that Tom is good at heart. And we, like his aunt and the community gathered for his mock funeral (Miller 71-72), forgive him.

Although Leslie Willis dismisses *Anne of Green Gables* as sentimental because Anne "suffers no real hardships" except over her initial reception and Matthew's death at the end of the novel (250), Anne does not have the security in her world that Tom has in his. Tom is at home in St. Petersburg, under the care of a doting, if at times punitive, aunt. But the orphaned Anne has already lost a series of homes. When she reaches Green Gables, she learns that Matthew and Marilla had wanted a boy to help with the farm, not a girl at all. Furthermore, although Marilla soon discovers that Anne is "smart and obedient, willing to work and quick to learn" (57), the girl is also a talkative, imaginative, hot-tempered redhead. Anne, like Tom, is presented as essentially good. But unlike Tom, if Anne is to have the home she so desperately wants, she must learn to control her behaviour.

This control, moreover, must come from her desire to please others rather than from a fear of punishment. When Anne's temper flares up over Mrs. Rachel Lynde's disparaging comments about her looks, for example, Marilla admits that her neighbour "is too outspoken. But," she adds, "that is no excuse for such behaviour on your part. She was a stranger and an elderly person and my visitor—all three very good reasons why you should have been respectful to her" (72). Although at first Anne refuses to apologize to Mrs. Lynde—the punishment Marilla lights upon—Anne eventually does so to please Matthew. As Matthew had immediately recognized, Anne is "one of the sort you can do anything with if you only get her to love you" (52). The threat of expulsion is always present, however, for as Muriel Whitaker points out, Marilla's favourite punishment when Anne has misbehaved is isolation, banishment, ostracism (53).

To secure a place in the community, Anne must learn "the importance of keeping fantasy and reality segregated," as Julie Fenwick points out (61). Tom, on the other hand, learns to translate his imaginary heroism into real heroism. If Tom were a "model boy" like his half brother Sid, he would not fight, play truant from school, sneak out at night, "hook" provisions, and so on. But without these boyish pranks, he would not have the courage and resourcefulness he needs to become a hero. Thus the ingenuity, self-sufficiency, and leadership Tom demonstrates when he, Joe, and Huck run away to Jackson's Island to become pirates are the same qualities he needs to find a way out when he and Becky become lost in the cave. Similarly, Tom's desire to act on his book-knowledge of buried treasure and the ways of robbers leads him and Huck to discover the whereabouts of Injun Joe and his treasure. As a result of these exploits, Tom becomes rich, by his standards, and wins the approval of Becky's father, the imposing Judge Thatcher. As Lyall Powers puts it, "the heroic game becomes impressively the Heroic reality" (321).

Anne's quest, on the other hand, leads her to heroic sacrifice: she gives up her hard-won scholarship to university to stay on the farm and care for Marilla. She is able to make this loving choice because she has learned to consider the rights and welfare of others without sacrificing her own individuality. As she tells Marilla on several occasions, Anne never does "the same naughty thing twice" (102). When her scrapes are her own fault—as in losing her temper with Mrs. Lynde, meddling with Marilla's brooch, and hitting Gilbert Blythe with her slate—Anne takes her punishment and mends her ways. But when her scrapes are not entirely her own fault—as when Diana gets drunk on mulberry wine or Anne puts liniment in the cake instead of vanilla—Anne also learns valuable lessons, for the willingness of Marilla and other adults to admit their own failings makes possible the sense of love and security that turn this initially hostile world into the home Anne so intensely desires. When her romantic views are "sabotaged by 'life' in incident after incident," Anne learns to distinguish romance from reality (Ross 46-48).

In the process of learning from her experiences, Anne is both transformed and transforms others (Whitaker 55). She overcomes Matthew's fear of females; awakens Marilla's undeveloped sense of humour; humbles the judgmental Mrs. Barry; sweetens the temper of Diana's crochety Aunt Josephine. By the end of the novel, even Mrs. Rachel Lynde, who is initially presented as the norm of the village, has become less rigid (Rubio 29). Anne is thus presented as a child who can exert some control over her environment by furnishing the "psychological, emotional, and imaginative dimensions which are lacking" in the adults' own lives (Rubio 35). In the process, as Whitaker points out, Anne has come to conform "pretty closely to the adult view of propriety" (52). By the time she reaches seventeen, Anne has become what Marilla wanted: "All I want is that you should behave like other little girls and not make yourself ridiculous" (89). But she has done so because this is what she too wants. Her essential nature, like her imagination, has been tempered by her trials, but not destroyed. This match between desire and fulfillment is possible because the world of Green Gables, like Anne herself, is essentially good. Integration into the community is thus itself the goal of Anne's heroic quest and her reward, earned through experience.

In contrast, neither Tom nor his world is transformed by his adventures. Although Robert Regan supports the view, originally put forward by Walter Blair, that the novel "trace(s) Tom's progress from childishness to maturity" (Regan 116), several critics disagree. They argue that because the adults of St. Petersburg are essentially childish, there is no impetus for Tom to change (Fetterley 300; Johnson 51; Miller 73; Whitley 60). Numerous incidents in the book support this contention. Thus Tom's trickery is echoed by Aunt Polly's attempt to catch him out, and Tom's showing off when Judge Thatcher visits the Sunday School by the antics of the staff:

> Mr. Walters [the Sunday School superintendent] fell to *showing off* with all sorts of official bustlings and activities. . . . The librarian *showed off*, running hither and thither with his arms full of books. . . . The young lady teachers *showed off*—bending sweetly over pupils that were lately being boxed. . . . The young gentleman teachers *showed off* with small scoldings and other little displays of authority. . . . (33) [emphasis mine]

Similarly, the fight that ends in the murder of Dr. Robinson is an adult version of Tom's fight, at the beginning of the book, with the new boy in town.

It is no wonder then that even after his harrowing escape from the cave and his recovery of the treasure, Tom returns to playing at robbers. The adult world is not portrayed as different from the world of childhood, and so there is no reason for Tom to grow up. Indeed, as Harold Aspiz remarks, "The town exists largely as a setting for Tom's adventures . . ." (147). In this respect, the worlds of Tom Sawyer and Anne of Green Gables are not similar, as Mary Rubio suggests (30), but radically different. If, as one critic suggests, Tom is not required "to sacrifice his boy's freedom in return for his success" (Regan 121), the reason may be that Twain "protects Tom from any experience that might seriously impair his 'unrestricted domination': boredom, humiliation, the serious threat of death, lasting or serious disappointment, growing up . . ." (Johnson 59). Tom's initiation thus consists of a series of adventures, not experiences that would lead to maturity (Johnson 51), and his rewards are correspondingly external.

I suggested earlier that these novels can be seen as presenting male and female models of heroism, Twain's novel celebrating individual exploits that lead to external rewards and Montgomery's celebrating a reciprocal process of internal change that leads to transformation of self and society. Robert Keith Miller points out that Twain saw himself as rebelling against the stereotype of the Model Boy portrayed in nineteenth-century children's books and creating instead a portrait of (in Walter Blair's words) "what a normal boy should be" (67). Montgomery's goal seems somewhat different. As we have seen, Anne's first task is to convince Matthew and Marilla that she is worth keeping even though she is not a boy. Anne's rivalry with Gilbert throughout the novel establishes their equality, in keeping with Montgomery's view of there being little difference between men and women (Burns 44-45). If we are tempted to read Anne's story as stereotypically that of the female who triumphs through self-sacrifice, we must remember that Gilbert is also forced to relinquish his chance for a university education because of his responsibility for his family.

This observation leads us to the possibility that the difference between the models of heroism portrayed in the two novels is not merely one of gender but also one of nationality. Tom's story, Lyall Powers argues, reflects the American dream and the American paradox: "The ideal hero is the stout individualist, the non-conforming natural man, American Rousseau, who yet lives snugly in suburbia as a regular fellow" (323). Does Anne then reflect the Canadian dream of social harmony with the recognition of the price we pay in individual sacrifice?

Works Cited

Aspiz, Harold. "Tom Sawyer's Games of Death." *Studies in the Novel* 27.2 (1995): 141, 13p. Online. AcademicSearch. 04 June 1999.

Burns, Jane. "Anne and Emily: L. M. Montgomery's Children." *Room of One's Own* 3.3: 37-47.

Fenwick, Julie. "The Silence of the Mermaid: *Lady Oracle* and *Anne of Green Gables.*" *Essays on Canadian Writing* 47 (1992): 51, 14p. MasterFILE. 7 June 1999 <http.//www.lrc.macewan.ca/research/databases/>.

Fetterley, Judith. "The Sanctioned Rebel." *Studies in the Novel* 3.3 (1971): 293-304.

Johnson, James L. *Mark Twain and the Limits of Power: Emerson's God in Ruins.* Knoxville: U of Tennessee P, 1982.

Miller, Robert Keith. *Mark Twain.* New York: Ungar, 1983.

Montgomery, L. M. *Anne of Green Gables.* Toronto: McGraw, 1968.

Powers, Lyall. "The Sweet Success of Twain's Tom." *Dalhousie Review* 53.2 (1973): 310-24.

Regan, Robert. *Unpromising Heroes: Mark Twain and His Characters.* Berkeley: U of California P,1966.

Ross, Catherine S. "Calling Back the Ghost of the Old-Time Heroine: Duncan, Montgomery, Atwood, Laurence, and Munro." *Studies in Canadian Literature* 4.1 (1979): 43-58.

Rubio, Mary. "Satire, Realism, and Imagination in *Anne of Green Gables.*" *L. M. Montgomery: An Assessment.* Ed. John R. Sorfleet. Guelph: Canadian Children's P, 1976. 27-36.

Towers, Tom H. "I Never Thought We Might Want to Come Back: Strategies of Transcendence in *Tom Sawyer.*" *Modern Fiction Studies* 21.4 (1975-76): 509-20.

Twain, Mark. *The Adventures of Tom Sawyer.* London: Penguin, 1986.

Whitaker, Muriel, "'Queer Children': L. M. Montgomery's Heroines." *L. M. Montgomery: An Assessment.* Ed. John R. Sorfleet. Guelph: Canadian Children's P, 1976. 50-59.

Whitley, John S. "Kids' Stuff: Mark Twain's Boys." *Mark Twain: A Sumptuous Variety.* Ed. Robert Giddings. London: Vision, 1985. 57-76.

Willis, Leslie. "The Bogus Ugly Duckling: Anne Shirley Unmasked." *Dalhousie Review* 56.2 (1976): 247-51.

14g Sample Non-Literary Research Paper

You will likely write research papers on non-literary topics in courses such as psychology and sociology, among others. For such assignments, you may be given a detailed topic that specifies a method of development or focus for your essay. Or you may simply be given a subject, for which you must then find your own focus. If so, review chapter 2, Gathering Material, for methods of exploring your subject and defining a focus.

When you write on a non-literary topic, your research includes finding facts as well as opinions about your subject. You must clearly indicate the source of these facts as well as the source of opinions from experts in the field, whether you use direct quotations or put the information into your own words. The following research paper shows how to give in-text citations and bibliographical references using the American Psychological Association (APA) format. For guidelines on APA format, see appendix C.

Sample Non-Literary Research Paper

Male Involvement in Social Services and Healthcare Volunteer Programs

by Sharon Cornelius

Volunteerism is the backbone of most communities, and involvement of volunteers of all ages and both genders is critical to the success of many programs. According to social services and healthcare agencies in the Parkland area, however, the number of male volunteers is dwindling and consequently compromising the scope of many volunteer programs. Understanding the trends affecting volunteerism in general, such as personal motivation, demographics, and economic issues, will help such agencies to devise strategies for increasing the potential number of male volunteers.

The local decline in male volunteers reflects a national trend. An analysis of Ontario hospital volunteers conducted by an International Year of the Volunteer Research team determined that women comprise 74% of the hospital volunteer base while men make up 26% (Handy & Srinivasan, 2002, ¶ 3). The report *Caregiving Volunteers: A Coming Crisis?* further substantiates the imbalance of women (78%) to men (22%) in caregiver volunteering. Male volunteers also start later in life—in their 50s and 60s—and 70% are retired (Phillips, Little, & Goodine, 2002, pp. 2–3). At WestView Health Centre in my own community of Stony Plain, men account for only 13% of the volunteers.

Why do so few men volunteer? In *Recruiting Male Volunteers: A Guide Based on Exploratory Research,* Stephanie T. Blackman discusses social perceptions of male roles as an impediment to volunteering, especially in healthcare programs. Blackman (1998–1999) indicates that one challenge for men is "overcoming the breadwinner syndrome." Although research participants noted that attitudes are changing, they still perceived that men are considered the breadwinners of the family and therefore would not have time to volunteer (1998–1999, Part 1, ¶ 2). Another challenge, according to Blackman, is that society does not think of men as "nurturers." She reports that research respondents felt women were better "nurturers," and men were more "aggressive," "independent," and "strong" (Part 1, ¶ 4).

These attitudes are reflected in the types of job assignments volunteers prefer. During an initial interview at the WestView Health Centre, for example, the volunteer coordinator outlines the various jobs new volunteers may choose. Interestingly, 45% of new volunteers prefer to drive clients to and from appointments or to assist with activities or outings in continuing care. These assignments are single events and the volunteer does not need to make a long-term commitment. This fits the lifestyle of the senior volunteers as they can pick and choose the extent of their involvement. The coordinator of volunteers also revealed that visiting clients in their home, playing cards, or going for a walk with a male client is not as appealing as driving clients. Volunteers, especially those under the age of 35, have mentioned feeling uncomfortable in the client's home. They often have difficulty starting and sustaining a conversation with the client. The younger volunteers prefer hands-on activities such as planting flower boxes, cutting wood for crafts, or cleaning out the client's storage areas.

These preferences reflect the ways in which social perceptions of male roles influence potential volunteers. Yet these perceptions may prevent men from volunteering in programs where they have a unique contribution to make. Hospice & Health Services, Inc. vigorously recruits male volunteers, for example, because they can share common life experiences and allow terminally ill men to face their fears without embarrassment (¶ 6). Luckily for patients in the Parkland area, male hospice volunteers are available at WestView Health Centre to provide this valuable support.

Social service agencies face similar challenges in attracting male volunteers. The Big Brother program across the country recruits men to work one-on-one with young males called Little Brothers, boys between the ages of 6 and 16 who are in need of a friend and a male influence in their life. Big Brothers are in great demand, and often all the requests cannot be met. *The Big Brothers Focus Groups: Final Report,* prepared for Big Brothers of Ontario in 1995, determined two main barriers to volunteering: lack of time and a fear of a close one-on-one relationship (Sage Research, 1995, p. 17). Interviewees worried, for example, that because they live busy lives, they might need to cancel meetings and disappoint the assigned Little Brothers. Others felt they could not make the required one-year commitment. One Big Brother in his 20s suggested that the time commitment be relaxed to 5 or 6 months, especially for university students (Sage Research, 1995, p. 20). In a finding consistent with Blackman's research, some men did not think of themselves as "nurturers." Prospective Big Brothers indicated they didn't want to be responsible for the way the Little Brother turns out (Sage Research, 1995, p. 21). Others worried that they might be paired with a "problem kid" (Sage Research, 1995, p. 25). *The Big Brothers Focus Groups: Final Report* noted that "Men with kids are more prone to choose a volunteer role that allows them to be with their own kids—such as Scouts, or sports teams" (Sage Research, 1995, p. 27). These men have a limited amount of time they can give, and if the choice is between helping with their own child's team and being a Big Brother, the former usually wins. All these factors contribute to the continuing dearth of male volunteers.

The perception that men are less nurturing than women, which was reported in both Blackman's study and *The Big Brothers Focus Groups: Final Report,* affects other social services programs. The Parkland Adult Literacy program, for example, does not actively recruit male volunteers. The goal of the program is to increase the literacy skills of students, to a level they have determined, by matching them with a volunteer tutor. Students come from many different walks of life, ethnic backgrounds, and, of course, from both genders. For the past three years, the fifteen volunteer tutors have included only three men. The program coordinator, who matches students with tutors, has discovered that students of both genders prefer a female tutor. This preference suggests that male students, particularly those from male-dominated ethnic groups, do not want to show their reading weakness to another man. The nurturing quality of the female tutors enhances the learning and completion rate of the students.

To increase men's involvement as volunteers in healthcare and social service programs, administrators must review and revamp their message, their methods of advertising, and the recruitment process to appeal to men. Recruiters should be knowledgeable about the current need for additional male volunteers. They should also be able to name the benefits and positive experiences that volunteering brings. Among the reasons people give for volunteering are developing new skills, adding their experience to a résumé, believing in the "cause," meeting new people, filling spare time, and feeling a sense of duty. Many people also want to give back to the community. John, an elderly male healthcare volunteer at the WestView Health Centre, made the following comment: "I volunteer because it will help with the total care of the patients. A member of my family was a patient in the Health Centre, and she received such great care. I want to give back to this facility" (personal communication, April 30, 2003). To attract more male volunteers, recruiters must ensure that their message appeals to men's personal motives for being involved.

Recruiters must also be aware of general trends in volunteering. The *2000 National Survey of Giving, Volunteering and Participating,* conducted by Volunteer Canada, discovered a number of changes since the 1997 survey. One significant change is that seniors as a group have less time available for volunteering because they travel or have multiple activities. Two groups are replacing seniors as new volunteers: young people who want to gain work-related skills, and new Canadians who want to develop work experience and to practise language skills (Volunteer Canada, 2002, ¶ 4).

These trends definitely apply to male volunteers in social service and healthcare programs. At WestView Health Centre, for example, a man in his early 20s volunteers in Diagnostic Imagery to prepare for his post-secondary education. Volunteering is one of the entrance requirements for the program he will be taking, and his volunteer experience has cemented his desire to pursue this field of work. Another man, also in his early 20s, continues to volunteer in the emergency department while he trains for the police department. The knowledge he gains of its inner workings will assist him when he is on active duty.

Focus groups can help to ensure that the agency's recruitment message appeals to the men being targeted and addresses their concerns. For example, Big Brothers used research participants of all age groups, current and potential Big Brothers, to create the message. The group agreed unanimously that the message must show the Big Brother's role as "fun" (Sage Research, 1995, pp. 30–31) and include sub-messages about friendship, time commitment, and lack of expense (Sage Research, 1995, pp. 31–33). Other organizations could use the same technique by simply pulling together a focus group to discuss the message.

Advertising is a powerful tool for volunteer agencies to convey their message to the community. Depending on the financial resources of the program, advertising could include television, radio, newspapers, and websites. Each of these outlets has pitfalls to be aware of. Television shows the "faces" of the organization but is very costly. In order to reach the target audience, television and radio spots should be aired during the times that men typically tune in: for example, during a sports game or the news. Free publicity from the local newspaper may depend upon the whims of the editor. To ensure that the complete and correct message gets printed, paid advertising is the best option. The World Wide Web increasingly connects communities; the challenge is to keep all the information current and relevant. In my experience, the best form of advertising is word of mouth. Coordinators could talk to current male volunteers and ask them to encourage a friend to become part of the team.

The interview process should also be reviewed. Because many potential volunteers work full-time, interviews may need to be held in the evenings or on weekends. Recruiters should explain the organization's mission, vision, and beliefs to enable potential volunteers to determine if their beliefs and values match those of the organization. Recruiters should also discuss time commitment, scope, and responsibilities of the various job assignments, keeping in mind the factors that affect male volunteerism.

Finally, if they want to increase the number of male volunteers, healthcare and social service agencies must stress the unique contribution men can make: as stated by Blackman (1998–1999), "One volunteer can create a ripple effect that may influence an organization, a client population, public opinion, and other volunteers" (¶ 3). Many healthcare and social service volunteer programs, not to mention the patient/client and the community, can benefit from an increased male volunteer base. It is now time for action.

Sample
Non-Literary
Research
Paper

References

Blackman, S. T. (1998–1999). *Recruiting male volunteers: A guide based on exploratory research.* Washington, DC: Corporation for National Service.

Handy, F., & Srinivasan, H. (2002). *IYV Research Program, Ontario hospital volunteers: Who they are and what they do.* Toronto, ON: Canadian Centre for Philanthropy.

Hospice & Health Services, Inc. *Hospice volunteers...making each day count...bringing light—and love—into people's lives.* Lancaster, Ohio. Retrieved April 27, 2003, from http://www.hhsfc.org/hhsfc.org/volunteer.htm

Phillips, S., Little, B. R., & Goodine, L. (2002). *Caregiving volunteers: A coming crisis?* Toronto, ON: Canadian Centre for Philanthropy.

Sage Research. (1995). *Big Brother focus groups: Final report.* Mississauga, ON: Sage Research Corporation.

Volunteer Canada. (2002). *Trends in volunteerism.* Retrieved May 6, 2003, from http://www.volunteer.ca/volcan/eng/volincan/trendsinvol.php

- UBC Writing Centre's Writers' Toolbox—tips on various aspects of writing an essay, with sections on argument and writing a rhetorical analysis.

  www.writingcentre.ubc.ca/workshop/toolbox.htm

- Advice on Academic Writing, University of Toronto—links to planning and organizing, reading and researching, using sources, and specific types of writing.

  www.utoronto.ca/writing/advise.html

- The University of Victoria Writer's Guide—especially useful for essays on literature with a link to literary terms; also summaries, logic.

  web.uvic.ca/wguide/

- The Purdue Online Writing Laboratory Research and Documenting Sources—includes research paper guidelines.

  owl.English.purdue.edu/handouts/research/index.html

- Directory of Academic Internet Resources—listings of best Internet sites for each subject.

  www.academicinfo.net

PART 4

BUSINESS WRITING

CHECKLIST | *Business Writing*

	OK	NEEDS WORK
1. Is your purpose clear?	☐	☐
2. Have you analyzed your audience and tried to meet your reader's needs?	☐	☐
3. Is there too much or too little information?	☐	☐
4. Is the organization effective?	☐	☐
5. Is the tone effective?	☐	☐
6. Is the information accurate and complete?	☐	☐
7. Are the explanations and details adequate?	☐	☐
8. Is the sentence structure appropriate?	☐	☐
9. Is the word choice effective?	☐	☐
10. Have you avoided outdated expressions?	☐	☐
11. Are the transitions between statements clear?	☐	☐
12. Is the format of the document correct?	☐	☐

CHAPTER 15

WRITING LETTERS, MEMOS, EMAILS, REPORTS, AND BROCHURES

All good business writers focus on plain, clear language that leaves no doubt about the intended message. They also try to gain readers' goodwill, both by the tone and style of writing and by keeping in mind the readers' needs and point of view.

15a Business Style
Analyzing Your Audience

Business writing often involves writing to someone you do not know personally. For this reason, you will need to make educated guesses about what your reader—a prospective employer, a grant committee, a student loans officer—needs to know. It's worthwhile to ask yourself these questions before you begin:

- What is my position in relation to this reader—taxpayer? employee? client? supplier?

- What tone, style, and format are appropriate for this relationship?

- How much background information does this reader need?

- What do I want my reader to do in response to this letter or report?

- How is my reader likely to respond to the message?

Your reader's expected response to your writing will help determine how you structure your message. Is your writing giving routine information or good news? If so, the reader is apt to react positively to your message, and you will begin directly with the nature of the message. Is the message going to disappoint the reader or attempt to persuade the reader to do something he or she may not want to do? If so, the reader is apt to react negatively to your message, and you will begin indirectly. You will begin with a buffer, a neutral statement that doesn't give the main message in the first paragraph. You will expand on the details in the body of the message. In both cases, you will end your message with the action needed, and if appropriate, a goodwill message.

Meeting Your Reader's Needs

To help your reader read quickly and respond favourably, you will need to write in language that is clear and easy to follow. Here are some suggestions:

15a

Business Style

- *Make sure your letter or report is complete, accurate, and precise.* Include all the background information (*who, what, when, where, why, how*) your reader will need to understand the context of your subject. Check all facts and figures. Telling your insurance agent that *The car skidded twenty metres* is more precise than saying *The car skidded a short distance,* but neither statement is accurate if the car actually skidded forty metres. In a report, include all the factual information and analysis required to support your conclusions and recommendations.

- *Make your writing clear and businesslike.*
  - Avoid outdated expressions, such as *with regard to your inquiry,* and contemporary bureaucratese, such as *prioritize our objectives* (set our goals) and *implement procedures* (take action).
  - Use short, familiar words to increase readability; use *find out,* not *ascertain,* and *use,* not *utilize.*
  - Avoid "tion" nouns such as *implementation* and *facilitation.* Reword the sentence and use verbs instead.
  - Use active verbs instead of passive verbs, unless you have a reason for choosing a passive verb. *We decided* is more direct than *It has been decided.* (See Active and Passive Voice, 20e.)
  - Avoid slang; you can generally use contractions (*can't, we'll*) except in formal reports.

- *Foster goodwill by keeping your tone friendly.*
  - Consider everything you write from the reader's viewpoint. Use *you* and *yours* more often than *I* or *we.*
  - Consider the benefits of what you say or propose for the reader, and include the reader's benefits in your message. For example, in chapter 16, Getting a Job, you will see that the cover letter needs to show an employer why your skills will help the company, not why you need the job.

- Be positive. Avoid drawing unnecessary attention to negative messages by using words such as *unfortunately, blame,* or *insist.*

- ***Keep your sentences and paragraphs fairly short.*** Average sentences in business writing are about twenty-two words, and paragraphs do not exceed eight to ten lines.

  - Put main points in short sentences. Use longer sentences to fill in details. Varying the length of your sentences will give your writing a more conversational tone.
  - Avoid stringing together a series of very short sentences (which can sound monotonous or aggressive), or a series of one-sentence paragraphs (which can make it difficult for a reader to see connections among your ideas).
  - Use lists with numbers (specific order) or bullets (no specific order) whenever they are appropriate. Introduce lists with a clear lead-in sentence. Be sure your list has parallel structure (see Faulty Parallelism, 18e).

Understanding Your Purpose

The purpose of some business writing is solely to convey or request information. Most business writing, however, has both an explanatory and a persuasive purpose. In addition to explaining or analyzing information, you may also want to persuade your reader to take action. Suppose you want to form a committee to plan for graduation celebrations. You will need to send a memo to your classmates with specific information about the work and time commitment that being on the committee would involve, but you will also want to give them some good reasons to participate. Thus your memo would have both an explanatory and a persuasive purpose.

In this chapter we will illustrate five kinds of business writing you are likely to do: letters, memos, emails, reports, and brochures/flyers. For more complete information, see Mary Ellen Guffey and Brendan Nagle, *Essentials of Business Communication, Fourth Canadian Edition* (Scarborough: ITP Nelson, 2003).

15b Business Letters

Requesting information, making complaints, and sending special messages (such as thank-yous, sympathy, and congratulations) are common reasons for writing letters. People are more likely to use emails, faxes, and the 1-800 number service to request information and order products. Most businesses place a high value on "special message" correspondence because of the goodwill it brings.

15c Business Letters: Format

Like other kinds of writing, business letters have their own conventions that raise particular expectations in a reader. By adhering to these conventions, you create a favourable first impression—one suggesting that you know what you are doing and should be taken seriously. Even if your handwriting is perfectly legible, type all business correspondence.

Here is the standard format for business letters. Left-justify all the parts of the letter, do not indent paragraphs, and leave a space between paragraphs. Every business letter should have the first six components.

1. ***Your address and the date***
Place this information in the upper left corner, single spaced. If you are using personal or company letterhead stationery that includes the address, leave a space and type the date below it. Do not include your name with your address.

123 Juniper Drive
Thompson, MN R7N 2K8
April 26, 2003

2. ***Your correspondent's name and address***
Place this information on the left margin, single-spaced. It should include everything you would type on the envelope.

3. ***The salutation (Dear . . .), followed by a colon***
If you do not know the name of the person to whom you are writing, use the title of the individual or department (*Dear Editor:* or *Dear Customer Relations Department:*) or the name of the organization (*Dear Starbucks:*). If you can, find out the name of a contact person and use it.

4. ***The body of the letter***
Your business letter will normally consist of three or four paragraphs. Business letters are seldom more than one page. If you need a second sheet, place the page number at the top. Never use the back of a page.

5. ***The complimentary closing***
Use *Yours truly* for more formal letters and *Yours sincerely* or *Sincerely* for less formal letters. Capitalize the first word of the closing. Place a comma at the end.

6. *Your signature*

Type your name below the signature.

7. *Enclosures*

Draw your reader's attention to any enclosures, such as a brochure or a cheque, by typing either *Enclosure* or *Enc.* beside the left margin after the signature. Indicate more than one enclosure like this: *Enc. 2.* Name an especially important enclosure in this way: *Enc.: contract.*

8. *Copies forwarded*

Use the notation *c* or *copy*, followed by either a colon or a period, to indicate that copies of the letter are being sent to other people:

> c: Mrs. Elizabeth Nelson
> copy: Dr. F. D. Schmidt

15d Sample Business Letter

In the following business letter, the numbers correspond to the eight components discussed above.

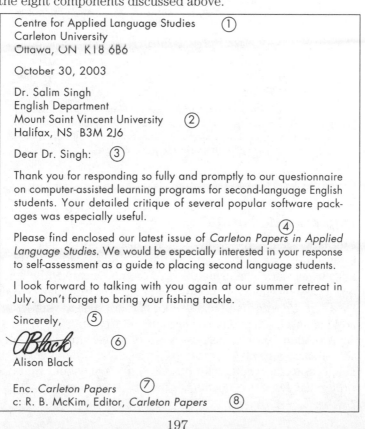

Centre for Applied Language Studies   ①
Carleton University
Ottawa, ON K1B 6B6

October 30, 2003

Dr. Salim Singh
English Department
Mount Saint Vincent University   ②
Halifax, NS B3M 2J6

Dear Dr. Singh: ③

Thank you for responding so fully and promptly to our questionnaire on computer-assisted learning programs for second-language English students. Your detailed critique of several popular software packages was especially useful.

Please find enclosed our latest issue of *Carleton Papers in Applied Language Studies*. We would be especially interested in your response to self-assessment as a guide to placing second language students.   ④

I look forward to talking with you again at our summer retreat in July. Don't forget to bring your fishing tackle.

Sincerely,   ⑤

Alison Black   ⑥
Alison Black

Enc. *Carleton Papers*   ⑦
c: R. B. McKim, Editor, *Carleton Papers*   ⑧

15e Memos: Format

Memorandums, or memos, are the usual form of communication between members of the same organization. Follow the guidelines for letter writing to organize the content of your memorandum. The format conventions are illustrated below. Notice that memos are not signed. Add your initials (by hand) after your name.

15f Sample Memo

DATE:	July 23, 2003
TO:	Susan Schnell, Franchise Manager [name and title of the person to whom the memorandum is sent]
FROM:	Carmen Ditopa [name of the writer] CD
SUBJECT:	Bunk Bed Safety [precise statement of the main focus]

Last week I received a letter from the Consumers' Advocates of Sarnia reporting complaints about the safety of children's bunk beds. These complaints included concerns about ladders that became detached from the bed frames and bunks that were not securely bolted together.

The most serious problems, however, occurred when sleeping children were caught between the guard rail and the mattress. The enclosed safety guidelines from Consumers' Advocates clearly show how a child can suffocate.

Please use these guidelines to check your stock and warn all sales personnel of the dangers posed by the models listed in the second enclosure. Sales staff should alert prospective buyers to the risks bunk beds may pose to children under six years of age.

Enc. 1.: safety guidelines
Enc. 2.: list of bunk bed models

15g Emails: Format

Emails are frequently used for communication within an office or between offices in the same company. Once used only internally, emails are increasingly used to communicate with clients quickly. Many emails are printed and filed, and they may be seen by others. Be sure your emails look as professional as your letters and memos. Each one needs careful proofreading.

Warning: Because business workers are becoming inundated with emails, you will want to consider whether or not your email is necessary or whether a phone call to a colleague would be preferable. Long documents are hard to read on email.

Follow these guidelines for your emails:

1. *The receiver*

The *To* line needs either the electronic address(es) only or the name(s) of the receiver(s) and the electronic address(es). Fill in the address of anyone receiving a blind or carbon copy.

2. *The sender*

The *From* line is filled in automatically on most computers. It should give your full name and your electronic address.

3. *The date*

The computer fills in the full date automatically.

4. *Subject line*

Make the subject line clear and specific so that the receiver knows what the message is about. Each email should only address one topic so emails can be filed appropriately.

5. *Salutation*

You may use a salutation such as *Hello Latisha,* or *Dear Andrew:*—or you may lead into the first sentence by using the receiver's name followed by a comma. Emails that are sent externally will look more professional with a salutation.

6. *Closing*

Although signing is optional, most people do sign emails after a close such as *Cheers, Best,* or *Regards.* Many writers include a signature block with their full name and contact information below it.

7. *Readability*

Use upper and lowercase letters as all caps are hard to read. Use bullets or numbers for lists, and leave a space between paragraphs.

15h Sample Email

To:	"Ivy Leung" <leungi@staffordhigh.ca>
From:	"Crystal Lucas" <clucas@offcentre.net>
Cc:	<ray@pacificoast.net>
Sent:	November 15, 2003

Subject: My talk with your students

Dear Mrs. Leung:

Yes, I will be happy to speak with your students about college life. I will tell them about residence life as well.

Will you please give me the following information so I can begin to prepare?
1. How many students do you expect?
2. Have they expressed any particular concerns?
3. Do you have a video projector available?
4. Which Friday in January will be best for you?

I will be glad to have an opportunity to see you again.

Best,

Crystal Lucas

15i Reports

The term **report** can refer to many kinds of communication, from an informal discussion over the telephone to a lengthy, formal document with a title page, table of contents, and bibliography. In most work situations, you will be given detailed guidelines for the content and the form of the reports you are expected to write. You can then adapt the more general information in this text to your particular task. Reports come in four forms:

1. fill-in-the-blank forms for routine reporting

2. memo reports for reports written within an organization

3. letter reports for reports written to another organization

4. manuscript reports for reports that stand alone with a title page and an accompanying letter or memo.

The first three reports are generally short, informal reports. Manuscript reports are formal reports of three or four pages or longer.

Use headings to identify major sections of your report for the reader. All headings must be parallel in wording (see Faulty Parallelism, 18e) and in the same font size and type.

Audience and Purpose

All reports are based on factual information presented in an organized form. The two general categories of reports are **informational** and **analytical.**

The information report provides details and data, such as weekly sales reports or progress reports on specific projects. It does not analyze any of the information presented. In contrast, analytical reports evaluate information in order to make recommendations, provide options, or attempt to solve problems. When crafting an analysis report, you may choose either to present your problem and fact-finding at the beginning and end with recommendations, or to begin your report with the recommendations, followed by the background, facts, and description of the problem.

If your audience has little knowledge about your topic, start with the background. For busy executives familiar with the subject, provide the recommendations first.

The more objective and credible your information is, the more useful it will be to your reader. Don't let your interests and biases (such as personal involvement with any of the participants) slant your presentation of the facts. Opinions have their place, but don't disguise them as facts.

15j Analytical Problem-Solving Reports

As its name suggests, a **problem-solving report** is appropriate when you want to analyze a problem and suggest ways to solve it. A dance student, for example, might write a report on the reasons for injuries to first-year students. A restaurant manager might write a report on the effects of staff reductions on the quality of service.

The more specifically you define the problem you want to solve, the more useful your report is likely to be. Try to narrow a general subject, such as security problems, to something more precise, such as *a 30-percent increase in locker room thefts in the last six months*.

A problem-solving report usually has three sections:

1. *Background*

Fill in enough information to give your reader a good sense of the context and the importance of the problem. How often does the problem occur? When and where does it occur? How many people are affected? What are the costs in money, efficiency, safety, prestige, morale?

2. *Analysis*

You should develop this section of your report through causal analysis. Make a list of all the factors contributing to the problem. Be sure to include both immediate causes (inadequate supervision contributes to theft by employees) and more remote causes (employees are dissatisfied with their wages and benefits and therefore some feel entitled to steal).

201

You can organize this analysis as a list of independent causes or as a chain of interdependent causes (low wages cause employee dissatisfaction; this dissatisfaction causes resentment against the employer; this resentment causes employees to steal). Depending on the complexity of the problem you are analyzing, you may want to combine both methods of developing a causal analysis. (For more information, see Explaining Causes and Effects, 6d.) Connect your analysis directly with the information in the background section so that your reader can see how your analysis explains the causes of the problem.

3. *Recommendations and implementation*

Suggest solutions to the problem you have analyzed. Your recommendations should follow logically from the analysis section. If you are suggesting a number of possible solutions, indicate which one is best and explain why. If appropriate, describe how the recommendations could be implemented.

15k Sample Problem-Solving Report

TO: Peter de Jong, Manager of the Marco Polo Restaurant
FROM: Lindsey Tomlinson, Dining Room Supervisor
DATE: January 31, 2004

SUBJECT: Serving Staff Injuries

Introduction

Since September 1, 2003, five of our fifteen servers have been injured on the job. Four of these injuries were minor (mostly cuts and burns), but one server sprained her wrist after falling on a wet floor. Although these injuries are certainly not life threatening, they are distressing and they seem to be increasing. We need to find ways to reduce them.

Analysis

Not surprisingly, most injuries occurred during our busiest times: the 11:30–1:30 lunch rush and the 5:30–8:30 dinner rush. Young and inexperienced staff find these times especially stressful, so they are more likely to make mistakes and get hurt. When I asked serving staff, both new and experienced, for their thoughts on the causes of injuries, they made the following observations:

1. Staff who have worked in other restaurants may not be as well trained as they say or assume they are.

2. When we are very busy, we ask staff to help out by doing jobs they are not adequately trained for. A new busboy, for example, may be asked to serve hot dishes.

3. Angry and demanding customers, as well as those who leave without paying their bill, upset serving staff who are then less careful about handling dishes, cutlery, and trays.

4. The ice machine leaks, so the floor around it is always slippery.

Recommendations

This feedback suggests that staff are well aware of safety problems and interested in helping to solve them. Here are some specific recommendations to consider:

1. Provide new servers with two training shifts whether or not they claim to be experienced. Focus on the most frequent causes of injuries: slips, spills, cuts, burns, and back strain.

2. Hold monthly safety meetings to give staff opportunities to voice their concerns and to learn safety tips from each other.

3. Remind all serving staff to ask for help if they don't know how to do a job or are having problems with customers. Provide staff with more opportunities to do a variety of jobs so they can help out when we are short-staffed.

4. Appoint a server to inspect the dining room for safety hazards (such as the leaking ice machine) at the beginning of each shift. Alert all serving staff to potential problems.

5. Repair or replace faulty equipment and furnishings promptly.

15l Brochures and Flyers

You may be one of the thousands of Canadians who create and run their own businesses at some point during their career, to earn money for your education, to freelance after you have gained experience, or to earn post-retirement income. Despite the invasion of television advertising, most businesses still rely on written communication to promote their products and services. Newspaper and magazine ads, promotional letters, brochures, and flyers are the most common types of persuasive pieces.

With only a limited budget and eager volunteers, you can produce a simple yet effective brochure that will get your business off the ground.

Creating a Brochure or Flyer

Complete these three stages in order to produce an effective brochure or flyer: create a framework, write the contents, and design the format.

Creating a Framework

Before you begin to write, answer the following questions to provide your framework:

1. What do you want the brochure to do for you (inform existing customers, find new customers, give information about new products or services, advertise a sale)?

2. Who is your target audience (households, other businesses, specific income levels or age groups)?

3. What needs does your product or service fill?

4. How will you use this piece (mail-out, drop-off, handout, leave-behind)?

5. What format will be most effective (full-page text, 6-panel–2 folds, half-page fold-over)?

Once you've answered the who, what, how, where, and why, you will know whether a brochure or a flyer is more appropriate, and you will be ready for the next stage.

Note: A flyer is either a full- or half-size, unfolded sheet (8 $\frac{1}{2}$ × 11 in.) with all the text on one side of the page. A brochure has one or two folds in the paper and the text is printed in columns on both sides of the page (8 $\frac{1}{2}$ × 11 or 8 $\frac{1}{2}$ × 14 in. is the typical size).

Writing the Contents

Marcia Yudkin, in her book *Persuading on Paper* (Haverford, PA: Infinity Publishing, 2001), outlines five steps to creating your piece:

1. ***Brainstorm ideas.*** For at least a week, jot down all ideas and thoughts. A thesaurus is a great tool for generating even more ideas. Allow enough extra time for these ideas to take shape.

2. ***Craft an attention-getting opener.*** This important first line helps you capture your readers' attention. These grabbers can be in the form of questions, news headlines, promises, or results (testimonials).

Ever Wondered How to Get More for Your Money?
Wake Up and Smell Our Coffee!

3. ***Spell out the offer or the action you want readers to take.*** Keep it simple and direct.

> This is a limited offer. Book your appointment by calling . . .
> Take advantage of our gift with purchase.

4. ***Select and arrange supporting facts and ideas gathered in Step 1 above.*** Provide details about your product or service that explain why people should buy from you. This is your chance to persuade your readers.

5. ***When you have produced a rough draft, get an unbiased second opinion.*** Make changes and then proofread carefully.

Brochures and Flyers

Designing the Format

Gather samples of other brochures and ads, and decide what you like and don't like. Visit your local copy shop and ask to see samples of paper. Pick out suitable paper in the weight and colour you think will get your message across.

The format needs to align closely with the tone and intent of the brochure. Choose the fonts, graphics, and layout that most closely match the content. It's a bit like choosing the right frame for a beautiful picture—isn't your content worthy of a great frame?

Because there are so many choices in a typical graphics package, remember to keep it simple. A clean, uncluttered look will have a more positive impact than too much text or too many graphics on the page.

TOO MANY CHORES & TOO LITTLE TIME FOR FUN?

**Give yourself a summer break—
Let Handy Hammers do those jobs for you!**

Plagued by weeds?
Worried about your plants during vacation time?
Frustrated with a falling-down fence?
Tired of spring cleaning?
Bored with tending your garden?
Concerned about leaky eavestroughs?

GIVE US A CALL

At your service, Shandy, Harry, June, and Ahmed are all eager to fix pesky problems and reduce those tiresome tasks so you'll have time for sun, surf, and relaxation. Our dedicated staff has a combined total of over 12 years' experience in household and yard maintenance. We guarantee our work—if you're not satisfied, we'll make it right!

FREE CONSULTATION & ESTIMATE
SPECIAL PRICES FOR SENIORS
REASONABLE RATES

CALL 555-6677 NOW & GET YOUR JUNE DISCOUNT

**Handy Hammers Home & Garden Care
123 Elm Street, Parkerville, ON M3C 1X1
Phone: 555-6677; Fax: 555-5544**

CHAPTER 16

GETTING A JOB

Since getting a job requires a great deal of effort, you must be organized and thorough in your approach. You must present yourself, on paper and in person, in a professional, businesslike manner. To prepare for the job search, you will need to create the following documents.

- résumé

- cover letter

- list of references

This section will guide you through each type of document, step by step, and give you examples to follow. You will also find tips for preparing for interviews.

16a Résumés

A résumé is a one- or two-page summary of your work experience and educational background, tailored to fit the requirements of each prospective employer. It's important and easy to make your résumé reflect each position you apply for. Simply type your choice of résumé, save it on disk, and modify it as needed, using the "cut and paste" feature of your computer.

A caution about professionally prepared résumés. While they look impressive, they are costly. Another drawback is that these documents sometimes inflate the applicant's abilities. In an interview, employers look for a match between the person they have seen on paper and the one facing them. Any discrepancy will raise questions about suitability. There is nothing wrong with getting some help to create the best portfolio you can; just be sure the words and descriptions fit with your personality and experiences. In other words, make it your own.

Contents of a Résumé

1. *Personal information*

At the top of the page, type your name, address, phone and fax numbers, and an email address. If any of these numbers are temporary, provide any permanent ones where you can also be reached.

2. *Objective or summary of skills*

If it's a part-time or summer job you're applying for, this statement is optional. However, if you are searching for a job that will provide experience to reinforce your career path, then include this information. Briefly describe your career goal and state the skills and abilities you would like to use.

> To broaden my administrative responsibilities in the health care field where my nursing background and effectiveness in dealing with people would be assets.

Alternatively, you may begin with a bulleted list of four or five key skills or abilities that your employer needs. Be sure your list is in parallel structure.

3. *Work experience and educational background*

These are the most important parts of the résumé. The way you present this information depends on the kind of résumé you are writing (see below), but your main purpose is to demonstrate that you can do the job you are applying for. Emphasize your achievements and the range of your responsibilities rather than merely giving your job title. List both work experience and education in reverse chronological order, listing the most recent first. List responsibilities in parallel structure, using past (or present) tense verbs. Include the names of the institution(s) you have attended and the degrees or certificates you have received. If you are a college or university student, you can omit information about your high school education.

List any work-related workshops, training sessions, and noncredit courses you have completed, because they indicate enthusiasm for your field. Indicate computer programs you use and any languages you speak. If your grades are high, list your grade point average.

4. *Interests, activities, recognition, and awards*

This personal information is optional in a résumé. You can include sports, hobbies, and awards to indicate that you have diverse skills and interests (some of which might be relevant to the job). These items may also indicate qualities that an employer would value, such as courage or perseverance. This information should be current, so don't include everything you have ever done. Your interests may provide an interviewer with an opening topic in an interview.

5. *References*

List names, addresses, and phone numbers of three people willing to provide references. Include their job titles and their relationship to you. Be sure to ask referees' permission before you include their names.

To choose your references, pick the people who can provide the best information about you for the type of job you're applying for—former employers, supervisors, and teachers. When you have an interview scheduled, it's a good idea to alert those on your list and remind them of skills and abilities you may want them to comment on, such as reliability, performance, and teamwork.

A frequently asked question about references is whether to include them on your résumé or just provide them when asked. Since most interviewers check references only after an interview, you may wish to take the references list to the interview. If you have room on your résumé, you may prefer to include them. If you have copies of favourable letters of recommendation, you can include one or two with your résumé.

Three Types of Résumés

There are three types of résumés: the *chronological,* the *functional,* and the *combination* résumé. Each has advantages and disadvantages.

The Chronological Résumé

Also known as the traditional résumé, this style presents your work experience and educational background in a chronological sequence from most recent to least recent. It is easy to read and prepare. Use this format if you have a consistent work record and steady employment. However, if you are new to the job market, haven't worked for some time, or have gaps in your work history, this type may not be the best because it quickly reveals these potential weaknesses.

The Functional Résumé

Headings for the functional résumé focus primarily on specific skills and accomplishments related to the prospective job, rather than the chronological listing of education and work experience.

If you've been away from the job market for a while, have an erratic work history, or have gained most of your experience from volunteer activities, then this format may be the best to emphasize your strengths. The functional résumé can use headings that emphasize the skills required in the position you are applying for. The major disadvantage of the functional résumé is that some employers find it dense and hard to follow. Even in a functional résumé, it's a good idea to include a brief employment history.

The Combination Résumé

As its name suggests, this résumé combines the features of the chronological résumé and the functional résumé. As in the functional résumé, you use skills and accomplishments as the major headings, but within these headings, you list the relevant information in a chronological sequence. The major advantage of a combination résumé is that you can present a more complete picture of yourself. The major disadvantage is that it is harder to organize. It may also be difficult to restrict to the maximum two pages.

16b Sample Chronological Résumé

Monique Tremblay used this résumé to get her first position in public relations after completing her degree at Mount Royal College in Calgary.

Monique Tremblay

#3, 10032-119 Street, Calgary, Alberta T5K 1M9
Home: 555-228-2910

Summary of Skills
- Experienced in a variety of public relations settings
- Enthusiastic and outgoing
- Strong writing and organizational skills
- Creative problem-solver and team-player

Education

2002–2003	**Bachelor of Applied Communications (Public Relations)** Mount Royal College, *Calgary, Alberta*
1997–2000	**Public Relations Diploma** Algonquin College, *Ottawa, Ontario*

Work Experience

January 5–
April 30, 2003
P/T

Account Coordinator, Shandwick
Canada, *Calgary, Alberta*
(Practicum Position)
- Wrote memoranda to clients.
- Booked a community tent throughout the summer for a city realtor, requiring research and correspondence with clients.
- Interpreted and entered marketing data.
- Planned program extensions for existing programs.

January 3–
April 25, 2003
P/T

Administrative Assistant, Alberta
Motion Picture Industries
Association (AMPIA), *Calgary, Alberta*
(Practicum Position)
- Was responsible for keeping track of all AMPIA Award entries (approx. 200), and silent auction donations in the database.
- Organized the silent auction with a committee.
- Assisted in preparing the program information.

September 2001–
September 2002

Marketing and Communications
Assistant, The Alberta College of Art
& Design, *Calgary, Alberta*
- As part of a team, organized and planned a major fundraising event. This involved taking ticket orders, organizing the silent auction, booking entertainment, planning party rentals, mailing out invitations, and working with a committee.
- Kept a fundraising database of approximately 8,000 names up-to-date and accurate.
- Organized/distributed an internal monthly newsletter.
- Organized/planned monthly President Luncheons promoting the College programs.

May 5–
August 24, 1999

Public Relations and Sponsorship
Liaison, Fringe Theatre Adventures,
Edmonton, Alberta
- Organized opening day ceremonies with a focus on the trade show and parade.
- Compiled over 100 individualized artist packages.
- Worked on Angels of the Fringe campaign, a fundraising venture with a $60,000 goal.

Professional Development

- Experienced with Microsoft Word and the Internet.
- Working knowledge of computer programs such as Raiser's Edge database program, PowerPoint, and Excel.
- Creative writing workshop certificate from Mount Royal College.
- Assistant Stage Manager of a Calgary theatre production, *Possible Worlds* (February and March 2003).

Personal Development

- Outdoor activities—skiing, softball, hiking
- Live theatre, music
- Travelling—travelled for four months to Thailand, Malaysia, and Australia

References and Portfolio upon Request

16c Sample Functional Résumé

A social worker changing jobs might prepare a résumé like this one.

Jason Singh

1235 Elm Street
Halifax, NS B3M 3J6

Ph: (555) 429-7854 Fax: (555) 429-7725
email: jsingh@iconn.com

Objective:
Personnel manager in a major retail firm where problem-solving, communication, and administrative skills would be assets.

Communication Skills:
- Set up and provided editorial assistance for an information newsletter for people on welfare. Achieved a readership of over 10,000 in the Halifax area.
- Delivered talks and lectures on family problems, organizational dynamics, and liaisons with government agencies. Regarded as an interesting and informative speaker.
- Wrote proposals for special projects requiring provincial government funding. Succeeded in securing an annual grant of $30,000 for special services to runaway teenagers.

Administrative Skills:
- Set up and directed a special project to assist runaway teenagers. Provided assistance to over 100 young people and their families.

- Hired, supervised, and assisted recent social work graduates in their first year of employment. Improved the efficiency and effectiveness of all employees.

Employment Highlights:
- Worked with a caseload of 150 families for five years.
- Counselled and provided practical assistance to parents and children.
- Had the reputation of offering skilled assistance to families in economic and emotional crisis.

Education:
- Bachelor of Social Work (Dalhousie University, 1996)
- Bachelor of Arts (major in sociology and English, Mount St. Vincent, 1994)
- Certificates from workshops in group dynamics, crisis intervention, and effective management skills

Activities:
- President, Toastmasters Club, 2001; member 1997–present
- Treasurer, Mount Pleasant Community Assoc., 1998–2003

Recognition and Awards:
- Volunteer Service Award, Westside United Church, 1998

References:

Dion Harris, Director
Youth Emergency Shelter
1310 Glengarry Avenue
Halifax, NS B5J 2P4
(555) 429-4221

Jean-Paul Sartre, Editor
No Exit
Box 1341, Postal Station B
Halifax, NS B2N 1J7
(555) 429-0000

Alastair MacLeod, Supervisor
Families in Transition
123 Boat Harbour Drive
Halifax, NS B2R 3P6
(555) 429-2957

16d Sample Combination Résumé

Sarah Daniels prepared this résumé for her first job in the travel field. She targeted areas of interest to her employer.

SARAH DANIELS

1920 Oak Street, Sudbury, ON L5S 0M9
Telephone: (555) 489-0715   email: sdaniels@compusmart.ca

Objective	A position in sales and marketing of tours and holiday packages

Education

September 2001 to September 2002	**Travel and Tourism Certificate** *Cambrian College, Sudbury, ON* *Courses completed: September 13, 2002* *Practicum: August 9–September 12, 2002* *Cumulative Grade Point Average: 3.45*
December 1999	**Front Page '98 Advanced Workshop** *Humber College, Toronto, ON*
September 1997 to August 1999	**Computer Information Systems Diploma** *Humber College, Toronto, ON*
September 1994 to April 1995	**Electrical Engineering Technology Certificate** *Cambrian College, ON*

Skills

- Proficient with the Apollo computer reservation system
- Familiar with Sabre computer reservation system
- Adept with Global/Matrix accounting system
- Skilled with word processing software such as Microsoft Office and Lotus 1-2-3
- Accomplished with graphics software such as Paint Shop Pro and CorelDRAW
- Trained at balancing bank deposits, bookkeeping, and administrative work
- Experienced in customer relations and retail store opening and closing procedures
- Capable of office machinery operation

Travel Experience

- Two-week independent bicycling adventure from Sudbury to Cape Breton, NS
- Tour of northern AB and the winter road from Ft. MacKay, AB, to Yellowknife, NWT
- Exploration of Yellowknife, NWT, and area (including activities such as snow-shoeing and dog-sledding)
- Independent travel through ON, PQ, NB, and NS
- Organized a weekend skiing trip for 50 to Banff, AB
- Cruised from Los Angeles, California, to Ensenada, Mexico

Work History

Administrative Assistant, Brown Family Dayhomes, Sudbury, ON
October 2000 to June 2001
- Completed bookkeeping and administrative duties
- Increased efficiency of administrative processes
- Introduced a new computer system for administrative tasks
- Improved administrative file organization

Web Page Designer, Shell Canada Limited, Toronto, ON
January 1999 to June 2000
- Examined and evaluated Human Resources department information
- Developed Human Resources department intranet pages for employee use
- Collected and summarized process flow data
- Created an interactive process flow website for internal and projected external use

Children's Entertainer and Balloon Artist, Just Clownin' Around, Sudbury, ON
September 1994 to December 1998
- Developed programs and performed at children's events and festivals
- Trained new employees and supervised others

Memberships

- President, Cambrian College Travel Club   2001–2002
- Council Member, Shell Web Council   1999–2000
- Publicity Director, Humber College Campus
  Student Association   1998–1999
- Editor, *The Chronicle,* Humber campus newspaper 1998–1999

Interests and Volunteer Work

Interests:
- travelling
- bicycling
- kayaking
- skiing (cross-country and downhill)

Volunteer Work:
- S.P.C.A. Walk A Dog participant
- Red Cross volunteer staff
- Head of Red Cross Blood Clinic organizing committee
- Travel Information Night organizing committee member and participant

215

16e Cover Letters

The cover letter accompanies your résumé when you apply for a job. Your aim in both pieces of writing is to create enough interest to secure an interview.

In your letter, you create interest principally by showing how your qualifications meet the requirements for the position. To achieve this purpose, you need a clear sense both of what your qualifications are and of what the job demands. Preparing your résumé will give you a good sense of your qualifications. To figure out what the job demands, first examine the job ad carefully. Note any particular skills and abilities required, such as a driver's licence or experience with a particular computer program. Second, find out as much as you can about the company and the position. Talk with anyone you know who has had a similar job or worked for the same employer. You may have to visualize yourself in the position and think through its demands. Then make a matching list of job requirements and your qualifications so that you can anticipate questions and provide answers in your cover letter.

You also create interest by the way you present yourself. Your letter should convey those aspects of your personality that are most appropriate for the job—your enthusiasm, initiative, personal warmth, experience in the field. But don't get carried away; this is a business letter. Choose your words carefully so that you don't sound too gushy, too pushy, or overly casual.

Warning: Proofread carefully. Mistake-ridden letters end up in the trash!

Contents of the Cover Letter

Job application letters usually have three parts:

1. An **introductory paragraph** stating the position you are applying for and indicating where you found out about the job. If possible, establish a connection with the employer by naming the person who suggested you apply. Express enthusiasm for the aims of the organization you want to join.

2. A **summary of your skills,** knowledge, and personal characteristics that are most relevant to the specific requirements for this position. This may take more than one paragraph. (See Sample Cover Letters, 16f.)

3. A **closing paragraph** referring to your résumé and indicating that you are available for an interview at the employer's convenience.

16f Sample Cover Letters

Sample Cover Letter I

Rita Alvarez wrote the following letter for a practicum position. It won her the practicum position as well as a permanent position after the practicum.

#103-112 West Park Avenue
Hamilton, ON L8S 1M5

July 4, 2003

Ms. Michelle Cranston
Ontario Motor Association—Hamilton
11220 19th Street
Hamilton, ON L5S 2T6

Dear Ms. Cranston:

The moment I have been waiting for is finally here! It's practicum time! When faced with the question of where I would like my first hands-on travel-industry experience to be, the answer was obvious. It has to be OMA.

The way your travel section is structured by having different stations, each with its own focus, allows your consultants to give clients their undivided attention and in-depth knowledge of particular areas. My year of travel in Asia and my fluency in Spanish and Italian would be resources I would be happy to share with your clients and staff. Your clients will find me efficient in creating the best travel plans for their needs.

Having had success with sales in the past, I look forward to using these skills within the travel industry. Because I enjoy the art of selling so much, I know that my sales skills will become a great asset to your company (not to mention my hard-working, professional attitude). My commitment to teamwork and my devotion to my job make me an ideal employee. I am confident that my love of learning, my interpersonal skills, my enthusiasm, and my training at Durham College make me exactly what you are looking for in a practicum student.

I look forward to meeting with you soon. You can contact me at (555) 308-9716 to arrange for an interview.

Sincerely,

Rita Alvarez

Rita Alvarez

Enclosure: résumé

Sample Cover Letter II

Cindy Chow's cover letter helped her gain employment upon completing her diploma.

2093 Granville Street
Vancouver, BC V6H 4D1

July 8, 2003

Jennifer Ormsbee
Manor Home Improvement Centre
300 Robson Street
Vancouver, BC V3H 5K1

Dear Ms. Ormsbee:

Working with London Drugs for nearly eleven years, I have developed a solid understanding of the sales industry. This environment has provided me with a strong background and knowledge of retail and its dynamics. I am very interested in applying my sales and customer service experience, along with my college education, in a challenging, varied, and demanding role as an employee for Manor Home Improvement Centre. I read of your need for a Junior Marketing Consultant on your website.

I will complete a two-year Management Studies Program at Capilano College in September of this year. In addition, I possess a bachelor of education from the University of British Columbia. I possess excellent interpersonal skills, communicating effectively with individuals at all levels. Throughout my work experience I have demonstrated my willingness and ability to familiarize myself quickly with applications, procedures, and policies, and to establish positive relationships with colleagues, managers, customers, and suppliers.

In my present position, a management training position, I have been responsible for overseeing stock personnel and cashiers while maintaining the smooth operation of the store. By listening and communicating with customers and other staff over the years, I have developed a keen understanding of the sales industry. As you can see on my attached résumé, I am energetic, resourceful, and committed to both company objectives and personal growth. I offer your team of professionals a highly motivated and professional approach to customer service and to the promotion of the home improvement industry.

I look forward to the opportunity to present further details of my qualifications in an interview. You may call me at (604) 514-9749.

Sincerely,

Cindy Chow

Cindy Chow

Enclosure

16g Letters of Recommendation

In addition to your résumé and cover letter, it's a good idea to include one or two letters of recommendation. If you make a habit of collecting them when you leave a job or complete a course, they will be readily available as attachments.

16h The Job Interview

Finally you get a call for an interview. You will need to prepare for it by finding out all you can about the company and the position. You will need to anticipate what questions you will be asked, as well as what questions you will need answered. And finally, you will need to practise for it to show yourself in the best light.

First, what do you know about the company? Check the company's website or annual report, or ask other employees of the company as long as they are not in the area you are applying for. You may call the receptionist, the Human Resources department, or the interviewer. Know how the company differs from its competitors.

Second, what skills is the company looking for? Analyze the position as carefully as you can, considering the technical and the interpersonal skills needed. Match your skills to those requirements. Consider difficult situations that could arise. If you are aware of areas of weakness or inexperience, consider how you would compensate or learn new skills.

Third, think of what you need to know about the position and the company. You may want to know about wages, when the job will begin, training or mentoring, benefits, or the dress code. Asking questions shows your interest and curiosity, so you want to be sure to ask a few. You will probably be asked if you have any questions toward the end of the interview. If you're not, tell the interviewer you have some questions. You want to be sure you will be happy with the position if you are offered it.

Lastly, how is the interviewer likely to structure the interview? Consider the interview as a formal conversation with a new acquaintance. You will begin with some general and light comments—the weather, common interests, the decor in the building or office, or even the traffic. You will then get to know each other better to see how your needs mesh. In an interview most questions fall into general categories—questions about yourself, about your strengths and weaknesses, past experience,

219

and your handling of past experiences. You may get a question that will make you squirm or you will have to think of an answer to a possible situation. Relax, think, and then speak. The interview will likely end with a summary, and either a plan to speak again or a time when you can expect to hear about the outcome.

Prepare for an interview by anticipating all details. The following guidelines will help:

1. Get a good night's sleep before the interview.

2. Plan what you will wear. Be sure your clothes are clean, conservative, and comfortable. Dress one notch above what you believe employees generally wear at the job.

3. Plan where you will park or how to get there. Arrive five minutes early.

4. Review your résumé and take two extra copies with you. Take samples of your work in a portfolio.

5. Shake hands firmly when you are introduced, smile, and make direct eye contact with each interviewer.

6. Don't ask for the position, but stress how you are suitable for it.

7. Think before you speak.

- Punctuation Guide from NASA's *A Handbook for Technical Writers and Editors*.
  stipo.larc.nasa.gov/sp7084/sp7084ch3.html

- Capitalization Guide from NASA's *A Handbook for Technical Writers and Editors*.
  stipo.larc.nasa.gov/sp7084/sp7084ch4.html

- Community Learning Network Career Resources—a collection of online resources on résumé writing, interview skills, success in the workplace, rights in the workplace, and Canadian career and job search centres. See Hunting Jobs; Writing Resumes and Cover Letters.
  www.cln.org/themes_index.html

- The Rensselaer Writing Center offers a variety of online handouts, including information on résumés and cover letters.
  www.rpi.edu/dept/llc/writecenter/web/handouts.html

- Professional Writing Handouts and Resources from the Purdue OWL.
  owl.english.purdue.edu/handouts/pw/index.html

- The Riley Guide: Employment Opportunities and Job Resources on the Internet.
  www.rileyguide.com

PART 5

PROOFREADING:
THE FINAL TOUCHES

CHECKLIST | *Proofreading*

	OK	NEEDS WORK

1. Have you corrected errors in
   sentence structure? ☐ ☐
   a. comma splices, fused sentences,
      fragments (18b, c, d)
   b. faulty parallelism, faulty
      subordination, mixed
      constructions (18e, f, g)

2. Have you corrected errors in
   the use of **modifiers**? ☐ ☐
   a. misused adjectives and
      adverbs (19a, b, c)
   b. misplaced and dangling modifiers,
      split infinitives (19d, e, f)

3. Have you corrected errors in the ☐ ☐
   use of **verbs**?
   a. verb forms (20a, b, c, d, e)
   b. subject-verb agreement (20f)

4. Have you corrected errors in the ☐ ☐
   use of **pronouns**?
   a. pronoun agreement (21a)
   b. pronoun form (21b, c, e)
   c. pronoun reference (21d)

5. Have you corrected errors in **punctuation**? ☐ ☐
   a. commas and semicolons (22a, b)
   b. quotation marks (22e)
   c. apostrophes (22h)
   d. other punctuation (22c, d, f, g)

6. Have you corrected errors in the use of ☐ ☐
   abbreviations, **capitalization**,
   and **numbers**? (22i, j, k)

7. Have you corrected errors in **format**? ☐ ☐
   a. in business writing (chapters 15 and 16)
   b. in MLA-style writing assignments
      (appendices A, B)
   c. in APA-style writing assignments
      (appendices A, C)

8. Have you corrected errors in **spelling**? ☐ ☐
   a. names, places, titles, other proper nouns
   b. homonyms, frequently misspelled words, typos

CHAPTER 17

PROOFREADING STRATEGIES

Proofreading involves looking for errors in sentence structure, grammar, punctuation, spelling, and format. Don't skip this last step, even if you are pressed for time or simply tired of a piece of writing. Poorly constructed sentences and slips in grammar can bring an A paper down to a B, or a D paper down to an F. Spelling errors in a résumé or cover letter can mean that you are not asked for an interview. Assure your reader of your competence by giving your writing a final polish.

To locate the rough spots in your writing, try these strategies:

- Leave your paper for at least a day. You will then be able to see what you actually wrote more clearly.

- Use the Proofreading Checklist to remind yourself of potential problems.

- Prepare a checklist of your own common errors. This list will help you focus on specific areas when you proofread.

- Read your paper aloud either to yourself or to a friend. Revise awkward or unclear sentences.

- Read your paper backwards, sentence by sentence. This strategy is especially good for highlighting sentence fragments and spelling errors.

- Use the spell checker and other correction features provided by your word-processing software. Customize the built-in dictionary to reflect Canadian spelling and usage.

- Don't forget to check the format of your document (including title page, quotations, and references, if any) before you print the final copy.

CHAPTER 18

PROOFREADING: SENTENCE STRUCTURE

18a Writing Good Sentences

Among other things, good writing is writing that "flows." Readers are quickly irritated by writing that doesn't flow because sentences are punctuated incorrectly or badly constructed.

This section will show you how to recognize and correct these common problems in sentence structure:

- comma splices
- fused sentences
- sentence fragments
- faulty parallelism
- faulty subordination
- mixed constructions

18b Comma Splice

When you're proofreading for errors in sentence structure, be especially careful to watch for **comma splices.** This error, sometimes called a *comma fault,* occurs when two main clauses are joined by only a comma.

COMMA SPLICE The wind whipped up dead leaves in the yard, violent drops of rain beat against the ground.

Recognizing Comma Splices

1. *Figure out whether your sentence contains two or more clauses.*
You can do this if you understand the difference between a clause and a phrase. A **clause** is a group of words with a subject and a verb.

she waved at the helicopter
when **she waved** at the helicopter

A **phrase** is a group of words without both a subject and a verb.

after waving at the helicopter
to wave at the helicopter
in the sky overhead

Note: Be alert when a pronoun occurs in a sentence (see chapter 21). The pronoun might signal the subject of a second clause.

Bhatia practised regularly, and so **she played** well for the concert.

Lateef celebrated when **he won** the figure skating competition.

2. *Figure out whether the clauses are main clauses or subordinate clauses.*

A **main clause** can stand alone as an independent sentence.

Marta stared in disbelief.

A **subordinate clause** cannot stand alone.

While Marta stared in disbelief

Adverbial subordinate clauses begin with subordinating conjunctions (*after, during, while, when, if, unless, until, because, although*). Other subordinate clauses begin with relative pronouns such as *that, which, who,* and *whom.*

3. *If the sentence contains two main clauses, are they joined by only a comma?*

If so, the sentence contains a comma splice.

Be especially careful to avoid comma splices when a main clause is followed by a subordinate clause and another main clause.

COMMA SPLICE	Tim completed a four-year degree in nursing, when he graduated, however, there were no jobs.
REVISED	Tim completed a four-year degree in nursing; when he graduated, however, there were no jobs.

Exercise 18.1

Underline the main clause(s) in each of the following sentences.

1. To prove your hypothesis, you must not falsify data or ignore contradictory evidence.

2. Clarence cut the questioning short with a caustic remark and a withering glance.

3. Furrowing her brow in concentration, Karen wound up for the pitch.

4. When he finished his project, Govind admired his handiwork: a two-storey birdhouse with a railed porch and cedar roof.

5. Hans scrubbed at the large blue stain on his shirt front, but he couldn't get it out.

Exercise 18.2

Mark the following sentences **CS** if they contain comma splices or **C** if they are correct.

1. When I worked as a cashier in a local supermarket, I dreaded the monthly special on quarter chicken legs.

2. The packages were poorly sealed, the three legs oozed raw chicken juices and blood.

3. The juices leaked all over the conveyor belt and all over my hands as I scanned and packed the chicken.

4. I was concerned about contamination, I sanitized the belt and my hands with antibacterial cleanser after each order.

5. Despite my best efforts to rid myself of the smell of chicken, my dog would practically knock me to the ground when I returned home.

Correcting Comma Splices

There are six ways to correct a comma splice.

1. ***Use a period to separate the two clauses.***

COMMA SPLICE   An enormous wave hit the boat, all those on deck were swept overboard.

REVISED   An enormous wave hit the boat. All those on deck were swept overboard.

2. *Use a semicolon to join the two clauses if they contain closely related ideas.*

COMMA SPLICE   Fish stocks have declined in the last ten years, fishing licences are now difficult to obtain.

REVISED   Fish stocks have declined in the last ten years; fishing licences are now difficult to obtain.

3. *Use a colon to join the two clauses if the second clause explains, expands, or emphasizes the first.*

COMMA SPLICE   After six months of treatment, Louisa was feeling much better, she now eagerly anticipated returnir.g to school.

REVISED   After six months of treatment, Louisa was feeling much better: she now eagerly anticipated returning to school.

4. *Use a semicolon and a conjunctive adverb, such as moreover, however, therefore, thus, or then to join the two clauses.*

18b

Comma Splice

COMMA SPLICE   Sean drifted out of high school without a diploma, he now has the job of his dreams.

REVISED   Sean drifted out of high school without a diploma; however, he now has the job of his dreams.

5. *Use a comma and coordinating conjunction (and, but, or, nor, yet, so, for) to join the two clauses.*

COMMA SPLICE   Peering through the darkness, they could see the lights of the settlement, they struggled onward.

REVISED   Peering through the darkness, they could see the lights of the settlement, so they struggled onward.

6. *Change one of the main clauses into a subordinate clause.* Put a comma after the subordinate clause if it comes first in the sentence.

COMMA SPLICE	You need more rest, you will get sick.
REVISED	If you don't get more rest, you will get sick.

Exercise 18.3

Revise the following sentences to eliminate all comma splices. Try a number of revision methods.

1. A loud crackling sound alerted Gerta to the fact that she had left the foil cover on the dish, both the meal and the microwave oven were ruined.

2. Alicia offered to replace my shift, when I called to confirm the arrangement, however, she had changed her mind.

3. As we waited in line, we heard Jason's unmistakable braying laugh, we hoped he wouldn't see us before we could disappear into the darkened theatre.

4. Tina groaned in dismay at the error message, she pulled out the massive user guide and started her search for help.

5. Neither team chose Maria, she took her ball and went home.

Exercise 18.4

Revise the following passage to eliminate all comma faults.

These days many people use their computers as stereo systems that not only play music but also go out and get the music they want to hear. In response, the major labels are experimenting with anti-piracy technology such as non-recordable CDs, they want to stop consumers from trading tunes on the Internet or burning recordable CDs. It's not clear how many non-recordable CDs have actually been released, however, the prospect has aroused considerable commentary. Some people say they have a right to burn their own CDs, the record companies are charging too much. Other people justify CD piracy by arguing that most of the money from sales goes to the companies, not the artists. In any case, it may not be possible to create a copy-proof CD that will still play in a computer. Trying to make one may annoy many consumers, the labels may decide it's not worth the risk.

18c Fused Sentences

A **fused sentence,** sometimes called a *run-on sentence*, occurs when two main clauses are written as one with no punctuation between them. The length of the sentence will not tell you whether or not it is fused. A sentence can be quite long without being run-on.

CORRECT   Wendy stopped and glared angrily at the mischievous children as another snowball flew by her head.

On the other hand, some fused sentences are quite short.

FUSED   Open the window I need some fresh air.

You can correct this error by using one of the following techniques:

1. ***Separate the two clauses with a period.***

   Open the window. I need some fresh air.

2. ***Use a semicolon to join the two clauses.***

   Open the window; I need some fresh air.

3. ***Use a comma and a coordinating conjunction to join the two clauses.***

   Open the window, for I need some fresh air.

4. ***Change one of the main clauses into a subordinate clause.***

   Open the window because I need some fresh air.

Exercise 18.5

Revise the following to eliminate all fused sentences.

1. Marvinder shifted slowly and repeatedly between forward and reverse she was therefore able to gain traction and move the car out of the mud.

2. Beatrice checked email three times a day she didn't want to miss any messages.

3. Watch where you're going you'll walk into the wall.

4. Without thinking, Delmar opened the side door and was startled by a shrieking siren he had forgotten to deactivate the alarm.

5. Washing four loads of shirts this morning was a chore even more daunting is the prospect of all that ironing.

Exercise 18.6

Revise the following paragraph to eliminate all fused sentences.

My final recommendation for becoming and staying a non-smoker is to eat Popsicles. Because you are taking on such a big commitment, you deserve a sweet treat now and then. Popsicles are low-calorie treats you will not gain weight. A Popsicle also gives you something to hold and put in your mouth just like a cigarette, but it is not a cigarette. You can choose any flavour you like when you have a really strong craving, you should not tear off the wrapper and plunge the Popsicle into your mouth because it will stick to your tongue and lips. If this happens to you, as it did to me, don't attempt to pull the Popsicle out it hurts. Have one of your support team come to your aid with warm water.

—*Athena Greba*

18d
Fragments

18d Fragments

A **fragment** is an incomplete sentence. In some contexts, such as informal personal letters, press releases, and advertising, a fragment is a good way to catch your reader's attention.

A wonderful occasion for all of us.

The best buy ever!

The end of the line for him.

A small step, but an important one.

If the rest of your sentences are grammatically complete, a fragment will stand out effectively for emphasis. On the other hand, if you mix unintentional fragments with intentional fragments, you'll confuse your reader and lose your intended emphasis.

Remember, too, that fragments will make your writing seem less formal. Unless you wish your work to appear somewhat casual, avoid fragments in reports, business letters, and essays. When you are proofreading for sentence fragments, watch for the following errors.

Recognizing Sentence Fragments

• *Phrases or subordinate clauses punctuated as complete sentences*

Sometimes the fragment belongs with the complete sentence that comes before or after it in the passage.

FRAGMENT

Bill could balance a glass of water on his head. Without spilling a drop. [The second construction is a prepositional phrase and, like all phrases, lacks a subject and a verb.]

COMPLETE SENTENCE

Bill could balance a glass of water on his head without spilling a drop. [The phrase has been joined to the sentence before it.]

FRAGMENT

Because there had been two major rent increases in the last two years. Maureen decided to look for a new apartment. [The first construction is a subordinate clause, not a complete sentence.]

COMPLETE SENTENCE

Because there had been two major rent increases in the last two years, Maureen decided to look for a new apartment. [The subordinate clause has been joined to the following sentence. There is a comma between the clauses because the subordinate clause is first.]

• *Sentences with missing verbs*

If you remember that every verb ending with *ing* must have an auxiliary in order to be a complete verb, you'll be less likely to write this kind of fragment.

FRAGMENT

The child frantically searching for her mother.

COMPLETE SENTENCE

The child was frantically searching for her mother.

Be especially careful with *being*, which is a participle, not a verb. Avoid the phrase *the reason being*. Use *because* instead.

FRAGMENT

The reason for her sore back being that she had fallen.

COMPLETE SENTENCE Her back was sore because she had fallen.

Exercise 18.7

Revise the following constructions to make them complete sentences.

1. Wendell driving around in circles, unable to find his date's house in the maze-like neighbourhood.

2. According to *The Hitchhiker's Guide to the Galaxy*, forty-two being the answer to the meaning of life, the universe, and everything.

3. After getting up to change channels himself because the remote control battery was dead. Brad sank back exhausted onto the couch.

4. Lydia, the last person I expected to quit school.

5. Angry at the parking attendant for writing up a ticket because the meter had expired.

Fragments

Exercise 18.8

Revise the following constructions to make them complete sentences. If the sentence is correct, write **C**.

1. Always quick to judge others, but he bridled at even the mildest criticism.

2. Open your booklets and begin the exam.

3. The fans cheering wildly as the defenceman raced down the ice.

4. Turning his head for an instant to look at his program, Brendan missed the winning goal.

5. A woman with fierce pride and a determined spirit.

6. The reason for the fire being a pot of hot oil left burning on the stove.

7. Last year Donald was the grand prize winner in the Bulwer-Lytton bad writing contest.

8. Tearing open the envelope and nervously removing the transcript of her final grades.

9. Although I could detect movement inside, no one answering my knock.

10. Because he didn't phone in or show up for work.

Exercise 18.9

Restore the following paragraph to its original form by eliminating all inappropriate sentence fragments.

> In life and in literature, people create alternate versions of reality. To avoid facing the unpleasant aspects of the lives they actually live. Or just to make their lives more exciting. In "Spy Story" by Filipino writer Jose Y. Dalisay, for example, Fred has convinced himself that he is a secret agent for the US Embassy. Thinking that everyone around him is a spy and up to no good. Fred creates some excitement in his otherwise boring job as a chauffeur. It's clear to most readers that Mr. Sparks, Fred's boss, is running a prostitution ring. Forcing Fred into the role of a pimp. But Fred imagines that Mr. Sparks is entertaining high-ranking American contacts to foil dangerous espionage activities. As well as commenting on our capacity for self-deception as individuals, "Spy Story," which has a significant political dimension. By setting his story in a seedy bar in the Philippines during the Cold War of the 1950s, Dalisay comments on the distortions of reality widely shared during this time of propaganda, spies, and secrets.

18e Faulty Parallelism

The principle of **parallelism** is that similar ideas should be expressed in grammatically similar ways. Whenever you use a coordinating conjunction (*and, but, or, nor, yet, so, for*), be sure to join grammatically equal words, phrases, or clauses.

> Her New Year's resolutions were to **quit smoking, lose weight,** and **exercise regularly.**

Faulty parallelism occurs when ideas of equal value are not expressed in the same grammatical form.

Avoiding Faulty Parallelism

- *Use the same part of speech for each item in a series of words.*

NOT   The family has wealth, reputation, and **is powerful.**

BUT   The family has wealth, reputation, and **power.**

- *Use the same construction for each phrase or clause in a series.*

Do not mix phrases and clauses, or even different kinds of phrases.

NOT   Maurice decided to complete his second
                       year at college, look for a job, and **then
                       he and Eva would get married.**

BUT   Maurice decided to complete his second
                       year at college, look for a job, and **then
                       marry Eva.**

• *Make sure that items in a bulleted or numbered list have the same grammatical form.*

NOT   1. Open the packet.
                       2. The contents should be poured into a
                          bowl.
                       3. Add one cup of water.

BUT   1. Open the packet.
                       2. Pour the contents into a bowl.
                       3. Add one cup of water.
                          [Note that each item in this list
                          begins with a verb.]

• *Include both elements in a comparison.*

NOT   My paper is as long as **Bill.**

BUT   My paper is as long as **Bill's** [paper].

• *Complete balanced constructions with grammatically similar sentence elements.*

NOT   The more I work on this assignment, **I
                       don't seem to accomplish much.**

BUT   The more I work on this assignment, **the
                       less I seem to accomplish.**

• *Make sure correlative conjunctions join grammatically similar sentence elements.*

The correlative conjunctions are *either/or, neither/nor, not only/but also, whether/or, both/and.*

NOT   Not only did the horse lose, **but the
                       right leg of the jockey was broken.**

BUT   Not only did the horse lose, but also **the
                       jockey broke her right leg.**

18e

*Faulty
Parallelism*

Exercise 18.10

Make elements in the following sentences parallel. If the sentence is correct, write **C**.

1. Robert can either work and save money for college, or he can take out a student loan.

2. The more I try to convince him otherwise, he is more determined to dye his hair green.

3. The Bennetts' house is smaller than their neighbour.

4. My car needs new paint, new tires, and the transmission is shot.

5. Not only did Marvin borrow my book without asking, but he also bent the cover and wrote in the margins.

6. The store went out of business because of inferior merchandise, their prices were high, and poor customer service.

7. Gina is both a skilled pianist and she is a talented baseball player.

8. Before becoming actors, some famous stars worked in other fields. For example, Harrison Ford was a master carpenter, and there is Michelle Pfeiffer, who was a cashier.

9. Some people keep repeating their mistakes; others keep making new ones.

10.
    - Graduated from Bishop Stratford High, 1998
    - Diploma in Automotive Repair, Mount Royal College, 1999
    - I took off to travel in Central and South America in 1999–2000
    - Completed my BS in Computing Science in 2004

Exercise 18.11

The errors in parallel sentence structure introduced into this passage make it wordy and confusing. Revise where necessary to make sentence elements parallel.

In an essay titled "The Pain of Animals," David Suzuki's subject is the pain humans inflict on animals by using them in scientific experiments, we hunt them, and some animals are kept in zoos. Suzuki's thesis is that we use animals for these purposes because their nervous systems are like ours and humans and animals have similar emotional responses. This similarity between humans and animals means, however, that animals feel fear and have pain feelings just as we do. Suzuki develops his essay by giving a series of examples of pain inflicted on animals in zoos and scientists perform experiments on them. He ends his essay with an account of his experience watching a film about the suffering endured by chimpanzees used for medical research. Their agony provides the strongest evidence for his argument that the similarities between chimpanzees and humans ought to make us more compassionate and we shouldn't be as exploitive in our treatment of animals.

18f Faulty Subordination

Faulty subordination occurs when you fail to differentiate less important ideas from more important ideas.

Avoiding Faulty Subordination

• *Check that you have attached the subordinating conjunction to the appropriate clause.*

Some common subordinating conjunctions are *before, after, since, while, when, if, unless, until, because, although.* You can signal the connections among your ideas more accurately by putting the less important idea in the subordinate clause and by beginning the subordinate clause with the appropriate conjunction.

NOT

He wanted to make a good impression, **because** he dressed carefully for the interview.

BUT

Because he wanted to make a good impression, he dressed carefully for the interview.

• *Use the most precise subordinating conjunction.*

Pay particular attention to your use of *since* and *as. Since* can mean *because,* but it can also mean *from the time that.* In some sentences, *since* is confusing. In such cases, it is best to rephrase the sentence.

CONFUSING

Since Sandy broke her leg, she hasn't been playing basketball.

CLEAR

Sandy hasn't played basketball since she broke her leg.

CLEAR	Because Sandy broke her leg, she hasn't been playing basketball.

As is another troublesome conjunction. Sometimes *as* means *because,* but it's clearer to use *as* to mean *during the time that.*

CLEAR	**As** the rain poured down, we made our way to the deserted cabin.

CONFUSING	**As** she cycles to work, she never gets stuck in traffic.

CLEAR	**Because** she cycles to work, she never gets stuck in traffic.

Note: Don't be afraid to begin a sentence with *because.* Just make sure to include a main clause in the sentence.

• *Limit the number of subordinate clauses in a single sentence.*

By piling subordinate clauses on top of each other you can make it difficult for the reader to judge how your ideas are related. Revise sentences with too many subordinate clauses by rephrasing the sentence or by reducing some of the clauses to phrases or single words.

18f

Faulty Subordination

NOT	**Because the committee could not reach a decision,** the project was stalled **because no one knew what to do next.**

BUT	The **committee's failure to reach a decision** stalled the project because no one knew what to do next.

NOT	The party **that wins the election, which will be held on November 10,** will set economic policies **that will affect the country** for the next ten years.

BUT	The party **that wins the November 10 election** will set the **country's** economic policies for the next ten years.

Exercise 18.12

Revise the following sentences to correct faulty or excessive subordination.

1. Since their home was badly damaged by fire, the Wongs have been living in a rented house.

2. Although Gina used the proper amount of bromine, the pool sides were still covered with algae although she also shocked the pool regularly with chlorine.

3. The fireplace that is in the basement has a pilot light that frequently goes out when snow blocks the outside vent.

4. Todd forgot to include his charitable receipts in his income tax return because his refund was delayed.

5. If you want to buy a computer, the person whom you should call is Roman, who is an expert on what are the best buys.

6. Craig isn't doing well in physics although he doesn't seem particularly concerned.

7. When I entered the building, I knew I was late for class when I heard the final bell.

8. Marina hates the taste of ketchup even though she likes ketchup-flavoured potato chips.

9. As I couldn't hear what he was saying, I asked him to speak up.

10. Since the air conditioner broke down, everyone has been complaining about the heat.

18g Mixed Constructions

Mixed constructions get their name because they mix incompatible grammatical units and thus produce sentences that will seem awkward to your reader. Mixed constructions result from the writer thinking of two similar sentences and then using parts of each in a single sentence. For example, let's say you have these two perfectly reasonable sentences in mind:

June is exhausted because she has three small children.

The reason June is exhausted is that she has three small children.

If you are not paying attention, you might lose track of what you are writing and produce a mixed construction:

MIXED   The reason June is exhausted is because she has three small children.

You can recognize awkward constructions like this by reading your work aloud to yourself or to a classmate. Here are some tips to help you avoid three common types of mixed constructions:

1. *Avoid* is when *and* is because *constructions.*

MIXED   **An example** of her snobbery **is when** she criticizes her neighbours for their un-grammatical speech.

REVISED   An example of her snobbery is **her criticism** of her neighbours' ungrammatical speech.

REVISED   She **reveals** her snobbery when she criticizes her neighbours' ungrammatical speech.

MIXED   **The reason** the brakes failed **is because** the brake fluid was accidentally removed.

REVISED   The reason the brakes failed is **that the brake fluid was accidentally removed.**

REVISED   The brakes **failed** because the brake fluid was accidentally removed.

Occasionally the subordinate clause appears before the verb.

MIXED   **Because he was always late** [subordinate clause] **was the reason** he was fired.

REVISED   **His habitual lateness** was the reason he was fired.

REVISED   Because he was always late, he **was fired.**

2. *Make sure you have a subject in the main clause.*

Remember that a prepositional phrase is never the subject of a sentence.

MIXED	In the article "Anorexia and the Adolescent" [prepositional phrase] explains Lilian Donaldson's views on the connection between self-starvation and the adolescent's need for control.
REVISED	In the article "Anorexia and the Adolescent," Lilian Donaldson [subject] explains the connection between self-starvation and the adolescent's need for control.
REVISED	The article "Anorexia and the Adolescent" [subject] explains Lilian Donaldson's views on the connection between self-starvation and the adolescent's need for control.

3. *Don't confuse questions with statements.*

MIXED	She wondered how long will it be until I see him again?
REVISED	She wondered how long it would be until she saw him again.
REVISED	She wondered, "How long will it be until I see him again?"

Exercise 18.13

Revise the following sentences to eliminate mixed constructions.

1. Geraldine asked her brother Ben how much longer will he be in the shower?
2. Because my dog ate my computer disk is the reason my paper is late.
3. Portaging is when you carry a boat overland between navigable lakes or rivers.
4. In Darrin's letter explained why he resigned his position.
5. The reason we cut our vacation short is because it rained for a solid week.

6. Without more donations means that the shelter will have to close.
7. Looking at his bank statement, Domenic wondered how did he spend so much money in only a month?
8. An example of Mary's thoughtfulness is when she cuts the lawn for her elderly neighbours.
9. In the theatre program lists all the actors in the play.
10. The next day is when Frank finally thought of a snappy comeback to Vincent's insulting remark.

18g

Mixed
Constructions

CHAPTER 19

PROOFREADING: MODIFIERS

19a Key Terms to Know

Adjectives modify nouns and pronouns (that is, they describe the physical, mental, and emotional qualities of the people, places, and things named by nouns and pronouns). Words that end with *ful, ish, less, like* (*thankful, foolish, helpless, childlike*) are usually adjectives.

> The quick brown fox jumped over the lazy dog. [*Quick* and *brown* modify *fox; lazy* modifies *dog.*]

Adverbs modify verbs, adjectives, and other adverbs (that is, they describe the manner or degree of the actions or qualities named by verbs, adjectives, and other adverbs). Many descriptive adverbs end in *ly* (a few adjectives, such as *friendly* and *lovely,* also end in *ly*). Some common adverbs, such as *very, always, not, well,* and *often,* do not end in *ly.*

> The cat stretched lazily in the sun. [*Lazily* modifies the verb *stretched.*]

> Dr. Lucas' lecture on the shortage of clean water in Ghana was extremely interesting. [*Extremely* modifies the adjective *interesting.*]

> The car went by too quickly for me to see who was in it. [*Too* modifies the adverb *quickly.*]

19b Comparative Forms of Adjectives and Adverbs

Most adjectives and adverbs have degrees of comparison (*pretty, prettier, prettiest; interesting, more interesting, most interesting*). If you are not sure of the comparative form of a particular adjective or adverb (should it be *clearer* or *more clear*?), consult your dictionary. Avoid using double comparisons, such as *more happier* or *most fastest.*

Some adjectives (such as *unique, perfect, empty*) express absolute concepts. One piece of pottery cannot be *more unique* than the rest, one math test cannot be the *most perfect* in the class, one glass cannot be *more empty* than another.

19c Troublesome Adjectives and Adverbs

• *Good, well*

Good is an adjective.

> I haven't seen a **good** movie for ages.

• *Well* is usually an adverb.

NOT	Declan **ran good** in the last race.
BUT	Declan **ran well** in the last race.

• *Well* in reference to health is an adjective.

> Jane hasn't been **well** since her bout of mononucleosis.

• *Bad/badly, real/really*

Bad and *real* are adjectives.

> This is a **bad** photograph of me.

> The huge boulder looks **real,** but it is actually made of papier-mâché.

Badly and *really* are adverbs.

NOT	The roof was damaged **bad** in the hailstorm.
BUT	The roof was **badly** damaged in the hailstorm.
NOT	Ben is **real** eager to begin his new job on Monday.
BUT	Ben is **really** eager to begin his new job on Monday.

• *Less* and *fewer,* both adjectives, are used differently. *Less* (the comparative of *little*) is an adjective used with items that cannot be considered as separate objects: *less* food, *less* kindness, *less* snow. *Fewer* (the comparative of *few*) is an adjective used with things that can be counted individually: *fewer* students, *fewer* courses, *fewer* responsibilities.

NOT	**Less** students have enrolled than we expected.
BUT	**Fewer** students have enrolled than we expected.

- Adjectives ending with *ing* and *ed*

If your first language is not English, you may find it confusing to decide on the correct meaning and appropriate ending for adjectives formed with an *ing* ending (present participle) or an *ed* ending (past participle of a regular verb).

She is **exciting.** [meaning that she causes others to feel excitement]

She is **excited.** [meaning that she herself feels excitement]

A good dictionary should help you decide on the correct ending.

- Articles (*a, an, the*)

Many languages do not have articles, and so learners of English often find this aspect of the language difficult. These guidelines may help:

1. Use the article *a* or *an* (before vowels) to indicate a noun in general terms (*a* meal, *an* orange).

2. Most proper nouns do not use an article. *The* is used with some plural proper nouns to indicate specific people (*the* Smiths) and geographical designations (*the* Rockies). *The* is also used with collective proper nouns referring to countries or groups (*the* United States of America, *the* United Kingdom, *the* CFL).

3. Use *the* to indicate a particular noun or one that has been mentioned earlier. (*The* photograph of *the* moon that I referred to is on page ten).

Exercise 19.1

Revise the following sentences so that adjectives and adverbs are used correctly.

1. He looked at me serious and began to speak.
2. The engine still runs good, but the body is badly rusted.
3. Less players have registered for hockey camp this summer.
4. The supervisor is real interested in your opinion of the proposal.

5. Clarence gets good grades in physical education, but he doesn't do so good in the chemistry.

Exercise 19.2

Revise the following sentences so that adjectives and adverbs are used correctly. If the sentence is correct, write **C.**

1. Lynette is the most liveliest member of my aerobics class.
2. You will feel considerable better after you have taken this medication.
3. The play went good in rehearsal, but opening night was a disaster.
4. Since landing a full-time job, Satpal has been able to afford more dressy clothes, but she has less social occasions on which to wear them.
5. The milk bottle in the refrigerator is completely empty.
6. Of the two reports, which is the more informative?
7. Eric answered all of the questions as honest as he could.
8. Although the hikers were real tiring, they decided to press on.
9. The door opened more easily after Jack adjusted the hinges.
10. Max is less happier living on his own than he was living at home.

19d Misplaced Modifiers

A **misplaced modifier,** as its name suggests, is in the wrong place. The resulting sentence is confusing and sometimes unintentionally amusing.

> Mr. Kowalski saw a horse by the side of the road on his way home from work.

Since Mr. Kowalski is more likely to be on his way home from work than the horse is, the prepositional phrase *on his way home from work* should be placed closer to *Mr. Kowalski* in the sentence.

> On his way home from work, Mr. Kowalski saw a horse by the side of the road.

Words such as *only, hardly, barely, nearly,* and *almost* are especially troublesome because they can easily be misplaced.

NOT	After a few lessons, James could **almost swim** the entire length of the pool.
BUT	After a few lessons, James could swim **almost the entire length** of the pool.
NOT	**I only want** a minute of your time.
BUT	I want **only a minute** of your time.

Note: Do not use *hardly* and *barely* with *not*.

NOT	**I can't hardly** hear you.
BUT	**I can hardly** hear you.
NOT	**She couldn't barely** hear the faint sound coming from the basket on the front steps.
BUT	She **could barely** hear the faint sound coming from the basket on the front steps.

19e Split Infinitives

19e

*Split
Infinitives*

An **infinitive** is *to* + a verb: *to think, to walk, to breathe.* A **split infinitive** occurs when a modifier (usually an adverb) is misplaced between *to* and the verb (*to quickly run*). It is best to avoid splitting an infinitive, especially when the resulting construction is awkward. You can correct a split infinitive by rephrasing the sentence.

SPLIT INFINITIVE	Marjorie needed time to **mentally prepare** for the exam.
REVISED	Marjorie needed time to **prepare mentally** for the exam.

Sometimes, however, a split infinitive sounds less awkward than when the modifier is relocated in the sentence.

The diners asked the man at the next table **to please stop** smoking his cigar. [Putting *please* anywhere else in the sentence would be clumsy.]

Exercise 19.3

Revise the following sentences to avoid split infinitives and to place modifiers as close as possible to what they modify.

1. Soak the shirt in cold water with the spaghetti sauce stain.

2. Sonia could almost run ten full circuits around the field.

3. Preserved in formaldehyde, the students examined the jar of tapeworms.

4. I promise not to unfairly judge you.

5. I had difficulty hearing the conversation standing by the band.

Exercise 19.4

Revise the following sentences to avoid split infinitives and to place modifiers as close as possible to what they modify. If the sentence is correct, write **C.**

1. The singer's fans couldn't hardly wait for the concert tickets to go on sale.

2. Properly cooked, you can eat hamburger without fear of food poisoning.

3. I want to thoroughly consider all my options before making a decision.

4. Greg has only enough money to cover this month's rent.

5. Seeing the accident ahead, the car pulled to the side of the road, and Tran got out to investigate.

6. We enjoyed the beautiful lawn and gardens eating our lunch on the patio.

7. You must be ill; you only ate half the pizza.

8. Jim heard the phone ring with his mouth full of toothpaste.

9. There is a family picture of our trip to Nassau on the hall table.

10. I asked him one final time to please stop pestering me.

19f Dangling Modifiers

Many types of phrases function as modifiers. Participial and infinitive phrases at the beginning of a sentence normally modify the subject of the following clause. **Participial phrases** are formed with the present or past participle of a verb.

Twisting in the wind, the kite rose higher.

Driven from their homes, the villagers set up camp in the hills.

Sometimes the introductory phrase suggests a participial form rather than stating it directly.

While [travelling] **in France,** we visited many wineries.

Infinitive phrases are formed with an infinitive (*to* + verb).

To swim well, you need to coordinate your stroke with your breathing.

To mend the tire, she had to find the leak.

Notice that in these examples, each phrase could be expanded into a clause with the same subject as the sentence following: *The kite* twisted in the wind. *The kite* rose higher.

Recognizing Dangling Modifiers

An introductory phrase that does not modify the subject of the following clause is called a **dangling modifier.**

DANGLING   **Driving down the mountain,** three
                    bears were seen.

                    To run a marathon, endurance must be
                    built up gradually.

Notice that if you expand these phrases into clauses, the subject is not the same as that of the following sentence: *We* were driving down the mountain. *Three bears* were seen.

Notice too that the verbs in the main clause are in the passive voice: *were seen, must be built up.* Introductory phrases are more likely to dangle when the verb is in the passive voice.

NOT   After discussing the case for days, a ver-
                    dict **was** finally **reached** by the jury.

BUT   After discussing the case for days, the
                    jury finally **reached** a verdict.

When you put the verb into the active voice, the phrase no longer dangles because the subjects are now the same (*the jury*). (For more on active and passive voice, see 20e.)

19f

*Dangling
Modifiers*

250

Exercise 19.5

Underline dangling modifiers in the following sentences. If the sentence is correct, write **C.**

1. Before signing a contract, a lawyer should go over it with you.

2. In the middle of the night, we were awakened by police sirens screaming down the street.

3. To reduce conflicts with their children, better listening skills are needed.

4. When in Rome, the social customs of the Romans should be followed.

5. Because they arrived early, the Chans had good seats for the concert.

Correcting Dangling Modifiers

When an introductory phrase dangles, you can revise the sentence in one of two ways. You can either expand the phrase to a subordinate clause or revise the main clause so that the introductory phrase logically modifies its subject.

NOT	Intending to finish the report by the end of the day, my plan was to work through lunch and coffee breaks.
BUT	Because I intended to finish the report by the end of the day, my plan was to work through lunch and coffee breaks.
OR	Intending to finish the report by the end of the day, I planned to work through lunch and coffee breaks.

You could correct the dangling modifier in the next sentence by changing the prepositional phrase to a clause, with the subject clearly stated.

NOT	After being honoured by sports writers and fellow athletes, the retired hockey star's name was inscribed in the Hall of Fame.

BUT	After the retired hockey star was honoured by sports writers and fellow athletes, his name was inscribed in the Hall of Fame.

Sometimes it is necessary to revise a sentence extensively to eliminate the dangling modifier.

NOT	Upon learning about the budget cutbacks, it was difficult for Ruth to hide her concern that her position would be abolished.
BUT	When Ruth learned about the budget cutbacks, she found it difficult to hide her concern that her position would be abolished.

Exercise 19.6

Correct each dangling modifier.

1. Walking into the room, a strange sight caught my eye.

2. While in high school, George's father was promoted and the family moved to Vancouver.

3. Exhausted by a heavy work schedule, a complete rest was recommended by the doctor.

4. To make a perfect omelette, the freshest ingredients are required.

5. After pleading earnestly, the curfew was extended to midnight.

Exercise 19.7

Correct each dangling modifier. If the sentence is correct, write **C**.

1. To have a chance at winning the lottery, a ticket must first be bought.

2. Hoping to catch the final inning of the baseball game on television, Michael left the office early.

3. Driven by arrogance and greed, Joe's friends were soon alienated from him.

4. After working so hard on the committee, our gratitude is definitely deserved.

19f

Dangling Modifiers

5. To extend your cable service, you may call any time during office hours.

6. While reading Stephen King's *Cujo,* my dog began barking in the backyard.

7. Concerned by the noise, I went outside to investigate.

8. Driving on the highway, Hank's car engine suddenly seized.

9. Staring intently at the small print, spots began to swim before my eyes.

10. To build a better mousetrap, the proper tools are essential.

Exercise 19.8

The following paragraph contains errors in the use of modifiers. Revise the passage to correct these errors.

Nineteenth-century workers couldn't hardly survive without spending long hours at demanding jobs. Farm workers and outside workers in the summer toiled from sunrise to sunset. Working shorter hours in the winter, less money was made. Shop employees were treated equally bad. To effectively meet the needs of their customers, shops stayed open real long hours—often fourteen to sixteen—with the same employees. The most dreadfulest conditions were in the factories. Treated as part of the machinery and forced to work at the pace of the machine, there was no time for talking or joking with other workers. Children as young as seven worked twelve-hour shifts and slept in factory dormitories. In England by the middle of the nineteenth century it was illegal to employ children under nine in textile factories, but most children were working full-time by the time they were thirteen or fourteen in 1900.

19f

Dangling Modifiers

CHAPTER 20

PROOFREADING: VERBS

Because the English verb system is quite complex, it's easy to make errors involving both verb tenses and verb forms.

20a The Principal Parts of Verbs

Each verb has four principal parts, from which all its other forms can be derived.

- The **infinitive** form (*to* + a verb) names the verb: *to walk, to run, to think.* The present tense is derived from the infinitive: *I **walk,** you **walk,** she **walks.***
- The **past tense:** *Yesterday I **walked** to school.*
- The **present participle:** *I **am walking** to school right now.*
- The **past participle:** *I **have walked** to school every day this week.*

  Regular verbs form the past tense and the past participle by adding *ed* to the infinitive: *walked, have walked; visited, have visited.*

  Irregular verbs form the past tense and the past participle in a variety of ways: *drank, have drunk; brought, have brought.* If you are not sure of the principal parts of an irregular verb, check your dictionary.

Auxiliary Verbs

20b Auxiliary Verbs

A number of verb tenses are formed by combining a participle with one or more **auxiliary verbs:**

am, is, was, were	*can, could, may, might*
be, being, been	*shall, will, should, would*
have, has, had	*ought to, have to, used to*
do, does, did	*supposed to*

20c Common Errors with Verbs

- *Using the past participle instead of the past tense*

NOT   I **seen** [past participle] him yesterday.

BUT   I **saw** [past tense] him yesterday.

- *Using an auxiliary verb with the past tense*

NOT   Ahmed **had went** to visit his parents in Manitoba.

BUT   Ahmed **went** to visit his parents in Manitoba.

OR   Ahmed **had gone** to visit his parents in Manitoba.

- *Using* being *as a main verb instead of* is *or* was

NOT   The reason **being** that I was already late.

BUT   The reason **is** that I was already late.

- *Using* of *to mean* have

NOT   He should **of** known better.

BUT   He should **have** known better.

- *Using too many* coulds *or* woulds *in* if/then *statements*

NOT   If you **would have asked** me, I would have helped.

BUT   If you **had asked** me, I would have helped.

- *Omitting verb endings*

Be sure the verb ending agrees with the subject of the sentence and that the tenses are consistent. (For more on these problems, see 20d and 20f.)

NOT   She **walk** to the video store.

BUT   She **walks** to the video store. [simple present tense]

NOT   After they **watched** the movie, they **walk** home.

BUT   After they **watched** the movie, they **walked** home. [simple past tense]

• *Misplacing prepositions that are part of phrasal verbs*

If English is not your first language, you may find phrasal verbs (verb + preposition that functions as part of the verb, such as *figure out, look up, take care of*) confusing. Keep the preposition with the verb.

NOT   He **looked** his brother **after.**

BUT   He **looked after** his brother.

Exercise 20.1

Revise the following sentences so that auxiliaries and principal parts are used correctly. If the sentence is correct, write **C.**

1. You should of did the dishes instead of playing computer games.
2. How could you have wore a hole in your new running shoes already?
3. Whenever Martin gets the urge to work, he lays down until he feels better.
4. If I would have known you were in town, I would have invited you to the party.
5. The reason being that they couldn't find a babysitter.
6. Yvette rung the doorbell and waited to be admitted.
7. Susan has not wrote to her parents in over two months.
8. If Tom had submitted the essay on time, he would not have lost marks.
9. I am positive that I seen Jocelyn at the concert, but she insists that she wasn't there.
10. Rosa has swum in that lake every summer since she was a child.

20d   Keeping Verb Tenses Consistent

Once you have decided on the tense—present, past, or future—of a particular piece of writing, be consistent. You may have to shift tenses to clarify time relationships, but don't do so unnecessarily. Use the present tense when you are writing about literature.

Note the use of the present tense in the following paragraph analyzing Stacey MacAindra, who is the central character in Margaret Laurence's novel *The Fire Dwellers*.

Stacey's inability to communicate with her husband and children is a manifestation of the "tomb silences" of her own parents. Again we see Laurence's concern with the past as a source of isolation, for Stacey's background does not give her the means to be fully open with others. Moreover, she is a victim not only of her own past but also of the past influences that shape her husband, Mac, who inherits his reticence and his tendency to misinterpret Stacey's remarks from a father who is himself often restrained and imperceptive. Because of their childhoods, both Stacey and Mac believe that "nice" people do not talk about fear or pain. Stacey understands the limitations of this belief, but her inability to free herself from its influence leads her to remark that everyone in her family is one-dimensional. This image conveys Stacey's feelings of dissociation from her husband and children.

Exercise 20.2

Revise the following paragraph to eliminate unnecessary tense shifts. Use the present tense. The paragraph deals with Thomas Hardy's novel *The Mayor of Casterbridge.*

It's important to see that Michael Henchard in Thomas Hardy's novel *The Mayor of Casterbridge* is a kind of Everyman figure. Like most of us, he is motivated by psychological forces that he did not recognize or understand. For example, he never seems to understand why he sells his wife and then remarried her. Henchard was also affected by external forces over which he, like the rest of us, has no control. During the 1840s when the novel was set, long-established agricultural practices were being modernized by machines and business practices are now much more complex. In addition to the forces of industrialization, Henchard, as a wheat trader, is especially vulnerable to natural forces such as the weather. After all, he made his living by predicting the harvest yields. Finally, Henchard is affected by chance and coincidence. It just happens that Farfrae, the man with exactly the skills Henchard needed, showed up when he is looking for an assistant manager.

20e Active and Passive Voice

English verbs have two voices: the **active** and the **passive.** In an active construction, the subject performs the action of the verb. In a passive construction, the subject is acted upon.

Edward made the announcement. [active]

The announcement was made by Edward. [passive]

When to Use the Active Voice

In most writing situations, it's best to use the active voice. Active constructions are usually clearer, more concise, and more forceful than passive constructions.

PASSIVE   The home owners were informed by the city that the weeds would have to be cleared from their lots immediately.

ACTIVE   The city informed the home owners that they would have to clear the weeds from their lots immediately.

When to Use the Passive Voice

Use the passive voice in the following circumstances.

- When you don't know the person or agent that performed the action.

  My bike was stolen last night.

  The streets of prairie cities are typically laid out on a grid.

- When you want to emphasize the person, place, or object acted upon rather than the agent performing the action.

  Mahatma Gandhi was born in 1869.

  Her sister was run over by a drunk driver.

- When you want to avoid blaming, giving credit, or accepting responsibility.

  Jeremy's two front teeth were knocked out by Paul's slapshot.

  The lowest bid was submitted by Megaproject Developments.

  "My ring is lost."

- When you want to sound objective, as in scientific, technical, and legal writing.

  The experiment was repeated with four groups of subjects.

  All construction work must be completed by November 15.

  The defendant was found guilty and sentenced to five years in prison.

20e

Active and Passive Voice

Note: Passive constructions distance you and your reader from your material. Don't use them merely to sound more formal. Your writing will be livelier and more engaging if you use the active voice whenever possible.

Being Consistent

Avoid mixing active and passive constructions in the same sentence.

NOT   A letter was written by the home owners saying the weeds would be cleared when they (the home owners) were good and ready.

BUT   The home owners wrote a letter saying they would clear the weeds when they were good and ready.

Exercise 20.3

Change passive constructions to active constructions where appropriate. If the passive voice is preferable, write C. Be prepared to defend your choices.

1. The light changed to amber before the intersection was reached by Oliver.
2. The municipal swimming pool was opened for the summer last week.
3. My directions were completely misunderstood by Burt.
4. After much lengthy debate, the meeting was finally adjourned.
5. The milk was spilled, but Marietta made no effort to wipe it up.
6. The building site has been shut down until all safety hazards have been eliminated.
7. Marcia was hurt by Sarah's careless remark.
8. After the lawn was trimmed and raked, we weeded the front flower bed.
9. Before setting out to write my exam, I searched for my good luck pen, but it couldn't be found anywhere.
10. The newspaper was delivered late again this morning.

20e

Active and Passive Voice

20f Making Subjects and Verbs Agree

The principle of **subject-verb agreement** is that singular subjects take singular verbs and plural subjects take plural verbs.

> This **ornament goes** on the top of the tree. [singular]

> The **lights go** on first. [plural]

Here are the most common causes of errors in subject-verb agreement:

- *A prepositional phrase separating subject and verb*

The subject and verb may be separated by a prepositional phrase (*of the workers, between the houses, across the field, including all team members, along with all his supporters*). The subject of the sentence is never located in the prepositional phrase.

> **One** of the workers **has filed** a complaint with the grievance committee.

> **Neither** of the women **wants** to press charges.

> **Mrs. Murphy,** along with her five noisy children, **attends** mass regularly.

- *Sentences beginning with* **there** *or* **here**

There or *here* may be the first word of the sentence, but neither will be the subject of the sentence. Look for the real subject after the verb.

> There **are** only five **bananas,** not enough for everyone.

> Here **come** the **Jackson twins,** just in time for dinner.

- *Subjects linked by paired conjunctions:* **either/or, neither/nor, not only/but also**

In sentences with paired conjunctions, the subject closer to the verb makes the verb singular or plural.

> Neither Reuben nor **his cousins were prepared** to kiss the bride.

> Not only the students but also the **teacher was delighted** by the unexpected holiday.

- *Subjects that may be singular or plural*

Collective nouns, such as *team, group, committee,* are considered singular when they refer to people or things acting as a unit.

Our **team is** on a five-day road trip.

The **herd has settled down** for the night.

Collective nouns are considered plural when they refer to people or things acting individually.

The **team do** not **agree** about the need for a new manager.

The **herd have scattered** in every direction.

Collective nouns of quantity (*number, majority, percentage*) are singular when preceded by *the*, plural when preceded by *a*.

The number of unemployed people **is increasing.**

A number of unemployed people **are** still **looking** for jobs.

The pronouns *all, none,* and *some* can be either singular or plural, depending on the noun to which they refer.

None of the cake **is** left.

None of the cookies **are** left.

Words joined by *and* are considered singular when they refer to a single unit or to the same person.

Bread and butter makes a fine basis for a sandwich.

My **neighbour and best friend has moved** to another city.

Exercise 20.4

Make subjects and verbs agree in the following sentences. If the sentence is correct, write **C.**

1. Neither Stephanie nor her sisters is available to help at the bazaar on Saturday.
2. The team have won the championship fours years in a row.
3. Neither of the applicants are willing to relocate to a branch office.
4. There goes the Pied Piper, along with all the children of Hamelin.
5. Fear of falling and of loud noises are instinctive.
6. Either the love birds or the goldfish make a suitable pet for an apartment resident.
7. The number of hamburgers sold has increased significantly this quarter.
8. The jury have been sequestered for three days.

9. Each of the committee members have made a different selection for Citizen of the Year.

10. Nothing I've seen in the last three clothing stores seem suitable for graduation.

*Making
Subjects
and Verbs
Agree*

CHAPTER 21

PROOFREADING: PRONOUNS

Pronouns substitute for nouns or other pronouns. The word to which the pronoun refers is called its **antecedent.**

> My **grandmother** goes bowling every Wednesday. Then **she** eats lunch at **her** fitness club. [*Grandmother* is the antecedent of *she* and *her*.]

We will discuss the five most common types of pronoun problems:

- pronoun agreement errors
- pronoun case errors
- errors with possessive pronouns
- pronoun reference errors
- shifts in pronouns of address

21a Pronoun Agreement

Errors in pronoun agreement occur when you don't match a singular pronoun with a singular noun or a plural pronoun with a plural noun. Pronoun agreement errors occur most frequently in the following situations.

Agreement with Singular Nouns

Pronoun agreement errors often involve using a plural pronoun to refer to a singular noun. Most often, the noun names a type of person (the alcoholic, the mature student, the typical worker) rather than an individual, as in the following example:

ERROR   The **alcoholic** may blame **their** drinking problem on unsympathetic family members.

There are four ways to avoid this kind of agreement error.

1. *Use a singular pronoun.*

   The alcoholic may blame **his** drinking problem on unsympathetic family members.

   Although this version is grammatically correct, the use of *his* is unappealing because it implies that all alcoholics are men.

2. *Use the phrase* **his or her.**

   The alcoholic may blame **his or her** drinking problem on unsympathetic family members.

   This correction works well in single sentences but becomes cumbersome when repeated frequently. Avoid using *he/she, s/he,* or *him/her* in any piece of writing.

3. *Make the noun plural.* Pluralizing is often the simplest and most effective way to ensure pronoun agreement.

   Alcoholics may blame **their** drinking problems on unsympathetic family members.

4. *Alternate masculine and feminine pronouns.* If you were writing about types of people, such as the teacher and his or her students or the doctor and his or her patients, you could alternate masculine and feminine pronouns by referring to the teacher or doctor as *he* in one paragraph and as *she* in the next paragraph. Alternating masculine and feminine pronouns paragraph by paragraph is much less confusing and distracting than alternating them within a single paragraph.

21a

Exercise 21.1

*Pronoun
Agreement*

Revise the following sentences to make antecedents and pronouns agree.

1. Every manager has been asked their opinion of the merger.

2. A new immigrant generally suffers from culture shock, no matter how well they have prepared for the move.

3. A daycare worker must ensure that their qualifications in basic first aid are current.

4. It is not unusual for even an experienced actor to suffer from stage fright before they begin a performance.

5. A customer service representative needs to remain calm and polite in their dealings with the public.

Agreement with Collective Nouns

Collective nouns are words such as *jury, team, band, audience, group, family, committee, congregation, herd,* and *flock* that refer to people or things taken together.

When a collective noun refers to people or things acting as a single unit, the collective noun takes singular verbs and singular pronouns.

The **jury was** unanimous in **its** verdict.

The **band was** doomed without **its** leader.

When a collective noun refers to people or things acting as individuals, the collective noun takes plural verbs and plural pronouns.

The **jury were divided** in **their** judgment of the defendant.

The **band were arguing** over **their** next number.

When a collective noun is followed by a prepositional phrase, be careful to match the pronoun with the collective noun and not with the noun inside the prepositional phrase.

A small **group** of hecklers made **its** impact on the meeting.

The stranded **herd** of horses lost **its** way.

Agreement with *Either/Or, Neither/Nor, Or, Nor*

Singular nouns joined by *either/or, neither/nor, or,* and *nor* are matched with singular pronouns.

Neither Farida nor Barbara has contacted **her** lawyer.

Either Mark or Craig will lend you **his** truck for the move.

Plural nouns joined by these conjunctions take plural pronouns.

Neither the students nor the teachers had time to collect **their** belongings when the fire alarm sounded.

When mixed singular and plural nouns are joined by these conjunctions, put the plural noun last and use a plural pronoun.

Neither the lead singer nor **the dancers** have been fitted for **their** costumes.

Pronoun Agreement

Exercise 21.2

Revise the following sentences where necessary to make antecedents and pronouns agree. If the sentence is correct, write **C**.

1. Neither the employees nor the supervisor believed that their position was wrong.

2. Either Sheryl or Jennifer will lend you her bicycle for the outing.

3. The herd of cattle left their grazing area and wended their way home.

4. Next week the safety committee will publish the results of their investigation.

5. If you need help with opening night at your restaurant, either Matt or Richard will offer their services.

6. The municipal government has issued their recommendations on property tax increases.

7. The weary group of tourists finally arrived at their hotel.

8. The class were packing their books in anticipation of the bell.

9. A family of bats has made their home in our attic.

10. I know you are curious, but neither Pierre nor Antoine wants me to tell you their plans for the weekend.

Agreement with Indefinite Pronouns

Singular Indefinite Pronouns

21a

Pronoun Agreement

The following indefinite pronouns are always singular. They take singular verbs, and any pronouns referring to them should also be singular.

everyone	*anyone*	*no one, one*	*someone*	*either*
everybody	*anybody*	*nobody*	*somebody*	*neither*
everything	*anything*	*nothing*	*something*	*each*

Here is a typical example of an agreement error with an indefinite pronoun:

Everyone in the office had put in **their** request for time off at Christmas.

Here *everyone,* which is singular, and *their,* which is plural, do not agree.

You could correct this error by using the strategies suggested above for singular nouns. Alternatively, you could rephrase the sentence to eliminate the pronoun altogether.

Everyone in the office had requested time off at Christmas.

Don't be misled by prepositional phrases. If a singular indefinite pronoun is followed by a prepositional phrase ending with a plural noun (*of the children, in the houses, under the benches*) the verb and any pronouns referring to the subject are still singular.

Neither of the drivers has contacted **her** insurance agent.

In this sentence, the antecedent of *her* is *neither*. Because *neither* is singular, the pronoun referring to it must be singular.

Plural Indefinite Pronouns
(*Many, Few, Several, Both*)

The indefinite pronouns *many, few, several,* and *both* take plural pronouns.

Both of the drivers filed claims with **their** insurance companies.

Singular or Plural Indefinite Pronouns
(*All, None, Some*)

The indefinite pronouns *all, none,* and *some* are matched with singular pronouns when they are followed by a prepositional phrase that contains a singular noun.

None of the furniture has been moved from **its** original position for years.

These pronouns are matched with plural pronouns when they are followed by a prepositional phrase containing a plural noun.

None of the chairs have been moved from **their** original positions for years.

Exercise 21.3

Revise the following sentences where necessary to make antecedents and pronouns agree. If the sentence is correct, write **C**.

1. Everyone purchasing these selected products is eligible to submit their name for the grand prize in the draw.

Pronoun Agreement

2. None of the witnesses on shore were prepared to risk their own safety to rescue the drowning man.

3. Each of the crafters is selling their best creations at the fall fair.

4. Neither of the men left their names when they called this morning.

5. Anyone interested in joining the canoe trip should send his or her payment to Harriet by the end of the month.

Exercise 21.4 Pronoun Agreement Review

Revise the following sentences where necessary to make antecedents and pronouns agree. If the sentence is correct, write **C**.

1. An experienced writer considers their readers' needs.

2. Neither of the suspects has confessed their involvement in the embezzlement.

3. The congregation is unanimous in its support of the new minister.

4. No one in the office has submitted their ideas on the proposal.

5. Some of the passengers stowed their baggage in the overhead bins.

6. After dissecting a frog in biology class, neither Stacey nor Veronica could eat their lunch.

7. A gambling addict may go deeply into debt to finance their habit.

8. All of the stolen money has been returned to its rightful owner.

9. An army marches on their stomach.

10. Everyone is expected to be on their best behaviour.

11. The band began its Canadian tour in Halifax.

12. Either Sandra or Brianne will give their oral presentation on Friday.

13. Neither of the two lost little boys knew their home address.

14. Every winner will have their picture in the newspaper.

15. Mr. Warden is a man who does their work without complaint.

Exercise 21.5 Pronoun Agreement Review

Revise the following paragraph to eliminate all errors in pronoun agreement.

A PowerPoint presenter arranges words and pictures into a series of pages that they project from a laptop computer onto a screen. Each of the screens typically has their heading followed by bullet points: six or seven words a line, six or seven lines a slide. Paragraphs and even sentences have too many words for a PowerPoint presentation, so the presenter must reduce their most complex ideas to little phrases. Of course, the bullet points eliminate the need for transitions, such as *because* or *on the other hand*, that might help a viewer understand connections among these phrases. The typical presenter hasn't noticed the absence of transitions. They have been so caught up in the technical features of PowerPoint that they have concentrated on the appearance of the text and the accompanying graphics. Never mind, if there are enough snappy visual aids, neither the viewers nor the presenter may notice that their presentation has the intellectual substance of a kindergarten show and tell.

21b Pronoun Case

The **subject pronouns** (*I, we, you, he, she, it, they*, and *who*) are used as the subject of a sentence or a clause. The **object pronouns** (*me, us, you, him, her, it, them,* and *whom*) are used as the object of a verb or a preposition. The most common error in pronoun case involves a confusion of subject and object pronouns.

NOT | **Her** and **I** are going to a movie tonight.

BUT | **She** and **I** are going to a movie tonight.

NOT | You can reach my wife or **I** at home after six o'clock.

BUT | You can reach my wife or **me** at home after six o'clock.

Subject Pronouns

Use subject pronouns in the subject position in the sentence. Don't be confused when the pronoun is part of a compound subject.

NOT | Frances and **me** went to the Farmers' Market on Saturday to buy vegetables.

269

| **BUT** | Frances and **I** went to the Farmers' Market on Saturday to buy vegetables. |

Don't be confused when the subject pronoun is followed by an explanatory noun (*we home owners, we students, we smokers*). The pronoun is still in the subject position.

| NOT | **Us** residents are presenting a petition to city council. |

| **BUT** | **We** residents are presenting a petition to city council. |

Use subject pronouns after comparisons using *than* or *as.*

| NOT | Peter is as tall as **me.** |

| **BUT** | Peter is as tall as **I.** |

| NOT | No one was more surprised than **her.** |

| **BUT** | No one was more surprised than **she.** |

Use a subject pronoun as the subject of an embedded subordinate clause. Be especially careful with *that* clauses.

| NOT | Ramesh said that **him** and his wife would be glad to help. |

| **BUT** | Ramesh said that **he** and his wife would be glad to help. |

Object Pronouns

21b

Pronoun Case

Use object pronouns as the direct or indirect object of a verb.

| NOT | The manager assigned Loretta and **she** to work a double shift. |

| **BUT** | The manager assigned Loretta and **her** to work a double shift. |

| NOT | Please let your mother or **I** know when you will be home. |

| **BUT** | Please let your mother or **me** know when you will be home. |

Use object pronouns in prepositional phrases.

NOT   Between you and **I,** there is something strange about our new neighbour.

BUT   Between you and **me,** there is something strange about our new neighbour.

NOT   The city replied to **we** home owners.

BUT   The city replied to **us** home owners.

Note: Don't use a **reflexive pronoun** (the pronouns that end in *self/selves*) as a substitute for a subject or object pronoun.

NOT   My family and **myself** will be going to Nova Scotia for a camping holiday.

BUT   My family and **I** will be going to Nova Scotia for a camping holiday.

NOT   Ms. Chang asked that all inquiries be directed to **herself** rather than to Mr. Morgan.

BUT   Ms. Chang asked that all inquiries be directed to **her** rather than to Mr. Morgan.

Who and *Whom*

Who is a subject pronoun. Use it to refer to a subject noun or pronoun.

Helen is the candidate. She is sure to win.

Helen is the candidate **who** is sure to win. [*Who* replaces *she*.]

Whom is an object pronoun. Use it after prepositions and to refer to an object noun or pronoun.

To whom do you wish to speak?

He is a lawyer. We can trust him.

He is a lawyer **whom** we can trust. [*Whom* replaces *him*.]

Exercise 21.6

Correct all errors in pronoun case in the following sentences. If the sentence is correct, write **C.**

1. Us workers must stand firm in our demand for safer conditions.
2. Him and me agree on hardly anything.
3. Todd is no more likely to know the answer than her.
4. Can you tell me who to contact about this insurance claim?
5. Please let Mrs. Wallace or I know your vacation plans.
6. James said that you can get additional copies of the newsletter from Serena or he.
7. Adrilla and myself share the same birthday.
8. Michael, Stephen, and him will be working for the same tree planting company this summer.
9. Olga told me that her and her sister haven't seen each other in years.
10. She is the kind of person who isn't afraid to express an unpopular opinion.

21c Possessive Pronouns

Use **possessive pronouns** (*my, mine, our/ours, your/yours, his, her/hers, its, their/theirs, whose*) to show ownership or possession. Pay especially close attention to the following points.

- Don't confuse the possessive pronoun *its* with the contraction *it's* (*it is*).

POSSESSIVE   The committee has tabled **its** report.

CONTRACTION   Don't call me unless **it's** an emergency.

- Don't confuse the possessive pronoun *your* with the contraction *you're* (*you are*).

POSSESSIVE   Did you bring **your** books?

CONTRACTION   **You're** late.

- Don't confuse the possessive pronoun *whose* with the contraction *who's* (*who is*).

| POSSESSIVE | I didn't hear **whose** name was announced as the winner. |
| CONTRACTION | I don't know **who's** calling. |

- Don't confuse the possessive pronoun *their* with the contraction *they're* (*they are*) or the adverb *there*.

POSSESSIVE	The Séguins are attending **their** family reunion in Regina.
CONTRACTION	**They're** staying with Cousin Denis and his family for two weeks.
ADVERB	They hope to see the whole family **there.**

- Do not use apostrophes with *hers, his, ours, yours,* and *theirs*.

    The battered canoe tied to the dock is **theirs.**

    This sweater must be **yours.**

- Add *'s* to indefinite pronouns.

    Everyone's assignments have been returned.

    Someone's keys were turned in to the receptionist.

Exercise 21.7

Correct all errors in the use of possessive pronouns in the following sentences.

1. It is anyones guess why Greg didn't show up for the interview.
2. Who's piece of chocolate cake is on the table?
3. I know that the suitcases are identical, but I'm certain this one is your's.
4. There's is the most beautiful garden in the neighbourhood.
5. The dog bared it's teeth and growled menacingly.

Exercise 21.8   Review of Pronoun Case and Possessive Pronouns

Correct all errors in pronoun case and possessive pronouns. If the sentence is correct, write **C**.

1. Please tell Nigel or myself if you need a ride on Saturday.

21c

Possessive Pronouns

273

2. Dale promised that him and his brothers would vacuum the pool before the barbecue.

3. No one is happier than me that you and her have won the scholarships.

4. The Vachons sold most of there furniture and moved into a condominium.

5. Do you know who's limousine is stopped at the light?

6. Justine claims that the idea was entirely her's.

7. Between you and I, she is not giving Ian his share of the credit.

8. Put everything back in its proper place.

9. The earliest that Dave and me can be there is noon.

10. Evangeline hopes that her boyfriend and herself are accepted by the same university.

Exercise 21.9 Review of Pronoun Case and Possessive Pronouns

Correct all errors in pronoun case and the use of possessive pronouns in the following passage.

Last February Peter and me decided to get married. We wanted to get married in June, so their were four months to plan the wedding. Although our wedding cost only $2000, it turned out beautifully. Here's how we did it.

First we made a list of everything we could do ourself. Me and my sister spent two weeks shopping every chance we got in Value Village stores and all the second hand vintage clothing shops. Luckily, I found the perfect dress for just under $50 and my sister found a gorgeous bridesmaid's dress for $100. I didn't mind that her's cost twice as much as mine because she said that her and her boyfriend might get married theirselves and she would wear that dress to the wedding. Peter was able to borrow his dad's dark suit, which his dad said looked better on Peter than it did on he. Peter's brother Tom had just gotten married, so he had a dark suit he could wear as best man. Having dealt with the clothing issue, we went to a pawnshop and bought two gold rings for $50 each.

Now we had to find a place to get married. We have a friend who's parents own a cottage near a local lake. They agreed to lend us there place for the weekend. For $200 we could rent canopies and tables to put on the lawn. Then I persuaded my mother to let Peter and myself raid her garden for lilacs, tulips, and daisies. They made lovely bouquets for all the tables.

Peter's Uncle Ted said that him and his friend, an amateur photographer, would take all the photographs. If we supplied the film, which cost about $100, he would print the photos with his own computer.

Now we had to find someone to marry us. We contacted a local marriage commissioner and discovered that the usual gratuity is $50. We had to give her another $50 to cover her travelling expenses. The marriage licence cost $50. So far, we had spent $700.

Its probably not surprising that food and liquor were our biggest expense. Because so many of our guests had allergies or were on special diets, we decided on a simple meal of chili, homemade cornbread, and huge salads, with beer and wine. For dessert, we had soy ice cream and a vegan wedding cake made by my father and I. Buying the food and liquor, and renting cutlery, glasses, and dishes cost about $700.

Of course, what's a wedding without music and dancing? No one knows more about the local music scene than Peter and myself, so we hired a band for $300. We didn't need to provide any of the sound equipment because the band said they would bring their's. Naturally, there were a few more miscellaneous expenses, but the total cost of our wedding was well under $2000. Between you and I, the wedding couldn't have suited we thrifty folks better if it had cost $20,000.

21d Pronoun Reference

When you are speaking, you can usually make yourself understood even if you use pronouns rather vaguely. When you are writing, however, you need to make the connections between pronouns and nouns clear to your reader. When this connection is unclear, you have made an error in pronoun reference.

Here are some of the most common errors in pronoun reference.

21d

Pronoun Reference

Confusing Pronoun References

This problem is most likely to occur in sentences containing indirect speech.

VAGUE	When Kevin told Ali that he was being laid off, he was very upset.
CLEAR	Kevin was very upset when he told Ali, "I'm being laid off."
CLEAR	Kevin told Ali, "You are being laid off." Ali was very upset.

Vague Use of *They* and *It*

Avoid using *they* if it doesn't refer to a specific noun in your writing.

VAGUE **They** say that a number of western democracies are shifting politically to the right.

CLEAR **Respected commentators** say that a number of western democracies are shifting politically to the right.

You can see a similar problem with *it* in this sentence.

VAGUE I spent hours working out a detailed budget, but **it** didn't solve my financial problems.

This sentence leaves your reader wondering what didn't help: the time you spent working on your budget? the budget itself? A revised sentence might read like this.

CLEAR I spent hours working out a detailed budget, but **this effort** did not solve my financial problems.

OR I spent hours working out a detailed budget, but **the budget itself** did not solve my financial problems.

Vague Use of *That, Which,* and *This*

21d

Pronoun Reference

In some sentences, *that, which,* or *this* refers to several different ideas.

VAGUE The cousins fought on different sides in the war, **which** tore their family apart.

What tore their family apart—the fact that they fought on different sides? the exploits? the war? A clearer version might read like this.

CLEAR The family was torn apart by the cousins' **decision** to fight on different sides in the war.

Exercise 21.10

Revise the following sentences to clarify vague pronoun references.

1. They say that nightmares are caused by anxiety.

2. Why do you tease your sister and call her names when you know it upsets her?

3. Natalie was disappointed when Nicole told her that she didn't get the job.

4. I rested and drank plenty of fluids, but it didn't make me feel better.

5. Maxine wanted to subscribe to the newspaper, but they said that home delivery was not available in her neighbourhood.

6. The cash register stopped working because a customer's child had turned off the main switch, but at the time Giselle didn't know it.

7. Raul added too much water to the dough and beat it mercilessly, which is why the pie crust is tough.

8. Rex is lazy, immature, and irresponsible, but that doesn't bother his friends.

9. I heard that Candace left her husband and children and ran away to Tahiti to paint. This greatly surprised me.

10. Mr. Carlson applied too much weed killer and overwatered the grass, which ruined the lawn.

Exercise 21.11

Revise the following paragraph to eliminate all vague and ambiguous pronoun references.

21d

Pronoun Reference

Vegans do not eat any animal products. This means that many of the foods most people enjoy, such as ice cream, mayonnaise, bacon and eggs, even toast with honey, are off limits. Because most prepared foods contain some animal products, eating out can be a real challenge, which is why many vegans cook at home and bring food with them when they go out. Of course, vegan cooking presents its own difficulties. When I became a vegan, I bought a cookbook with lots of delicious-looking recipes, but it didn't help. They put so many exotic ingredients in each recipe that I had to dash to the health food store before I could begin. Despite these obstacles, I'm glad to be a vegan. Now that they talk about so many diseases carried by cows, fish, and birds, who would want to eat meat even if they were killed more humanely.

21e Pronouns of Address

You establish your relationship to your reader by the **pronouns of address** you use (or don't use) in your first paragraph. If you want your readers to focus on you—your ideas, your experiences—use first-person pronouns (*I, me, my, mine*). If you want your readers to consider how your subject relates to them directly (as in sermons, advertisements, directions), use second-person pronouns (*you, your, yours*). If you use only nouns and third-person pronouns (*he, she, it, they*), you will encourage your readers to focus on your subject.

These sentences illustrate the different relationships you might establish with your readers in an article about word processors.

FIRST PERSON	When I first began to use a word processor, I lost several files.
SECOND PERSON	When you first begin to use a word processor, you may lose a few files.
THIRD PERSON	When they first begin to use a word processor, most people lose a few files.

Once you have established the basic pronouns of address for a piece of writing, do not shift abruptly and without reason to another set of pronouns.

NOT	When **you** first begin to use a word processor, **one** may lose a few files. [shift from second person to third person]
NOT	When **most people** begin to use a word processor, **you** may lose a few files. [shift from third person to second person]

Confusing pronoun shifts may occur from sentence to sentence as well as within sentences.

NOT	When **I** began to use a word processor, **I** lost several files. **You** find it hard at first to master the sequence of commands. [shift from first person to second person]

These shifts disrupt your relationship with your reader.

Correcting Pronoun Shifts

In the following example, the perspective shifts from the third person, *Conrad* (*his*), to the second person, *you*.

> **Conrad** has invested **his** money wisely because, as an oil rig worker, **you** always face the possibility of seasonal unemployment.

There are two ways to correct this error.

- Replace *you* with *he*.

> **Conrad** has invested **his** money wisely because, as an oil rig worker, **he** always faces the possibility of seasonal unemployment.

- Rephrase the sentence to eliminate the use of the pronoun.

> Conrad has invested his money wisely because oil rig workers always face the possibility of seasonal unemployment.

Exercise 21.12

Revise the following sentences to eliminate pronoun shifts. Where there are several possibilities, be prepared to explain your choice. If the sentence is correct, write **C.**

1. I dislike asking Pauline for help because you never know whether she will keep her promise.
2. Even when you are knowledgeable and competent, many sales associates find dealing with a difficult customer to be an unnerving experience.
3. When you see Simon, you will be surprised at the changes in his appearance.
4. The owners claim that you can hear their ancestor's ghost on his nightly tour of the old mansion.
5. Colin has agreed to have a root canal rather than an extraction because you don't want to lose a tooth that can be saved.

Exercise 21.13

Revise the following paragraph to eliminate all pronoun shifts.

> Participants will get a more effective workout in your next fitness class if you follow this advice. Novice participants should position themselves near the instructor so you can see and hear clearly. The participant near the front is also less likely to be distracted by other participants. We should give the class our full attention, so don't spend your time worrying about whether other people are watch-

ing you or whether you put enough change in the parking meter. Although one might be tempted to compensate for lack of ability with expensive exercise clothes, don't spend a fortune on exercise accessories. All participants really need is a T-shirt, shorts, running shoes, and a willingness to devote an hour to their own good health.

21e

Pronouns of Address

CHAPTER 22

PROOFREADING: PUNCTUATION AND MECHANICS

22a Commas

When you are proofreading for errors in the use of commas, remember the following two principles:

- **Single commas** are used to separate the items in a series of words, phrases, or clauses and to set off elements at the beginning or end of the sentence.
- **Pairs of commas** are used to enclose parts of a sentence.

Key Terms to Know

A **series** consists of three or more similar grammatical constructions.

> To complete grade twelve, Petra needs **English, chemistry,** and **physics.** [a series of nouns]

> Before leaving for the lake, Simon needs to **buy groceries, pack the camper,** and **pick up his children.** [a series of phrases]

> **If you can meet the entrance requirements, if you can find a sponsor,** and **if you can arrange your own transportation,** you can run in this year's marathon. [a series of clauses]

A **phrase** is a group of words without a subject and a verb (*around the corner, looking out the window, to finish the test on time*).

A **clause** is a group of words with a subject and verb.

A **main clause** can stand on its own as a sentence (*Sheila looked out the window*).

A **subordinate clause** cannot stand alone as a sentence (*After Sheila looked out the window*).

22a

Commas

Using Commas to Separate

Separating Items in a Series

Use a comma to separate words, phrases, or clauses in a series. Should you use a comma before the last item? Usage varies. We recommend putting a comma before the *and* or other conjunction that joins the last two items in the series, both to provide emphasis and to prevent misreading:

WITHOUT COMMA   I forgot to buy milk, orange juice, bread, peanut butter and jam. [does peanut butter and jam refer to one item or two?]

WITH COMMA   I forgot to buy milk, orange juice, bread, peanut butter, and jam.

- ### *Words in a series*

I forgot to buy **orange juice, milk, bread, peanut butter,** and **jam.** [unless you intended to buy a jar containing both peanut butter and jam]

Note 1: Do **not** put a comma between pairs of items considered a single unit.

The Prime Minister said that full employment, regional development, and **law and order** are the chief priorities.

Note 2: Do **not** put commas between adjectives that could not be joined with *and*.

James Cook was a highly skilled eighteenth-century navigator.

- ### *Phrases in a series*

The frightened puppy raced **through the door, down the hall,** and **under the bed.**

Listening to music, playing cards, and **eating peanuts** are my favourite recreational activities.

- ### *Clauses in a series*

Mohammed handles the budget, Judy handles customer complaints, and **Philip handles the advertising.**

Exercise 22.1

Add all necessary commas to the following sentences.

1. Lorraine packed two suitcases called a cab and headed for the airport.

2. The secret ingredients in my stew are eye of newt toe of frog wool of bat and tongue of dog.

3. We have agreed to put the armoire in the master bedroom the console in the hall and the pine desk in the study.

4. We'll need bread cheese cold cuts fruit and sodas for the picnic.

5. The diner complained that the meat was underdone the vegetables were soggy and the wine was sour.

Setting Off Main Clauses

Use a comma before the coordinating conjunctions *and, but, or, nor, for, yet,* and *so* when they join main clauses.

> The company sold off its unprofitable subsidiaries, **and** within six months its shares had doubled in value.

> Readers of the play may perceive Hamlet as slow to act, **but** on the stage the prince seems to rush headlong toward his death.

The comma is often omitted before *and* and *or* if the clauses are short or have the same subject.

> You stand in line and I'll find a table.

> They may achieve their goals or they may fail.

To prevent misreading, always use a comma before *for, so, yet* when used as coordinating conjunctions, since these words have other uses.

> The dog limped, **for** it was old. [coordinating conjunction]

> The dog limped **for** the door. [preposition]

Exercise 22.2

Add all necessary commas to the following sentences.

1. We must go now for our ferry leaves exactly at noon.

2. Freida knocked down the wall and David hauled away the rubble.

3. Liam is a painstaking editor yet a few small errors escaped even his sharp eye.

4. The Richardsons knew that they must replace the worn linoleum and repaint the walls a neutral colour or the house would never sell.

5. When Fiona first began working as a cashier she thought that she would never remember the PLU's for produce but she had soon memorized dozens of codes.

Setting Off Introductory Elements

• *After introductory subordinate clauses*

Use a comma after an introductory subordinate clause. These clauses begin with subordinating conjunctions such as *although, because, after, when, before, since,* and *while*.

> **Before anyone could stop the baby,** she had grabbed the edge of the tablecloth and pulled the dishes to the floor.

> **Because there has been so much rain,** the mosquitoes have been bad this year.

• *After introductory interjections*

Use a comma after mild interjections (*oh, well, my goodness, my*), and after *yes* and *no*.

> **My,** what a beautiful baby.

> **Yes,** the merchandise that you ordered last week has arrived.

• *After introductory transitional words and phrases*

The usual practice is to put a comma after transitional phrases such as *for example, on the other hand, in contrast*. Put a comma after conjunctive adverbs of more than two syllables: after *nevertheless,* but not after *thus*.

> **On the other hand,** many prairie grain farmers are in desperate straits.

> **Nevertheless,** people were optimistic that the economy would improve.

> **Thus** we need to work out a new system to deal with rural bankruptcies.

22a

Commas

Note: Do **not** use a comma after a subordinating conjunction.

NOT   **Although,** she was desperate for a cigarette, she was too intimidated to smoke.

BUT   **Although** she was desperate for a cigarette, she was too intimidated to smoke.

- *After introductory phrases of more than five words*

  Sitting patiently beside my neighbour's woodpile, Brutus stood vigilant guard over escaping field mice.

- *After any introductory element to prevent misreading*

  After the Smiths left, the Joneses turned out the porch light and retired for the evening.

  In the evening, darkness settled over the town.

Exercise 22.3

Add all necessary commas to the following sentences.

1. For example pizza has ingredients from all four food groups but it can also be high in fat.
2. During his years at university in Calgary Louis never took the opportunity to visit Banff or Lake Louise.
3. When Bret dropped the iron skillet on the tile floor he heard a sharp crack.
4. High above the planes flew in precise formation.
5. No I don't remember your lending me ten dollars.

Setting Off Elements at the End of a Sentence

Use a comma to set off a word, phrase, or clause at the end of a sentence that qualifies, contrasts with, or questions what comes before.

> A puppy is a perfect pet, **if you have lots of patience.** [qualifying clause]

> I ordered the chicken, not the squid. [contrasting element]

> You'll give me a hand, **won't you?** [question]

Setting Off Direct Speech and Quotations

Use a comma to set off direct speech and quotations from the rest of the sentence.

> Alice remarked, "The lights are on, but no one seems to be home."

> We see Hamlet's growing awareness of the burdens placed upon him when he says, "The time is out of joint. O cursed spite / That ever I was born to set it right!"

Note: Do **not** use a comma when a quotation is introduced with *that.*

> We see Hamlet's hostility when he says that Claudius is "A little more than kin and less than kind."

Exercise 22.4

Add all necessary commas to the following sentences. If the sentence is correct, write **C.**

1. It's best to feed a cold and starve a fever isn't it?
2. Nathan is constantly telling me that "he who hesitates is lost."
3. However I always counter "Look before you leap."
4. Time and tide wait for no man if you catch my drift.
5. Music has its charms to soothe the savage breast not the savage beast.

Using Pairs of Commas to Enclose
Enclosing Interruptions in the Sentence

Use a pair of commas to enclose words, phrases, or clauses that slightly interrupt the flow of the sentence. Such expressions include parenthetical remarks (*of course, indeed, for example*), transitions (*however, therefore*), interjections (*well, oh*), and nouns of direct address (*Henry, Mother*).

> I will, **as I have already told you,** investigate the matter fully.

> The events described in this story are true. The names, **however,** have been changed to protect the innocent.

> I'd say he weighs about, **oh,** 80 kg.

> This decision, **Kevin,** is for you to make.

Enclosing Nonrestrictive Phrases and Clauses

Use a pair of commas to enclose a nonrestrictive modifying phrase or clause. Nonrestrictive clauses and phrases function as adjectives, but their presence is not essential to identifying the noun they modify. Instead, they supply additional or supplementary information.

Nonrestrictive clauses and phrases usually modify **proper nouns**—nouns that name a particular person, place, or thing.

22a

Commas

NONRESTRICTIVE	Bob Edward, publisher of *The Calgary Eye-Opener,* was an influential and controversial figure until his death in 1922.
NONRESTRICTIVE	Clarence's Uncle David, who is an accomplished seaman, is planning to sail around the world.

Clauses beginning with *which* are more likely to be nonrestrictive than are clauses beginning with *that*.

NONRESTRICTIVE	In the story, which is about a seemingly ordinary village lottery, the horrifying nature of the prize is not revealed until the draw has been made.
RESTRICTIVE	I've lost the book that I intended to lend you.

Note: Do **not** use commas to enclose a restrictive phrase or clause that provides essential information in the sentence.

RESTRICTIVE	Men wearing straw hats are a rare sight today. [Only men wearing straw hats are a rare sight.]
RESTRICTIVE	All customers who install a smoke detector are eligible for a discount on insurance premiums. [Only customers who install a smoke detector are eligible.]
RESTRICTIVE	The one book that I am determined to read this summer is *War and Peace*.

Exercise 22.5

Add all necessary commas to the following sentences. If the sentence is correct, write **C**.

1. Thank you Mr. Sutherland for booking your vacation trip through our travel agency.

2. The people who live next door are covering their entire backyard in artificial grass.

3. Punch Dickins who won the Distinguished Flying Cross in World War I gained fame as a bush pilot in the 1920s.

4. Monty's python which hasn't eaten in a month has escaped from its cage.

5. Monty promised us however that we had nothing to fear.

Using Commas in Conventional Places

- Use a comma to separate the day of the month from the year.

Canada celebrated its centennial on July 1, 1967.

Note: The comma is optional when only the month and year are given.

Canada celebrated its centennial in July, 1967 [July 1967].

- Use a comma to separate the elements in geographic names and addresses.

Architect Douglas Cardinal designed the Museum of Civilization in Hull, Quebec.

The couple were married at St. Joseph's Basilica, 10044-113 Street, Edmonton, Alberta.

- Use a comma after the salutation in personal or informal letters and after the closing in all letters.

Dear Aunt Margaret,

Yours truly,

Sincerely yours,

Exercise 22.6 Comma Review

Add all necessary commas and delete unnecessary commas in the following sentences. If the sentence is correct, write **C.**

1. Have you stood in a winter storm at the corner of Portage and Main in Winnipeg Manitoba?

2. After Christmas the family ate turkey sandwiches turkey casserole and turkey croquettes for a week.

3. Repairing the defective component after the warranty has expired Mr. Fortino is not our responsibility.

4. When the signal on the microwave sounded Ted poured the wine and called his guests to the table.

5. The Sandersons are the only people who did not contribute money to the Victoria Day fireworks display.

22a

Commas

6. Whenever we go camping Father always says "If you don't fish where the fish are you'll be having hot dogs for supper."

7. Albert opened the window took a deep breath and composed his thoughts.

8. The one novel that I didn't read, was the basis for the essay question on the English exam.

9. Lucy Maud Montgomery the author of *Anne of Green Gables* was born in Clifton Prince Edward Island on November 30 1874.

10. Well you have certainly chosen a deep subject for your research paper.

11. To put the matter into its proper perspective I want you to consider the following factors.

12. Yes we do have that shoe style in your size.

13. I decided that Howard would bring the food Cliff would bring the drinks and you would bring the music.

14. The snow blockaded the door in deep drifts and icicles hung like spears from the roof.

15. Here is my estimate of the cost of paving your driveway. Taxes of course are not included.

16. Even during the day light could not penetrate the canopy of leaves.

17. Mr. Ramondo said "We're a few bricks short of a load but I think we have enough to build the fire pit."

18. Anyone who is caught stealing money will be fired immediately.

19. On a dark stormy night I like nothing better, than to curl up with a good novel.

20. Cynthia went back to university to study engineering, because she discovered, that her BA in linguistics was not highly marketable.

22b Semicolons

Use a semicolon in the following ways:

- By itself to join two closely related main clauses

  The storm struck with a destructive fury; the ship was broken by the violent wind and waves.

Note 1: Never use a semicolon to join a subordinate clause to a main clause.

NOT	Although it had snowed heavily during the night; the roads were clear by noon the next day.
BUT	Although it had snowed heavily during the night, the roads were clear by noon the next day.

Note 2: Avoid using a semicolon as a kind of big comma for emphasis.

NOT	Horrified, Nelson watched the tidal wave approach; knowing that his tiny boat could never withstand its force.
BUT	Horrified, Nelson watched the tidal wave approach, knowing that his tiny boat could never withstand its force.

- With a conjunctive adverb (*nevertheless, however, otherwise, consequently, thus, therefore, then, meanwhile, moreover, furthermore*) or with a transitional phrase (*in addition, as a result, for example*) to join main clauses

  The advertisement states that applicants with a degree in a related area are preferred; **nevertheless,** applicants with a diploma and relevant experience will be considered for the position.

- With a coordinating conjunction (*and, but, or, nor, for, yet, so*) when the main clauses contain internal punctuation

  Already late for work, I dressed hurriedly, ran out of the house, and jumped into the car; but when I turned the key, I heard only the ominous clicking sound of a dying battery.

- However, if you are joining two fairly short main clauses with a coordinating conjunction, a comma is a better choice.

NOT	Yvette longed to escape; yet she remained passive.
BUT	Yvette longed to escape, yet she remained passive.

- Instead of a comma between items in a series when the items themselves have internal punctuation

    The lottery prize includes the dream home, custom-built by a leading home builder; custom-made draperies, professional interior decorating, and exclusive furnishings; and free cleaning for one year.

Semicolons can be useful, but too many will give your writing a ponderous tone. If you're becoming addicted to the semicolon, you're probably relying too heavily on coordination to join your ideas.

    For several years, my computer has been working fine; now I'm having major problems. Perhaps a virus has infected the command system; the computer seems to be erasing files randomly. I'll have to be more careful to duplicate my material on backup disks; I'm losing too much valuable information.

You could improve this passage by introducing more subordination.

    Although my computer has been working fine for several years, now I'm having major problems. Perhaps a virus has infected the command system; the computer seems to be erasing files randomly. I'll have to be more careful to duplicate my material on backup disks because I'm losing too much valuable information.

For more information on joining sentences effectively, see Faulty Subordination (18f).

Exercise 22.7

Add semicolons where necessary to the following sentences.

1. Emilio wanted to be a famous astronaut he ended up operating the ferris wheel at the amusement park.

2. Zack thought that he had enough money in his account to pay for the new jeans however, his direct debit payment was not approved.

3. When the smoke had cleared from the oven, Lucas was afraid to open the door but, fortunately, a quick glance showed that the roast still looked edible.

4. Ashley is going camping with her family Erica has therefore agreed to take over the paper route for a week.

5. There was a heavy frost in the night as a result, farmers are concerned about the peach crop.

22b

Semicolons

Exercise 22.8

Add semicolons where necessary to the following sentences. Replace inappropriate semicolons with the correct punctuation. If the sentence is correct, write **C.**

1. Even though the skater was disappointed with the poor marks for artistic interpretation; he was pleased with the high marks for technical merit.

2. Clean the gardening tools after each use otherwise, they will rust.

3. Betty stood at the bus stop; patiently waiting for the children to come home from school.

4. When John graduated from university, he was fortunate to get a junior management position with an accounting firm; he then began setting aside money to repay his student loan.

5. The variety show will feature Vox Populi, a well-known local band, the Crazy Bones, a hilarious comedy act, and the Tumbling Turners, an acrobatic troupe.

22c Colons and Dashes

The **colon** and the **dash** can both be used to introduce a phrase or clause that explains or illustrates what precedes it.

> After the tenth day without food, the subject began to exhibit psychological debilitation: he had trouble concentrating and slept much of the time.

> I still love listening to the Beatles—they remind me of the sixties.

The colon is more appropriate for most formal writing situations. Use the dash when you want a more informal tone.

A pair of dashes can also be used to enclose parenthetical comments that slightly disrupt the flow of the sentence. By using dashes rather than commas or parentheses, you can set off these comments more emphatically from the rest of the sentence.

> The relationship between father and son—never very good—worsened as the son began to assert his independence.

Be careful not to overuse either the colon or the dash. Too many sentences containing colons will make your writing too formal and stilted. Too many sentences containing dashes will make your writing too choppy and informal.

22c

Colons and Dashes

Colons

Use a colon in the following situations:

- To introduce a list or series preceded by a complete main clause

  You will need the following equipment: a small tent, a sleeping bag, a camp stove, and several bottles of insect repellent.

- In a sentence introducing a list of items, you can use a colon after a verb when *as follows* or *the following* is strongly implied, as in this example:

  Our report includes:

  1. background information about the problem

  2. an analysis of its causes

  3. recommendations for solutions

  4. a detailed budget

Note: Do **not** use a colon with *such as* or *for example*.

NOT   The Robinsons brought back a number of souvenirs, such as: a red plush cushion with "Visit Niagara Falls" emblazoned on it, a slightly pornographic calendar, and two incredibly ugly beer mugs.

BUT   The Robinsons brought back a number of souvenirs, such as a red plush cushion . . .

- To introduce a concluding explanatory phrase

  She dedicated her research to one goal: finding the link between Einstein's theory of relativity and the theory of quantum mechanics.

- To join main clauses when the second clause restates, explains, summarizes, or emphasizes the first

  The movie was a complete waste of time: the plot dragged, the characters were boring, and the special effects were silly.

- To introduce a formal quotation. Both the sentence introducing the quotation and the quotation itself must be grammatically complete.

293

In Alice Munro's short story "Boys and Girls," the narrator gradually becomes aware of the full implications of being a girl: "A girl was not, as I had supposed, simply what I was; it was what I had to become. It was a definition, always touched with emphasis, with reproach and disappointment. Also it was a joke on me."

Note: Do **not** use a colon when the sentence introducing the quotation ends with *that* or is otherwise incomplete.

NOT   Hamlet shows a new acceptance of death when he says that: "There is a special providence in the fall of a sparrow."

BUT   Hamlet shows a new acceptance of death when he says that "There is a special providence in the fall of a sparrow."

- In biblical references (John 3:16)
- In time references (9:45, 12:05)
- Between the title and the subtitle of an article or a book
  A Harvest Yet to Reap: A History of Prairie Women

- After the salutation in a business letter

  Dear Business Manager:

  Dear Editor:

  Dear Ms. Bennett:

Dashes

Use a dash in the following situations:

- To indicate a sudden interruption or change of thought

  I left my briefcase—I remember it distinctly—right here by the front entrance.

  And then she said—but I see you've already heard the story.

- To emphasize parenthetical remarks

  Antonia worked hard—perhaps too hard—in spite of her illness.

- After a series at the beginning of a sentence

  Sports figures, entertainers, politicians—all have been invited to the wedding.

Colons and Dashes

- To set off a series that comes in the middle of a sentence

  It had everything—power, grace, beauty—that Chantal wanted in a car.

- To emphasize an expression that explains or illustrates

  Philip worked tirelessly toward his goal—an A in English.

Exercise 22.9

Add colons and dashes where appropriate to the following sentences. Where either is possible, be prepared to explain your choice.

1. Mae West offers an interesting perspective on making moral choices "When choosing between two evils, I always like to try the one I've never tried before."

2. I have registered in the following courses for the winter term Basic Calculus, Fluid Dynamics, and Introductory Drafting.

3. I am convinced I say this without reservation that Luke and Laura will never get back together.

4. None of the suspects Winken, Blinken, or Nod knew that they were under surveillance for stealing the sleeping pills.

5. My cat Puck is an excellent companion he is intelligent, affectionate and infinitely patient.

Exercise 22.10

Add colons and dashes where appropriate to the following sentences. Where either is possible, be prepared to explain your choice. If the sentence is correct, write **C.**

1. He had no means of escape all of the exits were blocked.

2. When Herb boasted that he was a "self-made man," Vernon replied, "That's the trouble with cheap labour."

3. Mrs. Christie you met her last week at the Doyles' party will host a murder mystery dinner at her country retreat.

4. Pottery, weaving, and willow furniture all will be for sale at the spring craft show.

5. The puppy was in a piteous state he was caked with mud, shivering uncontrollably, and close to starvation.

22c

Colons and Dashes

22d Parentheses and Brackets

Both **parentheses** and **brackets** serve to set apart certain information in a sentence or a paragraph, but they are used in different circumstances.

Parentheses

Use parentheses in the following situations:

- To set off supplementary material that interrupts the flow of the sentence

  The council finally agreed (but only after a heated debate) to the proposed amendments.

Note 1: Parentheses, dashes, and commas can all be used to set off nonessential information. When you enclose material in parentheses, you signal to your reader that it is relatively unimportant. Dashes tend to emphasize its importance, while commas will give it approximately equal weight.

Note 2: Do **not** use parentheses to enclose important information. In the example below, the parentheses are misleading because they suggest that essential information is incidental.

  Although he was only fifteen, Victor was sentenced to nine months in a juvenile detention centre. (This sentence was the result of his fifth conviction for theft over $1000 in two years.)

- To enclose explanatory material, such as bibliographical citations, brief definitions, and pieces of historical information

  The Celsius (centigrade) thermometer was invented by the Swedish astronomer Anders Celsius (1701–1744).

For information on in-text citations, see appendices B and C.

- To enclose letters or numerals in a list of items

  Each oral presentation will be graded on (1) delivery, (2) voice, (3) content, and (4) language.

- In general, resist the temptation to use parentheses too often. Information enclosed in parentheses interrupts the flow and meaning of a sentence. Too many of these interruptions will make your writing choppy and hard to follow, as in the following example.

*Parentheses
and Brackets*

Headhunting (often called an executive search) is the practice of seeking out (sometimes through advertising, sometimes through more direct approaches to individuals) senior, specialized employees (when no one with sufficient expertise is available within an organization) for business.

Rewritten with only one parenthetical comment, the paragraph reads much more smoothly.

Headhunting (as executive searches are often called) is the practice of seeking out specialized senior employees for business firms when no one with sufficient expertise is available within an organization. Headhunters may advertise these positions or approach prospective candidates directly.

Using Other Punctuation with Parentheses

- If the parenthetical remark is a sentence within another sentence, the parenthetical sentence does not begin with a capital or end with a period.

  The baby was sleeping (at least his eyes were closed) when I peeked into the room.

- If the parenthetical remark is a complete sentence that is not part of another sentence, capitalize the first word and put the end punctuation inside the closing parenthesis.

  After weeks of dull, cloudy weather, the first snowflakes began to fall on Christmas Eve. (The children had been convinced that Christmas wouldn't be Christmas without snow.)

- If the parenthetical construction within a sentence requires a question mark or exclamation mark, that punctuation goes inside the closing parenthesis.

  It is important for students to learn how to think (who can deny that necessity?), but they also need facts and information to think about.

Brackets

Use brackets in the following ways:

- To enclose explanatory material inserted into a quotation. These square brackets tell your reader that the material was not part of the original quotation.

In the essay "Grace before Meat," Charles Lamb says, "I hate a man who swallows it [his food], affecting not to know what he is eating. I suspect his taste in higher matters."

Note: The punctuation of the original sentence (the comma after *it*) goes outside the material enclosed in brackets.

- To show that you have changed a word (usually a verb or a pronoun) in a direct quotation so that it will fit grammatically with your sentence

    Old King Cole [is] a merry old soul / And a merry old soul [is] he.

- With the word *sic* (Latin for *thus*) to indicate that an error in spelling, grammar, or fact is part of the original quotation

    The newspaper headline read "Affects [sic] of cutbacks not yet known."

22e Quotation Marks

The main purpose of **quotation marks** is to acknowledge that you have used someone else's words. Use quotation marks in the following situations:

- Whenever you quote more than three consecutive words from any printed material. (For how to document your sources, see appendices B and C.)

    According to the article, many primatologists and psychologists believe that "chimpanzees have the capacity for self-awareness, self-consciousness, and self-knowledge."

- When you include comments made by someone you have interviewed. (For how to document interviews in a research paper, see appendices B and C.)

    According to Sharon Bush, records clerk in the registrar's office, "The completion rate for this course averages about 30 percent."

- When you include dialogue in a personal narrative or a short story. Indent the words of each speaker as you would indent separate paragraphs.

    "Do you have any plans to publish your autobiography?" the critic asked the novelist.
    "Actually, I was saving the best till last," remarked the author. "I might even arrange to have it published posthumously."
    "The sooner, the better," replied the critic.

Note: Remember that quotation marks set off direct speech. Don't use them with indirect speech.

| DIRECT SPEECH | The clerk asked the customer, "Will you pay cash, or shall I charge this purchase to your account?" |
| INDIRECT SPEECH | The clerk asked the customer whether she wanted to pay cash or charge the purchase to her account. |

- Use single quotation marks to indicate a quotation within a quotation.

  The witness testified, "I was present when the accused said, 'She'll pay for what she did to me!'"

Other Uses of Quotation Marks

- Put quotation marks around the titles of short works that have not been published separately, such as titles of chapters, short stories, articles, and most poems.

  His favourite Poe story is "The Fall of the House of Usher."

- When you want to draw your reader's attention to a word used in a special way, you can either underline the word to indicate that it is italicized (see Italics and Underlining, 22f) or put quotation marks around it.

  It's quite acceptable to begin a sentence with "because."

- Avoid using either quotation marks or italics merely to draw attention to slang or irony.

| NOT | My sister has become a real "couch potato." |
| NOT | Our "paperboy" is at least fifty years old. |

Exercise 22.11

Use quotation marks appropriately in the following sentences. If the sentence is correct, write **C.**

1. Two negatives make a positive, explained Ludwig. However, two positives don't make a negative.

   Yeah, right! replied Noam.

2. Heather said that she would pick Katie up from work and save Mother the trip.

3. According to an old Russian proverb, When money talks, the truth keeps silent.

4. I wish you would stop saying like and basically in every sentence. That habit drives me crazy, you know.

5. Virginia Woolf's essay The Death of the Moth is a thoughtful meditation on the nature of the life force.

Using Other Punctuation with Quotation Marks

When you close a quotation, should the end punctuation go inside or outside the quotation marks? Follow these guidelines:

- As a general rule, commas and periods go inside quotation marks; colons and semicolons go outside.

  Staring in disgust at the cans of escargots in the specialty section of the grocery store, Mr. Johnson remarked to his wife, "Let's can all the snails from the garden. We'll make a fortune." [The period is inside the quotation marks.]

  Facing Mr. Waters squarely, William replied, "That, sir, is not your concern"; he then walked resolutely out of the room. [The semicolon is outside the quotation marks.]

- When a quotation is a question or an exclamation, the question or exclamation mark goes inside the quotation marks.

  "Where are the snows of yesteryear?" she asked pensively.

  "Get out of my way!" the enraged customer bellowed as he pushed through the crowd.

- When the entire sentence containing the quotation is a question or an exclamation, the question or exclamation mark goes outside the quotation marks.

  What does it mean to say "A stitch in time saves nine"?

  The Great China Circus is now truly "the greatest show on Earth"!

- When a quotation ends a sentence, whatever punctuation is inside the quotation mark also ends the entire sentence. Don't add any other punctuation.

  Jane listened with growing horror as the voice from the attic screamed, "Please let me out!"

22e

Quotation Marks

Exercise 22.12

Use quotation marks appropriately in the following sentences. Be sure to punctuate each sentence correctly. If the sentence is correct, write **C.**

1. No, I won't move my car shouted the irate driver.
2. Aunt Eva is fond of saying that no one is responsible for making another person happy.
3. Was it Archimedes who said Give me a firm place to stand, and I will move the earth
4. The term portmanteau word refers to a word combining the sounds and meanings of two other words. For example, the word smog is a blending of the words smoke and fog
5. In today's English class we explored the attitudes to war expressed in Wilfred Owen's poem Dulce et Decorum Est and Randall Jarrell's poem The Death of the Ball Turret Gunner

Exercise 22.13

Use quotation marks and other punctuation appropriately in the following sentences.

1. What did Mother mean when she said The acorn never falls far from the oak tree
2. If fifty million people say a foolish thing noted Anatole France it is still a foolish thing
3. Hearing the familiar bell, the children ran into the street yelling We all scream for ice cream
4. The words chimpanzee, gorilla, and zebra all came into English from African languages.
5. Sitting alone in the darkened room, Steve morosely hummed the tune to Sam Cooke's Sad Mood

22f Italics and Underlining

Use **italic** script in typeset and word-processed material, or **underlining** in handwritten or typed material, for each of the following cases:

- For the titles of books, newspapers, magazines, pamphlets, plays, films, television and radio series, works of art, albums, or long musical compositions

The city library has purchased two sets of *The Canadian Encyclopedia.*

The police drama *Homicide: Life on the Streets* steadily gained popularity during its first few years.

- For the names of airplanes, ships, trains, and spacecraft

Note: Do not italicize or underline *the* or abbreviations that come before the name.

Captain James Cook commanded the H.M.S. *Resolution* on his second Pacific voyage.

- For foreign words and phrases that have not been accepted as English terms

Examples of these expressions include the following:

bon vivant (a person who enjoys food and drink)

casus belli (an event that brings about war)

tête à tête (an intimate conversation between two people)

Weltanschauung (a comprehensive concept of the universe and the relationship of humans to it)

- For words referred to as words, letters referred to as letters, and numerals referred to as numerals

The one word on the test that I couldn't define was *dipsomaniac.*

Don't forget to cross your *t*'s.

Is this an *8* or a *3*?

- For emphasis and clarity

I asked *who* you are, not *how* you are.

Late papers will *not* be accepted.

Note: Be cautious whenever you are tempted to use italics for emphasis. Like exclamation marks, italics lose their effectiveness if overused.

22g Hyphens

Hyphens are used as part of some compound words (*father-in-law, trade-in*). Other compound words are written as one word (*hairbrush, stepmother*) or as two words (*lawn bowling, token payment*). Because there is no pattern for forming compound words, and because compound words are constantly changing, your best source of current information is an up-to-date dictionary. You may find that dictionaries disagree on compound forms. Choose one spelling and use it consistently.

Use a hyphen in the following ways:

- With two-word numbers from twenty-one to ninety-nine

  There are **ninety-nine** bottles of beer on the wall.

- With numbers used as adjectives

  Is the tank **three-quarters** full?

  Atsuko, a **thirty-four-year-old** musician, made her television debut last night.

- With the prefixes *self* (*self-satisfied*), *ex* (*ex-husband*), and *all* (*all-purpose*); with prefixes that come before proper nouns (*anti-Catholic*); and with the suffix *elect* (*minister-elect*).

- To avoid an awkward combination of letters or to prevent misunderstanding: *re-cover* (cover again)

- To indicate that two or more prefixes or words share a common root

  Both **pre-** and **post-natal** classes are available.

  This course covers **eighteenth-** and **nineteenth-century** drama.

- To join two or more words that function as a single adjective conveying a single concept: *well-written essay, reddish-brown hair*

Note 1: If these constructions come after the noun, they are **not** hyphenated.

The essay is well written.

Her hair is reddish brown.

Note 2: If the group of words contains an *ly* adverb, do **not** hyphenate: *poorly conceived plan, frequently used reference book.*

22g

Hyphens

Hyphenating Words at the End of Lines

It's best to avoid dividing words at the end of a line if possible. Occasionally, however, you may not be able to squeeze all the letters on the line you are writing. Here are the guidelines to follow:

- Always hyphenate a word between syllables. The first part of the word must contain at least three letters. Try to divide the word in two approximately equal parts that convey the sense of the whole word (*butter-fly* not *but-terfly*).

- When a double consonant occurs at the end because you have added a suffix (*ing, ed*), divide between the two consonants (*let-ting not lett-ing*). If the root word ends in a double consonant, divide between the root word and the suffix (*bill-ing* not *bil-ling*).

- Include a single-letter syllable with the first part of the word (*regu-late* not *reg-ulate*).

- Do **not** hyphenate one-syllable words or words of five or fewer letters (regardless of the number of syllables). If possible, avoid hyphenating words of six letters.

- Do **not** hyphenate figures ($21.36, 123,000), dates (Dec. 10, 1926), abbreviations (UNICEF), or proper names (Albert Einstein, Calgary).

- Do **not** hyphenate the last word of more than two consecutive lines.

- Do **not** hyphenate the last word in a paragraph or the last word on a page.

Exercise 22.14

Add, change, or take out hyphens as necessary in the following sentences.

1. This neutral carpet can serve as an allpurpose floor-covering in any room.

2. You are looking particularly selfsatisfied after winning the job over twenty three equally-qualified candidates.

3. If you want to use gender neutral terms, use "workers" rather than "work-men" and "humanity" rather than "man-kind."

4. The ninety year old woman made her first parachute jump on the week-end.

22g

Hyphens

5. Julia's ex boyfriend returned all the compact-disks she had given him as presents.

Exercise 22.15

How would you hyphenate each of the following words if it appeared at the end of a line? If the word should not be hyphenated, write **C.**

1. iconoclast
2. crybaby
3. wrapping
4. faded
5. CUSO

6. railroad
7. thrilling
8. jimjams
9. memorize
10. radio

22h Apostrophes

Because plurals, possessives, and contractions that end in *s* sound the same, your ear is not a reliable guide for when and how to use an **apostrophe.** Instead, you need to know which of these forms you intend to create so that you can use the apostrophe appropriately. Remember, too, that if you're unsure of how to use an apostrophe, you are as likely to put it in the wrong place as to omit it in the right place.

- A **plural noun,** which is usually formed by adding *s* or *es,* indicates that more than one person, place, or thing is being discussed. Do not add an apostrophe when you wish to indicate a plural. Be especially careful with proper nouns.

PLURAL

All the **Joneses** congratulate you on keeping up with them. [The plural of *Jones* is formed by adding *es.*]

POSSESSIVE

The **Joneses'** car is in the garage. [The apostrophe indicates that the car belongs to the Joneses.]

- A **contraction** indicates that one or more letters have been omitted. The sense of the sentence will indicate whether the apostrophe signals possession or a contraction.

CONTRACTION

Your **report's** already three weeks late. [*report's = report is*]

POSSESSIVE

Your **report's** recommendations are out of line with current department policy. [The

305

apostrophe indicates that the recommendations belong to the report.]

- **Possessive pronouns** (*yours, hers, its, ours, theirs*) do not take apostrophes. Only nouns and indefinite pronouns (*someone, something, somebody, everyone, everything, everybody, no one, nothing, nobody, anything, anybody*) take an apostrophe to show possession.

NOT   These problems are **their's** to solve.

BUT   These problems are **theirs** to solve.

- *Its* is a possessive; *it's* is a contraction.

POSSESSIVE   The dog buried **its** bone in the garden.

CONTRACTION **It's** a serious problem.

Making Nouns and Indefinite Pronouns Possessive

- To make an indefinite pronoun possessive, add *'s*.

  This is **nobody's** business.

  Everyone's assignments have been marked.

- To make a singular noun that does not end with *s* possessive, add *'s*.

  The **child's** bike lay abandoned on the driveway.

  The **horse's** saddle is hanging on a nail in the barn.

- To make a singular noun that ends with *s* or *ss* possessive, add *'s* if the word is one syllable. Add only an apostrophe if the noun is more than one syllable.

  James's gloves are lying on the hall table.

  The **boss's** instructions are on her desk.

  The next **witness'** testimony is crucial to the defence.

  The **actress'** hopes were raised by the screen test.

- To make a plural noun that ends with *s* possessive, add only an apostrophe.

  All **students'** marks will be posted by the main office.

  There will be a meeting of the **girls'** hockey team on Wednesday.

22h

Apostrophes

306

- To make a plural noun that does not end with *s* possessive, add *'s*.

  Men's suits are on sale this week.

  The **children's** story hour has been cancelled.

- To make a compound noun possessive, add *'s* to the last word.

  Mario borrowed his **father-in-law's** lawn mower over the weekend.

- To indicate that two or more people own one thing (joint possession), add *'s* to the last name.

  Carmen and Roberta's restaurant opened last month.

- To indicate that two or more people own things separately (separate possession), make all the names possessive.

  Ralph's and **Howard's** cars are in for repairs.

Note: Possessive nouns do not always refer to people. They can also refer to animals or objects.

  The **sun's** rays are very strong today.

  Today's news is better.

  This **society's** children have special needs.

Exercise 22.16

Add all necessary apostrophes to the following sentences.

1. Helens and Stephanies projects both won honourable mentions at this years science fair.
2. Several patrons cars were vandalized in the mall parking lot.
3. Nobodys pecan pie is as good as yours.
4. Mens and womens cross trainers are advertised in the stores flyer.
5. Annes sister-in-laws mail was delivered to the wrong address three days in a row.

22h

Apostrophes

Other Uses of the Apostrophe

- To form the plural of letters, add *'s*. Italicize or underline the letter but not the *s*.

  Pay particular attention to the long *o's* in this poem.

- To form the plural of words referred to as words, add *'s*. Italicize or underline the word but not the *s*.

   There are five *a lot*'s in this one paragraph.

- To form the plural of abbreviations, add *'s*.

   She has two **MA's**, one in English and one in history.

- You have a choice in forming the plural of numerals and dates. Add *'s* or *s* alone.

   His family emigrated from Scotland in the **1920's** [1920s].

   What are the chances of rolling nothing but **2's** [2s] in a dice game?

Exercise 22.17

Add all necessary apostrophes to the following sentences.

1. For some reason, I can never remember that *vacuum* has two *u*s and only one *c*.
2. Its important to respond to your hostess invitation promptly and courteously.
3. Lester and Marys puppy chewed up three pairs of shoes in less than a week.
4. Justins parents cottage is badly in need of a new roof.
5. Someones pen was left on the desk.
6. I need to buy some apples and bananas for the childrens lunches.
7. Short pauses in your oral presentation are perfectly acceptable. Dont fill the space with *um*s and *uh*s.
8. Janet paid a months rent in advance before moving into her apartment.
9. Wont you have more tea and another of Grandmother Mildreds ginger snap cookies?
10. The books cover has been torn in half.

Abbreviations

22i Abbreviations

Abbreviations are appropriate in scientific and technical writing and in footnotes and bibliographies. In most other kinds of writing, use abbreviations sparingly. If you wish to abbreviate a term that you intend to use repeatedly, write the term out in full the first time you use it, and then use the abbreviation.

American Sign Language (ASL) is the first language of many deaf children. Because ASL has a different grammatical structure from English, deaf children who use ASL must learn English as a second language.

The following guidelines cover the appropriate uses of abbreviations in nontechnical writing.

Names of Dates and Times

- Write out the names of months and holidays.

  Hanukkah comes in the darkest part of December.

- Use *a.m.* (*ante meridiem*) to refer to exact times before noon and *p.m.* (*post meridiem*) to refer to exact times after noon. Note that these abbreviations are not capitalized.

  The meeting began at 9:07 a.m. and concluded at 5:31 p.m.

- Use *BC* (Before Christ) to refer to dates before the birth of Christ. Put *BC* after the date. Use *AD* (*Anno Domini*) to refer to dates after the birth of Christ. Put *AD* before the date. Stop using *AD* when you can assume that your reader knows that the event did not take place before the birth of Christ, usually for any date after AD 500.

  Julius Caesar, who unified the Roman Empire under his dictatorship, was assassinated in **44 BC.**

  Hadrian's Wall, completed in **AD 123,** was constructed to prevent northern tribes from invading Roman Britain.

If you prefer, use BCE (Before the Common Era) and CE (Common Era). Both of these abbreviations follow the year.

Units of Measurement

Write out metric words such as *gram, metre,* and *kilometre* when you use them without numerals.

  Speed limits are now given in **kilometres** per hour.

Abbreviate these words when you use them with a numeral. Don't put a period after the abbreviation.

  Combine **10 g** flour with **1 l** milk.

22i

Abbreviations

Scientific and Technical Terms

Some commonly known scientific and technical terms are usually abbreviated.

DNA (deoxyribonucleic acid)

DDT (dichlorodiphenyltrichloroethane)

AIDS (Acquired Immune Deficiency Syndrome)

Common Latin Terms

Although it's useful to know the following Latin abbreviations, it's usually better to omit them or replace them with English equivalents. If you use them, note where the periods go.

e.g. *exempli gratia* (for example)

i.e. *id est* (that is)

etc. *et cetera* (and so forth)

Be especially careful with *etc.* Using it at the end of a list suggests that you have run out of ideas. Instead, end the list with an inclusive phrase like "and other..." or begin the list with the phrase *such as* or an equivalent expression.

NOT   The Niagara region grows apples, peaches, pears, **etc.**

BUT   The Niagara region grows apple, peaches, pears, **and other fruits.**

OR   The Niagara region grows fruits **such as** apples, peaches, and pears.

The Ampersand (&)

Never use this symbol in general writing. Use the ampersand only when you are copying the name of an organization or following APA documentation style.

He works the night shift at the local **A&W.**
Maccoby, E. E., **&** Jacklin, C. N. (1974) . . .

22j Capitalization

All proper nouns are capitalized. A proper noun names a specific person, place, or thing.

Meet me at the main entrance of **The Bay.**

22j

Capitalization

Use capitalization in the following way:

- For kinship terms such as mother, father, brother, sister when they are part of a name (as in *Mother Teresa, Grandfather McGregor*) or when they are used as a substitute for the proper name. Do not capitalize kinship terms preceded by a possessive adjective (*my, our, your, her, his, their*).

  Is **Baba Kostash** going to the dance?

  Is **Grandfather** going to the dance?

  We are going with our father and mother.

- For titles used as part of a person's name.

  I have a meeting with **Professor Qureshi** this afternoon.

  I get along well with two of my **professors** this term.

- For the names of directions (*north, south, east, west*) when they are part of a proper name or refer to a region.

  It has always been his ambition to travel to the **North.**

  The house faces **north.** [*North* names a direction, not a region.]

- For the names of planets, stars, and other heavenly bodies. Do not capitalize *sun* and *moon*. Do not capitalize *earth* when it is modified by *the*.

  The astronauts saw **Earth** from their spaceship.

  Unless we act now, all the waters of **the earth** will be polluted.

- For the names of institutions, organizations, political parties, and branches of government. Do not capitalize words such as *party, college,* or *university* unless you are using the term as a shortened version of the full name.

  Faryl has a **university** degree in biology.

  Tim will complete his final year at **Capilano College** this spring.

- For nationalities, languages, religious groups, religions, sacred and religious names.

  Canadian, Cree, Protestant, Taoism, the Koran, the Bible

- For days of the week, the months, holidays, events. Do not capitalize the names of seasons.

  Monday, January, New Year's Eve, the Middle Ages, summer, winter, spring, fall

22j

Capitalization

- For the names of specific courses. Do not capitalize the names of general subjects, except languages.

Psychology 101, **Chemistry** 400

I studied **English, French, drama, math,** and **sociology** in my first year of university.

Other Occasions for Capitalization

- Capitalize the first word in a quotation if the quotation is a complete sentence. If the quotation is not a complete sentence, do not capitalize the first word.

The instructor turned to me and said, "Please give me your views on the opening scene in *Macbeth*."

Susan remarked that she would rather be "poor and healthy" than "rich and sick."

- Capitalize the first, last, and all important words in the titles of books, short stories, plays, poems, articles, newspapers, magazines, movies, and musical compositions.

"Back in the USSR"   *River of the Brokenhearted*
"To an Athlete Dying Young"   *The Globe and Mail*

22k Numbers

Numerals are appropriate and preferred in scientific and technical writing. In general writing, however, certain conventions determine the use of numerals or words to express numbers.

Numerals

Use numerals in nontechnical writing in the following cases:

Numbers

- *To provide a series of numbers*

In 1986, **250** children were involved in the school lunch program. By 1987, the number had increased to **300** children. Last year, **350** children were eating lunch at school.

- *To express a number that would take more than two words to spell out*

Last year the shelter for battered women helped **259** women and their children.

- *To express exact times of the day and with **a.m. and p.m.***

  We'll begin the meeting at **9:15** sharp.

  The plane from Toronto will arrive at **8:03 a.m.**

- *To express exact sums of money*

  This wonderful car can be yours for only **$2999.99.**

- *To express dates.* Years are always expressed in numerals; centuries should be written out.

  The events between **1939** and **1945** affected the rest of the **twentieth century.**

You can use *st, nd, rd, th* with numerals in dates if you do not give the year, but these abbreviations are not essential.

  The concert is scheduled for August 20th [or August 20].

- *To express addresses*

  2939 107 Street; #976, 10098 Elm Street; P.O. Box 12

- *To express percentages and decimals*

  29%, 87 percent, 3.9 cm

- *To express page, line, verse, act, and scene numbers in literary works.* See appendix B for more information.

  Act 3, Scene 2, lines 23–38 **or** 3.2.23–28

  John 1:1–5; 1 & 2 Corinthians

Words

Use words in place of numerals in these instances:

- *For numbers that can be spelled out in one or two words*

  At least **fifty** people were invited to the party.

- *To express approximate numbers used with money, times of the day, and measurements.* In these cases, the whole of the round number should be expressed in words. If the number is VERY large, a combination of numerals and words can be used.

  I used to be able to buy a huge bag of candy for less than **ten cents.**

22k

Numbers

313

Every day she gets up at around **five o'clock** to do her homework.

By the end of this century, **10 billion** people will compete for space and food on the earth.

- ## *When you begin a sentence with a number*

   Thirty percent of first-year students need some form of financial assistance.

Note: Use a combination of words and numerals as necessary to prevent confusion.

NOT   He ordered **2 10 cm** pieces of wood.

BUT   He ordered **two 10 cm** pieces of wood.

Exercise 22.18

Correct all errors in the use of numerals or words to express numbers in the following sentences. If the sentence is correct, write **C.**

1. He bought 4 250-page packages of binder paper at the beginning of the term.
2. 15 percent of those polled responded that they were still undecided about how they would vote in the election.
3. At least 20 customers have returned the sheets because they were labelled the wrong size.
4. Including the PST and GST, the chocolate bar costs $1.14.
5. Some sports analysts say that Wayne Gretzky was at his peak playing with the Edmonton Oilers in the nineteen eighties. Gretzky retired from professional hockey in nineteen ninety-nine.

Numbers

- Guide to Grammar & Writing, Capital Community College—links to word- and sentence-level topics, among others; includes interactive quizzes.
  www.ccc.commnet.edu/grammar

- UBC Writing Centre Online Resources—links to Purdue University On-Line Writing Lab; The Rensselaer Writing Center; University of Victoria Writer's Guide; Rutgers University Guide to Grammar and Style.
  www.writingcentre.ubc.ca/online_resources.html

- UBC Writing Centre's Writers' Workshop—links to dictionaries, grammar and composition resources, general writing references.
  www.writingcentre.ubc.ca/workshop/reference.htm

- University of Maine Writing Center—links to grammar and mechanics guide, writing resources, dictionaries, thesauruses, foreign language dictionaries, citation format guides, ESL resources, composition and rhetoric resources.
  www.ume.maine.edu/wcenter/

- Hypergrammar, University of Ottawa Writing Centre—online grammar handbook.
  www.uottawa.ca/academic/arts/writcent/hypergrammar/

- Useful Writing Links, Queens University Writing Centre—links to grammar resources, ESL-related resources, dictionaries, reference resources, among others.
  qsilver.queensu.ca/~wcentre/usefulinks.html

Web Links

- Advice on Academic Writing, University of Toronto—links to style and editing resources, grammar and punctuation resources, ESL answers, among others.
  www.utoronto.ca/writing/advise.html

- Wilfrid Laurier University Writing Centre—links to resources on sentence writing, grammar, ESL, among others. **www.wlu.ca/writing/handouts.shtml**

- University of Wisconsin-Madison Writing Center, Writer's Handbook—links to resources on grammar and punctuation, improving your writing style, among others. **www.wisc.edu/writing/Handbook/index.html**

General Writing Resources
- If you log on to **www.altavista.com** and type "online writing" in the SEARCH box, you will find dozens of sites for online writing resources.

Web Links

APPENDICES

APPENDIX A

FORMAT CONVENTIONS

A1 Formatting: Writing Assignments

The presentation of any writing assignment creates your reader's first impression and ensures that your ideas are clearly communicated. Take time to proofread and format your paper properly, using the following guidelines.

- *Typing*

Strive to produce a clean, professional-looking paper. Most instructors prefer papers to be typed and some insist on it (publishers accept only typed material). If you are allowed to submit handwritten papers, use blue or black ink.

When keyboarding, make sure the print is legible. Avoid last-minute printer problems by planning ahead and printing your essay at least one day before it is due. Use a standard 12 cpi Times Roman font. Avoid fonts and typographical devices that create a cluttered look.

Proofread your final hard copy and, if necessary, make neat corrections in ink. Even if someone else does your word processing, you are responsible for any errors.

- *Paper*

Use standard white computer paper or, if you are handwriting, lined paper of approximately the same size ($8^1/_2 \times 11$ in.). Use only one side of the page.

- *Word-processing functions*

Become familiar with your computer's default settings and the functions with which to change paragraph format (indenting, spacing), to insert automatic page numbers, to sort and format works cited or reference entries, and so forth. Do not use your computer as you would a typewriter: for example, do not leave two spaces between sentences as this can cause problems if a sentence falls at the end of a line—your next line may start one space in from the intended margin.

- *Spacing*

Always type double-spaced to allow room for comments. Many readers prefer handwritten work to be double-spaced for the same reason. Others prefer handwriting single-spaced on wide-lined paper.

- *Margins*

Adequate margins make your text more readable and give room for comments. The default margins on most word-processing programs are adequate. If you need to set margins, leave 4 cm ($1^1/_2$ in.) on the top and left sides and 2.5 cm (1 in.) on the bottom and right.

- *Title*

Your title should make the subject of your paper and the assignment you have chosen clear to your reader. The title of an essay is often a short form of the thesis. Or it may suggest the subject and arouse interest. Never use labels such as "Essay #1" or "Personal Essay."

- *Title page*

Determine the documentation style you will use for your essay. Then see appendix B (MLA) or appendix C (APA) for title-page guidelines and sample title pages.

- *Pagination*

In both the MLA and APA documentation styles, all pages are numbered at the top right corner. See appendices B and C for examples.

- *Bibliography*

End your paper with your list of references (APA) or works cited (MLA), if required. Be sure to number these pages.

- *Fastening*

Use a staple or paper clip to fasten the pages. (Some instructors and editors object to staples; all object to straight pins and other hazardous devices.)

- *Copies*

If you are using a word processor, make two backup copies: one on your hard drive and one on a disk. Set your computer's backup function to ten minutes or so, and overwrite revisions as necessary. If you are handwriting, make a photocopy of your paper in case the original is lost.

• *Compatibility*

Be aware of possible incompatibilities between the word-processing program you use at home and other computers you may be using to print or submit your work. Computer labs often don't allow disks to be brought in from the outside because of the danger of spreading viruses. If you submit work electronically, through a course tool such as WebCT or by email attachment, ensure that your instructor will be able to convert your documents.

A2 Documentation: General Guidelines

Whenever you use quotations, facts, or ideas from other sources, whether in a research paper or any other kind of writing, you must clearly indicate what you have borrowed, and you must do so in two places. Use parenthetical references (called *in-text citations*) to acknowledge your sources within your paper, AND include a list of those sources at the end of your paper to provide more complete bibliographical information.

Documenting your sources is important for two reasons. First, it enables your reader to check statements that you have made or to look up more information on your subject. Second, it ensures that you do not take credit for information that is not your own (see Taking Notes, 14c, and Documenting Sources, 14d). For these reasons, knowing what to document is just as important as knowing how to do it.

• You **don't** need to document the source of commonly known pieces of information, such as the fact that the earth is the third planet from the sun, or the source of familiar quotations, such as St. Paul's statement that it is "better to marry than to burn" or Hamlet's "to be or not to be" soliloquy, when you use them as allusions.

• You **do** need to document quotations from primary and secondary sources.

• You **do** need to document the source of all facts, ideas, and opinions that you have taken from other sources *whether or not* you have quoted directly. Be especially careful to acknowledge the source of statistics. Don't make the mistake of thinking that you can avoid having to acknowledge the source of your information by changing the wording slightly. Failure to cite your references in this situation is still plagiarism.

There are two main systems of documentation. The Modern Language Association of America (MLA) is the accepted authority for documentation in the humanities (for example, English, film studies, or philosophy). The American Psychological Association (APA) is the accepted authority for documentation in education, the social sciences (for example, psychology, sociology, or anthropology), and many fields in the physical sciences. See appendices B and C, respectively, for more information on these documentation styles.

A3 Quotations: General Guidelines

Although you will need to acknowledge any sources of information you use, you don't always need to quote your sources directly. In fact, you shouldn't include quotations in non-literary essays unless the exact wording seems important. Alternatives are paraphrasing and summarizing (for more information, see chapter 14, Research Papers). When you analyze works of literature, however, you should use quotations to support each point you make.

It takes skill and practice to use direct quotations effectively. Here are some general points to remember.

- *Use brief quotations to support points.*

Make all the major points in your own words and use brief quotations to support them. Do not rely on the quotation to make the point for you; your reader may interpret the quotation quite differently from the way you do. Often you can shorten a quotation by expressing most of it in your own words and quoting only the crucial part.

- *Use quotations in context.*

Do not take quotations out of context and use them to mean something other than what the writer intended, as in this example.

Original Text
"The movie was entertaining, but it simplified the more interesting complexities of the novel."

Misleading Extract
"The movie was entertaining ... [creating] interesting complexities."

• *Clarify the context for quotations.*

Introduce each quotation with a sentence that makes its context clear. Be sure to identify the speaker and the circumstances of the comment. Do not string several quotations together; introduce each one separately. Be sure each quotation fits grammatically with the sentence that introduces it.

Weak Example
"It is a truth universally acknowledged, that a single man in possession of a good fortune, must be in want of a wife" (1). This quotation is a good example of Jane Austen's irony because single women need to marry, not single men.

Weak Example
The opening sentence of *Pride and Prejudice* is ironic because "It is a truth universally acknowledged, that a single man in possession of a good fortune, must be in want of a wife" (1).

Strong Example
The ironic opening sentence of Jane Austen's *Pride and Prejudice* introduces the central concern of the novel—the economic necessity for women to marry: "It is a truth universally acknowledged, that a single man in possession of a good fortune, must be in want of a wife" (1).

• *Punctuate quotations appropriately.*

Pay close attention to punctuation before the quotation. If the introductory material ends with *that,* use no punctuation.

> The editorial in this morning's paper states **that** "If the Canadian dollar rises, exporters suffer; if it falls, importers suffer" ("Chasing the Dollar," *Daily Express,* Nov. 24, 2003, A13).

When the introductory material ends with words such as *states, says, argues, remarks,* and so forth, use a comma.

> The editorial in this morning's paper states, "If the Canadian dollar rises, exporters suffer; if it falls, importers suffer" ("Chasing the Dollar," *Daily Express,* Nov. 24, 2003, A13).

Finally, use a colon after a grammatically complete sentence introducing a quotation that is also a complete sentence.

The editorial in this morning's paper captures the dilemma of the Canadian economy: "If the Canadian dollar rises, exporters suffer; if it falls, importers suffer" ("Chasing the Dollar," *Daily Express,* Nov. 24, 2003, A13).

Notice that the end punctuation follows the parenthetical citation.

Whenever you summarize, paraphrase, or quote, determine the documentation style you will be using for your essay and see appendix B (MLA) and appendix C (APA) for guidelines and examples.

A3

APPENDIX B

DOCUMENTATION: MLA SYSTEM

B1

As mentioned in appendix A2, the main system of documentation in the humanities is the one developed by the Modern Language Association of America. Students would use this system for papers in English, film studies, and philosophy courses, among others.

The material in this appendix is a brief summary of the most common items required for documentation in MLA. Your college or university library may have printed and electronic summaries, and there are numerous Internet sites that post style sheets for MLA users. For more advanced work, consult the explanations and examples in the current sixth edition of the *MLA Handbook for Writers of Research Papers*. This work is available online through several websites (see part 4, Web Links).

B1 Formatting Your Essay

The general guidelines for formatting (appendix A) apply to essays in MLA style. Unless your instructor asks for a separate title page, prepare the first page of your paper as follows.

- Create a header that includes your last name and an automatically inserted page number. (This header will appear on all pages of your essay.)

- Beginning on the first line of double-spaced text, and flush with the left margin, type your name.

- On the next and subsequent lines type your instructor's name, your course number, and the date.

- Next, centre the title of your essay.

- Immediately below the title, begin your essay text.

Here is a scaled-down example of the first page of an essay in the MLA style.

Carol Lin

Professor Smith

English 101 (XXX)

8 October 2003

Language and Structure in Sharon Olds's "The Victims"

Sharon Olds's poem "The Victims" plays with forms of the verb "to

take." The infinitive and its forms have multiple meanings, but two dis-

tinct ones resonate throughout Olds's poem, helping to structure the

B2

B2 In-Text Citations

In-text citations serve two purposes: they provide enough information to allow your reader to locate full bibliographical references in your list of works cited; and they give page numbers (or, for some electronic sources, paragraph numbers) for quoted, paraphrased, and summarized material.

- The basic format consists of putting the last name of the author(s) and the page or paragraph number(s) in parentheses immediately after the quoted or paraphrased material.

  In the world of Alice Munro's short stories, no one is innocent (Caplan 23).

- If you have included the name of the author(s) in your introduction to the quotation or paraphrase, give only the page or paragraph number(s) in parentheses.

  Caplan argues that in the world of Alice Munro's short stories, no one is innocent (23).

- If you refer to more than one work by the same author, include a shortened version of the title.

  In a recent article, Caplan argues that the question of identity is central to Munro's fiction ("Self-Creation" 77).

- For works with two or three authors, give the last names in the order they appear on the title page. For works with more than three authors, give only the first author's last name and add *et al.* (meaning "and others").

> The development of the bourgeois family can be traced in the novels of the nineteenth century (Seligman and Urbanowitz 112–113).

> The editors of this anthology provide helpful comments on prosody (Beaty et al. 2004).

For works where no author is given, use the title or a shortened form that begins with the word under which the entry appears in the list of works cited.

> A *Daily Express News* editorial calls the film "a gross distortion of history" ("Crusade").

Sample In-Text Citations

In the following entries, pay special attention to punctuation surrounding the passage and the in-text citations.

Quotations

• *Short quotations of prose (author not previously identified)*

If the quotation is not more than five lines, incorporate it into your sentence. Do not change the capitalization. If the quotation is obviously incomplete, do not put an ellipsis (three spaced periods) before or after it. Put the in-text citation after the quotation, followed by the end punctuation for the sentence.

> Elizabeth's pride in her own intelligence is obvious in her remark that she would "never ridicule what is wise and good" (Austen 50).

• *Short quotations of poetry (author previously identified)*

Incorporate three lines or less of poetry into your sentence. Punctuate exactly as in the original. Use a slash, with a space before and after it, to indicate line divisions. Put the line reference in parentheses after the quotation. If you are quoting from a play with act, scene, and line numbers, give these in your reference.

> Claudius realizes that Hamlet is neither lovesick nor mad: "Love! His affections do not that way tend, / Nor what he spake, though it lacked form a little, / Was not like madness" (3.1.156-158).

- **Long quotations of prose or poetry**

Use a long quotation only when you will be making detailed comments on the passage. Use paragraph formatting functions to indent the long quotation 1 in. from the left- and right-hand margin. Check with your instructor as to his or her preference for double- or single-spacing. Do not use quotation marks unless the quotation includes dialogue. Put the citation in parentheses after the final punctuation at the end of the long quotation.

> John Donne begins "The Sun Rising" by complaining that the sun has awakened him and his beloved:
> Busy old fool, unruly sun,
> Why dost thou thus,
> Through windows, and through curtains, call on us?
> Must to thy motions lovers' seasons run? (1–4)

- **Quotation from a secondary source (written by a critic or scholar about a work of literature)**

In this example, notice the single quotation marks around two words that, in the original passage, were emphasized by double quotation marks.

> As James L. Johnson points out, "Tom's world is one in which 'adventure' replaces 'experience'" (51).

Paraphrased or Summarized Material

- **Paraphrase or summary from primary text (author not previously identified)**

This excerpt is from an essay that refers to more than one work by Margaret Atwood.

> A severe thunderstorm passing directly overhead reminds Iris of the advice that Reenie would give the girls: every piece a dire warning calculated to instill fear (Atwood, *Blind Assassin* 135).

- **Paraphrase or summary from secondary source (author not previously identified)**

Paraphrasing and summarizing, important alternatives to quoting directly, challenge you to use your own words.

> Tom is not changed by his encounters with Muff Potter, Dr. Robinson, and Injun Joe, even though encounters such as these would ordinarily affect how a person sees the world (Johnson 51).

B3 List of Works Cited

At the end of your paper, on a separate sheet entitled Works Cited, present a list of sources. In most cases, your list of works cited should include only the works you have actually cited in your paper. If you consulted a reference, but did not cite it in your work, do not include it on the list.

B3

- Make sure you include every work you refer to in a form your readers can find. If you have cited an essay in an edited collection, for instance, the bibliographical entry should appear under the name of the author of the essay, not under the name of the editor.

- List the entries alphabetically according to the author's last name. If a work has more than one author, keep the names in the order they are given and alphabetize according to the first name in the list.

- If the author is not given, alphabetize according to the first word in the title (not *The, A,* or *An*).

- Double-space within the entry and between entries. The first line of each entry should start at the left-hand margin. Indent subsequent lines by five spaces by using the hanging indent function on your computer. Do not number bibliographical entries.

In the following examples, note both the order of information and the punctuation. For a model of the MLA system of documentation, see the sample research essay, "*Tom Sawyer* and *Anne of Green Gables:* Two Models of Heroism" (14f).

Sample Works Cited Entries

Print Sources

- *Article*

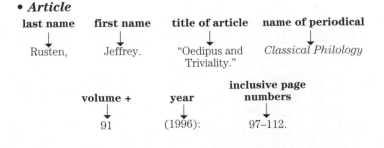

If each issue in the volume starts with page one, give the issue number as well: 91.1 (1996).

- *Book*

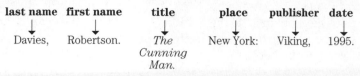

Note 1: If the city of publication is not well known or could be confused with another city of the same name, add the abbreviation for the province, state, or country (Paris, TX). If several places are listed, give only the first.

Note 2: Give only a short form of the publisher's name (McClelland, not McClelland and Stewart Inc.).

Note 3: Some instructors may prefer that you underline titles rather than italicize as shown here.

- *Part of a book*

Put the editor's name (if applicable) after the title and the inclusive page numbers of the part you are citing at the end.

Cohen, Leonard. "Suzanne Takes You Down." *The HBJ Anthology of Literature.* Eds. Jon C. Stott, Raymond E. Jones, and Rick Bowers. Toronto: Harcourt, 1993. 632–33.

Ellman, Richard. "The Critic as Artist as Wilde." *Oscar Wilde.* Ed. Harold Bloom. New York: Chelsea House, 1985.

Atwood, Margaret. "Uglypuss." *Bluebeard's Egg.* Toronto: Seal, 1984. 67–93.

- *Subsequent work by the same author*

Type three hyphens in place of the author's name. Continue as for the appropriate entry.

———. "Unearthing Suite." *Bluebeard's Egg.* Toronto: Seal, 1984. 240–58.

- *Multiple authors or editors*

Invert the order of the first name only.

Barnet, Sylvan, and Hugo Bedau. *Critical Thinking, Reading, and Writing: A Brief Guide to Argument.* 4th ed. New York: Bedford-St. Martin's, 2002.

When there are more than three names, use only the first name and *et al.*

Beaty, Jerome, et al., eds. *The Norton Introduction to Literature.* 8th ed. New York: Norton, 2002.

- **Reference books**

If the article is signed, the author's name comes first; if not, the title of the article comes first. If the reference work, such as an encyclopedia, is well known, omit the place of publication and the publisher, but include the edition (if given) and the year. If the work is arranged alphabetically, omit the volume number and the page number.

B3

"Biological Effects of Radiation." *Encyclopaedia Britannica*, 1998 ed.

Electronic Sources

The format for citing material you access through a portable electronic database (such as a CD-ROM), through an online database, or through the Internet does not differ much from other citations. You include everything you would give for the print version of your source, but you also need some additional information.

1. *The publication medium*—This information is important because versions of the same material published in various media (CD-ROM, diskette, magnetic tape) may not be identical.

2. *The name of the vendor*—This is required if the information provider has released different versions of the data to more than one vendor.

3. *The date of the electronic publication*—For an online database, indicate both the date of its publication and the date you looked at it, since material online may be changed or updated frequently.

You may not be able to find all of the required information. Cite what is available.

- **CD-ROMs and other portable databases**

Portable databases are electronic media that you can carry around, such as CD-ROMs, diskettes, and magnetic tapes.

1. *Periodically published databases on CD-ROM*—Many periodicals (scholarly journals, magazines, and newspapers) and reference works such as annual bibliographies are now available on CD-ROM as well as in print versions. Begin your entry by following the guidelines for citing the print version. Then give the title of the database, the publication medium, the name of the vendor (if relevant), and the electronic publication date.

Feaver, William. "Michelangelo." *Art News* 94 (1995): 137–38.

database	medium	vendor	electronic pub. date
↓	↓	↓	↓
Art Index.	CD-ROM.	SilverPlatter.	1995.

2. *Books on CD-ROM*—Cite these publications as you would the print version, but add the medium of publication.

B3

    medium
      ↓
The Oxford English Dictionary. 2nd ed. CD-ROM. Oxford UP, 1992.

3. *Publications on diskette or magnetic tape*—Cite these publications as you would books, but add the medium of publication.

Kriya Systems Inc. *Typing Tutor III with Letter Invaders for the IBM PC*. Diskette. New York: Simon and Schuster, 1984.

• **Online databases**

Online databases are available only through computer services (such as Dialog, CompuServe, Prodigy), or by subscription through your college or university library. Give all the information you would for the appropriate print version. Then add the name of the database, the name of the computer service or network, and the date you accessed the material.

Schiff-Zamano, Roberta. "The Re/membering of Female Power in *Lady Oracle*." *Canadian Literature* 112 (1987): 32–38.
MLA Bibliography 1963–1989. Dialog. 8 Aug. 1995.

         ↑   ↑   ↑
    database   **network date accessed**

Be sure to check with your instructor and the library staff at your educational institution about preferences for citing online databases. Your local library's URL, for example, will be easier to access than the originating library, as prescribed by the *MLA Handbook*.

• **Internet sources**

When you obtain research materials directly through your favourite search engine, include as much of the usual information as you can, the date you accessed the website, and the URL (Universal Resource Locator) or electronic address.

URL Access—Professional or Organizational Home Page

Literary Landscapes. Home page. Collect Britain Putting History in
   Place. 18 Sep. 2003 <http://www.collectbritain.co.uk/galleries/
   litlandscapes/doorway.cfm?author=wordsworth>.

URL Access—Articles in Online Periodicals

Sinopoli, John. "A Pact with God, A Pact with the Devil." Rev. of *Mercy
   Among the Children,* by David Adams Richards. *Varsity Review.*
   18 Sep. 2003 <http://www.varsity.utoronto.ca/archives/121/oct16/
   review/apact.html>.

Other Material

• *Film or video recordings*

Include the title, the director, the distributor, and the date. Add
any other information that is relevant to the discussion (such
as the names of the principal actors or the costume designer)
just before the distributor and the date. For videocassettes and
similar recordings, give the original release date and put the
medium (videocassette, filmstrip) before the name of the distributor.

Anne of Green Gables. Dir. Kevin Sullivan. Perf. Megan Follows
   and Colleen Dewhurst. Videocassette. Sullivan Films, 1986.

If, instead of the film itself, you are citing the work of a director, actor, or screenwriter, begin your entry with that person's name.

• *Interview*

Give the name of the person interviewed, the type of interview
(personal, telephone, email), and the date.

Brandt, Di. Personal interview. 3 Feb. 1996.

APPENDIX C

DOCUMENTATION: APA SYSTEM

The system of documentation developed by the American Psychological Association (APA) is the accepted authority for research papers in education, health care, the social sciences (psychology, sociology, anthropology, and so forth), and many fields in the physical sciences. Students in a wide range of studies use this system of documentation for their papers.

The material in this appendix is a brief summary of the most common items required for documentation in APA. Your college or university library may have printed and electronic summaries, and there are numerous Internet sites that post style sheets for APA users. For more advanced work, consult the explanations and examples in the current fifth edition of the *Publication Manual of the American Psychological Association.*

C1 Formatting Your Research Paper

The general guidelines for formatting (appendix A) also apply to student papers using the APA system of documentation. More rigorous formatting and stylistic requirements apply to papers that will be published in professional journals.

- All pages of your paper should include a header, referred to as the **manuscript page header.** Include one or two of the most significant words in your title, as well as the computer-generated page number, in this automatic text. This header will appear on the title page and on all subsequent pages of your paper, including the references page.

- The next item on the title page is the **running head.** At the top-left margin, type an abbreviated version of your title in uppercase letters. The running head can be a maximum of 50 characters. The running head appears *only* on the title page.

- Centre the rest of the information on the title page both horizontally (centre align) and vertically (use print preview to judge). The official APA format calls for the writer's affiliation, but student papers usually include course information as in our sample below. Present this information in double-space format:

- the title of your paper
- your name
- the course and section number
- the instructor's name
- the date

Here is a scaled-down title page for the sample APA research essay that appears in chapter 14.

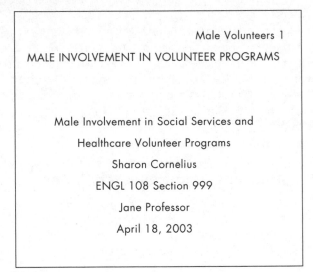

Male Volunteers 1

MALE INVOLVEMENT IN VOLUNTEER PROGRAMS

Male Involvement in Social Services and

Healthcare Volunteer Programs

Sharon Cornelius

ENGL 108 Section 999

Jane Professor

April 18, 2003

C2 In-Text Citations

The basic information to be documented is the last name(s) of the author(s), the date, and the page or, for unpaginated electronic sources, the paragraph number.

- Place parenthetical references to your sources immediately after quoted or paraphrased material.

- When you paraphrase an idea, give only the author's last name and the year of publication at the end of your sentence. (Note that in the APA system, name and date are separated by a comma.)

A recent study suggests that while depression and substance abuse are associated, it is not necessarily the depression that comes first (Wu, 2002).

- If you include the author's name in the sentence introducing the reference, put the year of publication immediately after the author's name.

  In another study, Wu (2002) reports that while depression and substance abuse are associated, it is not necessarily the depression that comes first.

- If you are quoting directly, put the page number after the year in the parenthetical citation, with *p.* or *pp.* For electronic text, paragraph numbers identified by the symbol ¶ may be used in place of page numbers.

  (Wu, 2002, p. 45)

  (Hardy & Srinivasan, 2002, ¶ 3)

C2

- If you are citing a work that is discussed in another work, name the original work; then cite the source you consulted and give the date for that source.

  Singh's study (as cited in Robertson, 2000) . . .

  . . . (Singh, as cited in Robertson, 2000).

- If you are repeating the same source in the same paragraph, omit the year of publication and include only the author's name in parentheses for the second and subsequent citations.

- If you will be referring to more than one work written in the same year by the same person, use the year of publication and a lowercase letter that identifies the order of the work in the references.

  (Gibaldi, 2001b)

- If the work has two authors, cite both names every time you refer to the work. If the work has fewer than six authors, cite all the authors in your first in-text citation. In subsequent references, include only the surname of the first author followed by *et al.* and the year. If the work has more than six authors, cite only the surname of the first followed by *et al.* and the date in all in-text citations.

- If the author of the work is not identified, give a short version of the title in your in-text citation.

- Spell out the name of corporate authors in every in-text citation.

(National Film Board, 1996)

Sample In-Text Citations

The following examples demonstrate various ways of integrating material from common sources into your APA paper.

Quotations

- **Short quotations**

If a quotation is short (40 words or fewer), incorporate the quotation, with regular (double) quotation marks around it, into the text of your paper. Put the final punctuation for the sentence after the parenthetical citation. This example uses ellipses to indicate words omitted, and square brackets to indicate changes. The original passage includes a quoted portion; in the example, these words are enclosed with single quotation marks.

> A research question may be difficult or easy to answer directly; an example of a research question with a "final, definitive answer…[is] 'How does penicillin destroy bacteria?'" (Troyka, 2004, p. 131).

- **Long quotations**

Use a long quotation only when the original passage contains ideas or statistics that cannot be paraphrased easily. Do not enclose the passage in quotation marks. Indent the quotation 1 in. from the left-hand margin. Check with your instructor as to his or her preference for double- or single-spacing for the quotation. Put the citation in parentheses after the final punctuation at the end of the quotation. Introduce the quotation appropriately, as in the following example.

> F. C. Donders, a Dutch physiologist (1818–1889), invented mental chronometry, a method of measuring mental processes. Early psychologists eagerly adopted this new technique.
>
> > Precisely because it was a quantitative method, [mental chronometry] helped to ensure the scientific stature of experimental psychology as apart from qualitative philosophical psychology. It took the mind out of the armchair and into the laboratory. (Leahey, 2000, p. 225)

- ***Quotation from a professional article***

This quotation is taken from a full-text article retrieved from a database. The original print version is reproduced in the electronic file, allowing you to refer to the page instead of a paragraph number.

> Lonsdale (2002) reminds us that a 1943 experiment found that "marginal thiamine deficiency produced bad behavior that would be traditionally thought of as psychological in character if it occurred spontaneously" (p. 86).

- ***Indirect quotation***

When you quote a passage that has been quoted in your source, be careful to indicate both writers clearly. Give the page number from your source (in this example, Leahey's book) and list this source in your references.

> Ulric Neisser (as cited in Leahey, 2000) considered computer models of cognition as "simplistic" and not "satisfactory from the psychological point of view" (p. 505).

Paraphrased or Summarized Material

- ***Paraphrase or summary***

Often it is preferable to explain a writer's ideas in your own words or shorten a passage. Name the author (with date) to make it clear that the paraphrased or summarized material reflects another writer's, and not your own, ideas. The *APA Manual* encourages but does not require the page (or paragraph) reference for paraphrased or summarized passages. You can't go wrong if you include it as a courtesy to your reader. The examples below demonstrate appropriate paraphrase and summary of the quotations shown above.

Paraphrase

> Lonsdale (2002) reminds us that a 1943 experiment found that bad behaviour can be caused by a slight thiamine deficiency. Prior to this discovery, it was thought that sudden, unexplained bad behaviour was related to a psychological problem (p. 86).

Summary

> F. C. Donders, a Dutch physiologist (1818–1889), invented mental chronometry, a method of measuring mental processes. As Leahey

(2000) explains, early psychologists were keen to use Donders' technique because it allowed mathematical, empirical inquiry and thus gave them the status of scientists rather than philosophers (p. 225).

C3 List of References

At the end of your paper, on a separate sheet entitled References, present a list of all the works you have cited.

C3

- Alphabetize the entries according to the last name of the principal author (the one that appears first on the title page). Alphabetize government and corporate publications by the name of the government department, institution, or business where they originated, such as Statistics Canada, Royal Ontario Museum, or BC Hydro. For publications where no author is given, such as unsigned newspaper pieces and encyclopedia entries, alphabetize by the title, disregarding *A, An,* and *The.*

- Double-space within the reference and double-space between references. Begin the first line of each reference at the left margin; indent subsequent lines by one tab (use a hanging indent).

- Capitalize only the first word of the title and of the subtitle of books and articles. Do not put quotation marks around the title of articles. Use italics for titles of books and other separately published works.

Sample Reference Entries

Print Sources

- ***Article***

Do not use *p.* or *pp.* for page numbers of journal articles, but do use them for magazine and newspaper articles.

name	initial	date		title of article
↓	↓	↓		↓
Baumeister, R.		(1990).		Suicide as an escape from the self.

title of journal	volume	issue	inclusive pages
↓	↓		↓
Psychological Review,	*97*(1),		90–113.

- **Book**

name initial date   title   place of publication publisher

Katz, J. (1991). *Seductions of crime.* New York: Basic Books.

- **Part of a book**

  name initial date   title of article or chapter

  Adam, K. (1994). Suicidal behavior and attachment. In M. B.

     editor(s)   title of book

  Sperling & W. H. Berman (Eds.), *Attachment in adults*

  inclusive page nos.   place   publisher

  (pp. 275–298).   New York: Guilford.

- **Government documents and reports**

The basic elements are similar to other APA reference entries. If a government catalogue, report, or publication number is given, put it in parentheses after the title. Always cite a government department from the most general to the most specific (department>agency>division>committee>subcommittee).

Individual Writer Given

Day, D. M. (1995). *School-based violence prevention in Canada: Results of a national survey of policies and programs.* (Catalogue No. JS4-1/1994-2E). Ottawa: Solicitor General Canada, Ministry Secretariat.

Department as Author and Publisher

Statistics Canada. (2002). *Human activity and the environment, annual statistics.* Ottawa: Statistics Canada, Environment Accounts and Statistics Division, System of National Accounts.

- **Subsequent work by the same author**

If you have used more than one source by the same author, arrange the works by year of publication, starting with the earliest. Arrange two or more works by the same author in the same year alphabetically by the title (disregard *A, An,* or *The*). Add lowercase letters beside the year, within the parentheses.

Freud, S. (1963a). *An autobiographical study* (J. Strachey, Trans.). New York: W. W. Norton. (Original work published 1925.)

Freud , S. (1963b). *A general introduction to psycho-analysis* (J. Riviere, Trans.). New York: Simon & Schuster. (Original work published 1920.)

Bowlby, J. (1977). The making and breaking of affectional bonds. *British Journal of Psychiatry, 130,* 201–210.

Bowlby, J. (1980). Attachment and loss. Vol. 3, *Loss, sadness, and depression.* New York: Basic Books.

C3

- ### *Multiple authors*

Give last names followed by initials for all authors, in the order in which they appear in the publication. Use a comma and an ampersand to join the last two authors in the entry.

Wharf, B., & McKenzie, B. (1998). *Connecting policy to practice in the human services.* Toronto: Oxford.

- ### *Reference books*

If no author is given, begin with the title of the entry.

Dinosaurs. (1993). *Collier's Encyclopedia.* New York: Collier.

Electronic Sources

- ### *CD-ROMs and other portable databases*

1. If there is a print version that's the same as the electronic version, cite the print version.

2. If there is no print equivalent, start with the author, date, and title as for print versions.

3. Put the type of medium (CD-ROM, electronic data tape, computer program) in square brackets after the title.

4. If you are citing a bibliographic database, give the location and name of the producer and distributor.

- ### *Online databases*

Give the author, date, article title, journal title, and volume and issue number as for a print version. Follow with the date of retrieval and the database name. If the author is not given, begin with the title followed by the date.

Lonsdale, D. (2002). High calorie malnutrition. *Journal of Nutritional and Environmental Medicine, 12*(2). Retrieved September 17, 2003, from MasterFILE database.

Anorexia nervosa—Part 1: How the mind starves the body, and what can be done to prevent it. (2003, February). *Harvard Mental Health Letter, 19*(8). Retrieved September 26, 2003, from Health Reference Center Academic database.

- **Internet sources**

When you obtain research materials directly through your favourite search engine, begin with the usual information, and then state the date you accessed the website and the URL (Universal Resource Locator), or electronic address. When giving an electronic address or URL, do not end with a period. Stray punctuation will interfere with retrieval.

URL Access—Daily Newspaper Article Retrieved Through an Internet Search

Scott, P., & Crowson, S. (2003, September 30). Reserve victim 'just a good boy': Youngster, 13, faces murder rap. *Calgary Herald.* Retrieved September 30, 2003, from http://www.canada.com/calgary/calgaryherald

URL Access—Document Created by a Private Organization

MADD Canada. (April 23, 2003). *Checklist shows little done to fight impaired driving.* Retrieved September 30, 2003, from http://madd.ca/news

Other Material

- ***Films, videotapes, audiotapes, slides, charts, works of art***

Give the titles of the originator and primary contributors in parentheses after the name, and the medium of publication in square brackets after the title.

originator   **and/or primary contributors**
  ↓   ↓
Kilbourne, J. (Writer), & Lazarus, M. (Producer/Director).

medium
  ↓
(1987). *Still killing us softly* [Videorecording].

- ***Interview***

In APA documentation, personal communications—letters, interviews, email—are cited parenthetically in the text and not given in the list of references.

For a model of the APA system of citations and references, see the sample research paper, "Male Involvement in Social Services and Healthcare Volunteer Programs" (14g).

For more information and references not covered here, consult the *Publication Manual of the American Psychological Association*, 5th ed. Available online through several websites (see part 4, Web Links).

C3

APPENDIX D

WRITING ESSAY
AND SHORT-ANSWER EXAMS

D1 Preparing for Exams

You can help to prepare for exams by taking these steps.

- Review the overall purpose and direction of the course. If the instructor emphasized the acquisition of one or more skills, such as the ability to analyze a piece of writing, review the terms and procedures appropriate to those skills.

D2

If the instructor emphasized the acquisition of a body of knowledge, such as the nature of a particular historical period or different theories of human behaviour, decide which three or four units of material seem most important and learn this material thoroughly.

- Outline the relevant chapters of textbooks or your notes, set yourself a question about each unit, and practise writing out the answer. Writing the information will help you remember it better than merely reading it over.

- Make notes about similarities and differences among events, theories, works of literature. Comparison questions are frequently set on exams because they cover more material and emphasize important concepts in the course.

- Memorize key names, dates, facts, and so forth. The more specific information you give, the better your answer will be, as long as the information is relevant.

D2 Tips on Writing Exams

- Look over the whole exam paper and decide how much time to spend on each section. If one section of the exam is worth 60 percent, for instance, plan to spend 60 percent of the available time on it.

- If you have a choice of questions or essay topics, first note any restrictions (such as not writing twice on the same subject or work) and then select accordingly.

- Answer easier questions first. That will give you confidence. It will also allow your mind to work subconsciously on the harder questions before you tackle them.

- Read the directions for each question carefully. Often they will suggest a focus for your response and provide directions on how to develop it. In the topic *Why is the "right of return" such an important issue in Israeli-Palestinian peace talks?,* the key issues are *right of return* and *Israeli-Palestinian peace talks.* To develop your answer, you would need to use both definition and causal analysis.

D3

D3 Planning and Writing Essay Exams

Planning

1. Read the topics carefully. Pay particular attention to **direction words** (*compare* means "analyze both similarities and differences") and **specialized terms** (*point of view* means the narrative perspective from which a novel or a story is told).

2. Use invention techniques such as brainstorming, freewriting, and discovery questions to come up with ideas (see chapter 2). Once you have some ideas on paper, work out an outline (see chapter 3). Be sure that each part of your outline is directly relevant to your essay topic. **Continue to plan your essay until you have worked out your thesis and the topic sentences for all your middle paragraphs.**

Writing

1. Give your essay a title. It will help you to remain focused on your topic.

2. Write a short introduction. In an exam essay, you can limit your introduction to naming your subject and stating your thesis.

3. Begin each middle paragraph with a topic sentence that states the main idea of that paragraph.

4. Develop your ideas fully within your essay and include details and examples to support them.

5. Check your essay carefully for errors in grammar, spelling, and punctuation. Proofreading errors will cost you marks.

D4 Responding to Short-Answer Questions

The most common types of short-answer questions ask you to define a term or concept (for guidelines, see 6c), to analyze an excerpt, or to identify and explain the significance of a particular item, such as a person, a text, an object, or an event.

Analyzing an Excerpt

Exam questions of this sort usually ask you to explain how a specific part of a literary work contributes to the whole. A good answer will include the following:

1. The title of the work and the name of the author.

2. The context of the excerpt: explain where it occurs in the work.

3. An explanation of how the excerpt is relevant to the central ideas in the work as a whole.

4. The most important stylistic features of the excerpt including some of the following: diction, imagery, sentence length and structure, sound patterns, rhythm.

Sample Literature Exam Question

Question

Explain the significance of the following excerpt in relation to the theme and structure of *Hamlet* as a whole.

Excerpt

> Within a month,
> Ere yet the salt of most unrighteous tears
> Had left the flushing in her gallèd eyes,
> She married. O, most wicked speed, to post
> With such dexterity to incestuous sheets!
> It is not, nor it cannot come to good.
> But break my heart, for I must hold my tongue.

Superior Answer

This excerpt from Hamlet's soliloquy in act 1, scene 2 of Shakespeare's play *Hamlet* provides our first insight into the Prince's state of mind. At this point, the ghost has not appeared to him, so he does not know that Claudius has murdered his father. Yet, even without this knowledge, he is deeply disillusioned by the hasty marriage of his mother to his uncle. He describes his mother's tears as "unrighteous" and condemns the marriage as incestuous, unnatural, an idea that echoes throughout the play in suggestions that Denmark is a diseased kingdom. He accuses his mother of lust and later generalizes this accusation to include all women, even Ophelia. We see his distress in the emphasis given to the words "She married" and in the exclamation "O, most wicked speed." His awareness that he cannot openly express his opposition to the marriage intensifies the pressure he is under and prepares us for the "antic disposition" he will later assume to disguise his feelings.

Weak Answer

In this excerpt, *Hamlet* is clearly very upset that his mother has married his uncle so soon after his father's death. Hamlet cannot understand how his mother can be crying at one minute and hopping into bed with her brother-in-law the next minute. He even accuses her of incest. Hamlet's negative feelings about his mother and his uncle are a big issue in the whole play.

Identifying and Explaining an Item

Exam questions of this sort usually ask you to demonstrate both specific knowledge about the item in question and an understanding of why it is important. A good answer will include the following.

1. A brief summary of basic information about the item (*who, what, when, where*).

2. A clear explanation of the item's causes, effects, or role in a larger context. Give as much specific information as possible: names, dates, places, events, and so forth.

Sample History Exam Question

Question: Briefly identify the following: *War Measures Act*

Superior Answer

The *War Measures Act,* passed in 1914, gave the federal Cabinet emergency powers to govern by decree during "war, invasion or insurrection." The Act was invoked during both world wars to justify regulations that limited the freedom of Canadians, including the internment of 20,000 Japanese Canadians during the Second World War. The *War Measures Act* has been invoked only once during peacetime. Prime Minister Trudeau, declaring a state of "apprehended insurrection," invoked the Act during the October Crisis of 1970 in response to the kidnappings of British trade commissioner James Cross and Quebec Minister of Labour and Immigration Pierre Laporte by the FLQ. Regulations promulgated under the Act banned the FLQ and permitted more than 450 people to be arrested or detained without charge. Although government officials defended these measures as necessary to combat terrorism, Quebec nationalists and civil libertarians accused the federal government of unwarranted infringement of civil liberties. Opposition to this use of the *War Measures Act* contributed to the popularity of the separatist Parti Quebecois, which won the Quebec provincial election in 1976.

D4

Weak Answer

The *War Measures Act* allowed the government to use emergency powers during both world wars. It became well known when Prime Minister Trudeau used the *War Measures Act* against terrorists in the October Crisis. A lot of people thought Trudeau was justified at the time, but later it seemed that he might have used the Act for political purposes.

In comparison with the superior answer, the weak answer contains few specific facts and no discussion of the effects of the *War Measures Act.*

APPENDIX E

GLOSSARY OF GRAMMATICAL TERMS

Active Voice

A construction in which the subject performs the action of the verb.

Lightning **struck** the enormous tree.

In the passive voice, the sentence would read:

The enormous tree **was struck** by lightning.

Adjective

A word that modifies a noun or pronoun. An adjective can express quality (*red* balloon, *large* house, *young* child) or quantity (*one* apple, *many* peaches, *few* pears). Other words or grammatical constructions can also function as adjectives, including present and past participles (*skating* party, *torn* shirt) and subordinate clauses (the woman *who is chairing the meeting*).

Adjectives change form to show degrees of comparison—positive, comparative, superlative (*clean, cleaner, cleanest*).

Adverb

A word that modifies or describes a verb (run *quickly*), an adjective (*extremely* heavy), or another adverb (eat *very* slowly). Adverbs usually answer the questions *how, when, where,* or *why.* (They whispered *how*? / They whispered *quietly*.)

Phrases (walked *into a room*) and clauses (He couldn't speak *because he was angry*) can also function as adverbs.

Adverbs change form to show degrees of comparison—positive, comparative, superlative (*quickly, more quickly, most quickly*).

Antecedent

The noun to which a pronoun refers. The antecedent usually, but not always, comes before the pronoun.

The **dancers** [antecedent] are rehearsing **their** [pronoun] routine.

Appositive

An explanatory word or phrase that follows a noun or pronoun.

Martha, **my closest friend,** is visiting from Halifax.

Auxiliary Verb

A verb that helps to form the tense or voice of another verb (*have been* practising, *should have* phoned, *was* consulted).

Case

The form of a noun or pronoun that shows its relationship to other words in a sentence.

Possessive case [nouns and indefinite pronouns]: **Bill's** car, **nobody's** business.

Subject case [personal pronouns]: **She** and **I** left early.

Object case [personal pronouns]: Give the message to **him** or **me**.

Clause

A group of words containing a subject and a verb. **Main clauses** can stand on their own as grammatically complete sentences.

He didn't finish dinner.

Subordinate clauses, sometimes called dependent clauses, often begin with subordinating conjunctions such as *because, although, while, since, as, when.*

Because he was in a hurry, he didn't finish dinner.

Other subordinate clauses begin with relative pronouns, such as *who, which,* and *that.* These subordinate clauses function as adjectives or nouns.

The man **who didn't finish dinner** is in a bad mood. [adjective clause]

She wished **that the ordeal would end.** [noun clause]

Comma Splice

A sentence structure error in which main clauses have been joined by a comma alone, or by a comma and a conjunctive adverb.

The party is over, everyone has gone home.

The party is over, **therefore** everyone must go home.

Complex Sentence

A sentence containing one main clause and one or more subordinate clauses. See *Clause.*

If we can't fit everyone in the car, we'll take the bus.

Compound Sentence

A sentence containing two or more main clauses. See *Clause.*

We can't fit everyone in the car, so we'll take the bus.

Compound-Complex Sentence

A sentence containing two or more main clauses and one or more subordinate clauses.

> Before the storm broke, Mary put away the lawn chairs and Shistri closed the windows.

Conjunction

A word or phrase that joins words, phrases, or clauses. See *Conjunctive Adverb, Coordinating Conjunction, Correlative (Paired) Conjunction,* and *Subordinating Conjunction.*

Conjunctive Adverb

An adverb used with a semicolon to join main clauses in a compound or compound-complex sentence. Common conjunctive adverbs include *therefore, however, nevertheless, otherwise, thus, furthermore, moreover.*

> I must hurry; **otherwise,** I'll be late for class.

Coordinating Conjunction

A word used to join ideas of equal importance expressed in the same grammatical form. The coordinating conjunctions are *and, but, or, nor, for, yet, so.*

> He was down **but** not out.

> The weather was good, **but** the facilities were terrible.

Coordination

The stylistic technique of using coordinating and correlative conjunctions to join ideas of equal importance. See *Coordinating Conjunction* and *Correlative (Paired) Conjunctions.*

> The battery is dead **and** all four tires are flat.

> **Neither** the fridge **nor** the stove is working.

Correlative (Paired) Conjunctions

A pair of conjunctions used to join ideas of equal importance expressed in the same grammatical form. The correlative conjunctions are *either/or, neither/nor, both/and, not only/but also.*

> **Not only** are these apples expensive **but** they are **also** of poor quality.

> These apples are **both** expensive **and** of poor quality.

Dangling Modifier

A modifying phrase that is not logically connected to any other word in the sentence.

> **Turning green,** the pedestrians crossed the street.

Definite Article

The word *the,* which specifies the noun it is describing: *the* book, *the* baby, *the* opportunity of a lifetime.

Fragment

A phrase or subordinate clause punctuated as if it were a complete sentence.

> And last, but not least.

> Although it seemed like a good idea at the time.

Fused Sentence (also called *Run-on Sentence*)

The error of writing two main clauses as if they were one, with no punctuation between them.

> It's cold today my ears are freezing.

Indefinite Article

The words *a* and *an,* which do not specify the nouns they describe: *a* book, *a* breakthrough, *an* amazing feat.

Infinitive

To + a verb: *to run, to walk, to think.* See *Split Infinitive.*

Interjection

A word or phrase thrown into a sentence to express emotion.

> **"Oh great,** we're going on a picnic!"

> **For Pete's sake,** I knew that already.

Some interjections can stand on their own as complete sentences.

> "Wow!" "Ouch!" "Hurray!"

Misplaced Modifier

A modifying word, phrase, or clause that has been put in the wrong place in the sentence.

> **Lying in the driveway,** Mr. Jones drove over the bicycle.

Mixed Construction
(also called an *Awkward Sentence*)

The error of mixing incompatible grammatical units.

> **An example of this is when** she daydreams constantly.

> The more he learns, **he doesn't seem to remember much.**

Modifier

A word, phrase, or clause that changes or qualifies the meaning of a noun, pronoun, or verb.

Restrictive modifiers provide essential information and are not enclosed in commas.

Teenagers **who take drugs** need help.

Nonrestrictive modifiers provide additional information and are enclosed with commas.

Susan, **who has been taking drugs for several years,** needs help.

Mood

The form of the verb that shows whether the speaker is stating a fact (indicative mood: He *wants* some food), giving a command or making a request (imperative mood: *Give* him some food), or suggesting a possibility or condition (subjunctive mood: If we *were to give* him some food).

Noun

A word that names a person, place, thing, quality, idea, or activity. A **common noun** is not capitalized and refers to any one of a class: *woman, cat, city, school.* A **proper noun** is capitalized and refers to a particular person, animal, place, thing: *Linda, Fluffy, Guelph, Westlane Elementary School.* A **collective noun,** such as *herd, flock, family, community, band, tribe,* is considered singular when the group is acting as a unit and plural when the group members are acting as individuals.

The band is on an extended trip.

The band are unpacking their instruments.

Object

A word, phrase, or clause that receives the action of the verb or that is governed by a preposition.

Stephen lent me his pen. [*Me* is the indirect object of the verb *lent; pen* is the direct object.]

She has already left for work. [*Work* is the object of the preposition *for.*]

Parallel Structure

A construction in which ideas of equal importance are expressed in the same grammatical form.

His analysis is **precise, thorough,** and **perceptive.** [parallel adjectives]

What he says and **what he means** are completely different. [parallel clauses]

Participle

A verb form that can function as a verb or as an adjective. Present participles are formed by adding *ing* to the present tense. Past participles of regular verbs are formed by adding *ed* to the present tense.

When combined with an auxiliary verb, participles become the main verb in a verb phrase (*is laughing, has been dancing, could have finished*).

As adjectives, participles can modify nouns and pronouns (*smiling* face, *running* water, *chipped* tooth, *sworn* testimony; *frowning*, he addressed the assembly).

Parts of Speech

Types of words, such as nouns, verbs, and adverbs. See *Adjective, Adverb, Conjunction, Interjection, Noun, Preposition, Pronoun, Verb.*

Passive Voice

A construction in which the subject is acted upon by the verb.

The water **was tested** for contaminants by the researchers.

In the active voice, this sentence would read:

The researchers **tested** the water for contaminants.

Preposition

Prepositions include such words as *by, between, beside, to, of,* and *with*. A preposition, its object (usually a noun or a pronoun), and any words that describe the object make up a prepositional phrase (*toward the deserted beach*). These phrases can function as adjectives (the man *with the red beard*) or as adverbs (walked *down the road*, tired *of waiting*).

Pronoun

A word that substitutes for a noun.

Indefinite pronouns *everybody, everyone, everything, somebody, someone, something, nobody, no one, one, nothing, anybody, anyone, anything, either, neither, each, both, few, several, all*
Personal subject pronouns *I, we, you, he, she, it, they*
Personal object pronouns *me, us, you, him, her, it, them*
Possessive pronouns *my, mine, our, ours, your, yours, his, her, hers, its, their, theirs*
Reflexive/Intensive pronouns *myself, ourselves, yourself, yourselves, himself, herself, itself, themselves*
Relative pronouns *who, whom, which, that, what, whoever, whomever, whichever*

Pronoun Agreement

The principle of matching singular pronouns with singular nouns and pronouns, and plural pronouns with plural nouns and pronouns.

The **committee** forwarded **its** recommendations.

Everyone has made **his or her** views known to the nominating committee.

Pronoun Reference

The principle that every pronoun should clearly refer to a specific noun. See *Antecedent*.

Tom told Hussein that **he** had won the scholarship. [pronoun reference unclear]

Tom told Hussein, "**You** won the scholarship." [pronoun reference clear]

Pronoun Shift

The error of shifting abruptly and with no logical reason from the expected personal pronoun.

I didn't like working in the complaints department because **you** were always dealing with dissatisfied customers.

Split Infinitive

A form of misplaced modifier in which an adverb is placed between *to* and the verb.

to **quickly** run

Subject

The word or group of words that interact with a verb to establish the basic meaning of a sentence or clause. Subjects are nouns, pronouns, or constructions that function as nouns.

Costs are rising.

To argue with him is a waste of time.

Cleaning the garage is not my idea of a pleasant way to spend the weekend.

Subject-Verb Agreement

The principle of matching singular subjects with singular verbs and plural subjects with plural verbs.

He has his work cut out for him.

They have their work cut out for them.

Subordinating Conjunction

A word used to begin a subordinate clause—a clause that expresses an idea of subordinate or secondary importance. Subordinating conjunctions include words such as *although, because, before, since, while, when, if, until*. See *Clause*.

Subordination

The stylistic technique of expressing less important ideas in subordinate clauses and phrases.

> **Although I am angry with you,** I am still willing to listen to your side of the story.

Tense

The form of the verb that shows its time (past, present, future).

Tense Shift

The error of shifting abruptly and with no obvious reason from one verb tense to another.

> Hamlet **was** angry when he **confronts** his mother.

Verb

A word that indicates action (*run, jump, breathe*), sensation (*feel, taste, smell*), possession (*have, own*), or existence (*are, were, seem, become*). A verb phrase consists of a main verb (a past or present participle) and one or more auxiliary verbs. For more information on verb phrases, see *Participle* and *Auxiliary Verb*. For more information on verbs, see *Tense, Mood, Active Voice, Passive Voice,* and *Subject-Verb Agreement*.

E

APPENDIX F

ANSWER KEYS

Chapter 18

Exercise 18.1

1. you must not falsify data or ignore contradictory evidence

2. Clarence cut the questioning short

3. Karen wound up for the pitch

4. Govind admired his handiwork

5. Hans scrubbed at the large blue stain; he couldn't get it out

Exercise 18.2

1. **C**
2. **CS**
3. **C**
4. **CS**
5. **C**

Exercise 18.3

Because sentences containing comma splices can be corrected in a number of ways, these sentences suggest only one of a number of possible revisions.

1. A loud crackling sound alerted Gerta to the fact that she had left the foil cover on the dish; both the meal and the microwave oven were ruined.

2. Alicia offered to replace my shift; when I called to confirm the arrangement, however, she had changed her mind.

3. As we waited in line, we heard Jason's unmistakable braying laugh. We hoped he wouldn't see us before we could disappear into the darkened theatre.

4. Tina groaned in dismay at the error message; then she pulled out the massive user guide and started her search for help.

5. Neither team chose Maria, so she took her ball and went home.

Exercise 18.4

These days many people use their computers as stereo systems that not only play music but also go out and get the music they want to hear. In response, the major labels are experimenting with anti-piracy technology

F1

356

such as non-recordable CDs **because** they want to stop consumers from trading tunes on the Internet or burning recordable CDs. It's not clear how many non-recordable CDs have actually been released**; however,** the prospect has aroused considerable commentary. Some people say they have a right to burn their own CDs **because [, for]** the record companies are charging too much. Other people justify CD piracy by arguing that most of the money from sales goes to the companies, not the artists. In any case, it may not be possible to create a copy-proof CD that will still play in a computer. Trying to make one may annoy many consumers, **and so** the labels may decide it's not worth the risk.

Exercise 18.5

1. Marvinder shifted slowly and repeatedly between forward and reverse; she was therefore able to gain traction and move the car out of the mud.
2. Beatrice checked email three times a day because she didn't want to miss any messages.
3. Watch where you're going, or you'll walk into the wall.
4. Without thinking, Delmar opened the side door and was startled by a shrieking siren. He had forgotten to deactivate the alarm.
5. Washing four loads of shirts this morning was a chore; even more daunting is the prospect of all that ironing.

Exercise 18.6

My final recommendation for becoming and staying a non-smoker is to eat Popsicles. Because you are taking on such a big commitment, you deserve a sweet treat now and then. Popsicles are low-calorie treats**, so** you will not gain weight. A Popsicle also gives you something to hold and put in your mouth just like a cigarette, but it is not a cigarette. You can choose any flavour you like. **When** you have a really strong craving, you should not tear off the wrapper and plunge the Popsicle into your mouth because it will stick to your tongue and lips. If this happens to you, as it did to me, don't attempt to pull the Popsicle out. **It** hurts. Have one of your support team come to your aid with warm water.

Exercise 18.7

1. Wendell **drove** around in circles, unable to find his date's house in the maze-like neighbourhood.
2. According to *The Hitchhiker's Guide to the Galaxy,* forty-two is the answer to the meaning of life, the universe, and everything.
3. After getting up to change channels himself because the remote control battery was **dead, Brad** sank back exhausted onto the couch.
4. Lydia **is** the last person I expected to quit school.

5. **The driver was** angry at the parking attendant for writing up a ticket because the meter had expired.

Exercise 18.8

1. **He was** always quick to judge others, but he bridled at even the mildest criticism.
2. **C**
3. The fans **cheered** wildly as the defenceman raced down the ice.
4. **C**
5. **She is** a woman with fierce pride and a determined spirit.
6. The reason for the fire **was** a pot of hot oil left burning on the stove.
7. **C**
8. **She tore** open the envelope and nervously **removed** the transcript of her final grades.
9. Although I could detect movement inside, no one **answered** my knock.
10. Because he didn't phone in or show up for work, **Garry lost his job.**

Exercise 18.9

In life and in literature, people create alternate versions of reality to avoid facing the unpleasant aspects of the lives they actually live or just to make their lives more exciting. In "Spy Story" by Filipino writer Jose Y. Dalisay, for example, Fred has convinced himself that he is a secret agent for the US Embassy. **Thinking that everyone around him is a spy and up to no good, Fred creates some excitement in his otherwise boring job as a chauffeur.** It's clear to most readers that Mr. Sparks, Fred's boss, is running a prostitution ring **and forcing** Fred into the role of a pimp. But Fred imagines that Mr. Sparks is entertaining high-ranking American contacts to foil dangerous espionage activities. **As well as commenting on our capacity for self-deception as individuals, "Spy Story" has a significant political dimension.** By setting his story in a seedy bar in the Philippines during the Cold War of the 1950s, Dalisay comments on the distortions of reality widely shared during this time of propaganda, spies, and secrets.

Exercise 18.10

1. Robert can either work and save money for college or take out a student loan.
2. The more I try to convince him otherwise, the more determined he is to dye his hair green.
3. The Bennetts' house is smaller than their neighbour's.

4. My car needs new paint, new tires, and a new transmission.

5. **C**

6. The store went out of business because of inferior merchandise, high prices, and poor customer service.

7. Gina is both a skilled pianist and a talented baseball player.

8. Before becoming actors, some famous stars worked in other fields. For example, Harrison Ford was a master carpenter, and Michelle Pfeiffer was a cashier.

9. **C**

10. • High school diploma, 1998
    • Diploma in Automotive Repair, 1999
    • Travel in Central and South America, 1999–2000
    • BS in Computing Science, 2004

Exercise 18.11

In an essay titled "The Pain of Animals," David Suzuki's subject is the pain humans inflict on animals by using them in scientific experiments, **hunting them, and keeping them in zoos.** Suzuki's thesis is that we use animals for these purposes because their nervous systems **and emotional responses** are like ours. This similarity between humans and animals means, however, that animals feel fear and **pain** just as we do. Suzuki develops his essay by giving a series of examples of pain inflicted on animals in zoos and **in scientific experiments.** He ends his essay with an account of his experience watching a film about the suffering endured by chimpanzees used for medical research. Their agony provides the strongest evidence for his argument that the similarities between chimpanzees and humans ought to make us more compassionate **and less exploitive** in our treatment of animals.

Exercise 18.12

1. Because their home was badly damaged by fire, the Wongs have been living in a rented house.

   Or

   The Wongs have been living in a rented house since their home was badly damaged by fire.

2. Although Gina used the proper amount of bromine and shocked the pool regularly with chlorine, the pool sides were still covered with algae.

3. The pilot light in the basement fireplace frequently goes out when snow blocks the outside vent.

4. Because Todd forgot to include his charitable receipts in his income tax return, his refund was delayed.

5. If you want to buy a computer, call Roman, who is an expert on the best buys.

6. Although Craig isn't doing well in physics, he doesn't seem particularly concerned.

7. When I entered the building and heard the final bell, I knew I was late for class.

8. Even though Marina hates the taste of ketchup, she likes ketchup-flavoured potato chips.

9. Because I couldn't hear what he was saying, I asked him to speak up.

10. Everyone has been complaining about the heat since the air conditioner broke down.

Exercise 18.13

1. Geraldine asked her brother Ben how much longer he would be in the shower.

2. Because my dog ate my computer disk, my paper is late.

3. Portaging is carrying a boat overland between navigable lakes or rivers.

4. In his letter, Darrin explained why he resigned his position.

5. The reason we cut our vacation short is that it rained for a solid week.

6. Without more donations, the shelter will have to close.

7. Looking at his bank statement, Domenic wondered how he had spent so much money in only a month.

8. Mary shows her thoughtfulness when she cuts the lawn for her elderly neighbours.

9. The theatre program lists all the actors in the play.

10. The next day Frank finally thought of a snappy comeback to Vincent's insulting remark.

Chapter 19
Exercise 19.1

1. seriously	3. fewer players	5. do well, chemistry
2. runs well	4. really interested	

Exercise 19.2

1. liveliest	4. fewer social occasions
2. considerably better	5. is empty
3. went well	6. **C**

Exercise 19.3

1. Soak the shirt with the spaghetti sauce stain in cold water.

2. Sonia could run almost ten full circuits around the field.

3. The students examined the jar of tapeworms preserved in formaldehyde.

4. I promise not to judge you unfairly.

5. Standing by the band, I had difficulty hearing the conversation.

Exercise 19.4

1. The singer's fans could hardly wait . . .

2. You can eat properly cooked hamburger . . .

3. I want to consider all my options thoroughly . . .

4. **C**

5. Seeing the accident ahead, Tran pulled the car to the side of the road and got out to investigate.

6. Eating our lunch on the patio, we enjoyed . . .

7. . . . you ate only half the pizza.

8. With his mouth full of toothpaste, Jim heard . . .

9. On the hall table there is a family picture . . .

10. **C**

F2

Exercise 19.5

1. Before signing a contract

2. **C**

3. To reduce conflicts with their children

4. When in Rome

5. **C**

Exercise 19.6

1. Walking into the room, I saw a strange sight.

   Or

   When I walked into the room, a strange sight caught my eye.

2. While George was in high school, his father was promoted and the family moved to Vancouver.

3. Because Maurice was exhausted by a heavy work schedule, the doctor recommended a complete rest.

4. To make a perfect omelette, you require the freshest ingredients.

5. After Theresa pleaded earnestly, her parents extended her curfew to midnight.

Exercise 19.7

1. To have a chance at winning the lottery, you must first buy a ticket.

2. **C**

3. Driven by arrogance and greed, Joe soon alienated his friends.

4. After working so hard on the committee, Bernard definitely deserves our gratitude.

5. **C**

6. While I was reading Stephen King's *Cujo,* my dog began barking in the backyard.

7. **C**

8. While Hank was driving on the highway, his car engine suddenly seized.

9. As I stared intently at the small print, spots began to swim before my eyes.

10. To build a better mousetrap, you need the proper tools.

Exercise 19.8

Nineteenth-century workers **could hardly** survive without spending long hours at demanding jobs. **In the summer,** farm workers and outside workers toiled from sunrise to sunset. Working shorter hours in the winter, **they made less money.** Shop employees were treated equally **badly. To meet the needs of their customers effectively,** shops stayed open **really** long hours—often fourteen to sixteen—with the same employees. The most **dreadful** conditions were in the factories. Treated as part of the machinery and forced to work at the pace of the machine, **factory workers** had no time for talking or joking with their mates. Children as young as seven worked twelve-hour shifts and slept in factory dormitories. **By the middle of the nineteenth century it was illegal in England** to employ children under nine in textile factories, **but in 1900** most children were working full-time by the time they were thirteen or fourteen.

Chapter 20

Exercise 20.1

1. should have done

2. have worn

3. lies

4. had know

5. The reason is

6. rang

7. has not written

8. **C**

9. saw

10. **C**

Exercise 20.2

It's important to see that Michael Henchard in Thomas Hardy's novel *The Mayor of Casterbridge* is a kind of Everyman figure. Like most of us, he is motivated by psychological forces that he **does** not recognize or understand. For example, he never seems to understand why he sells his wife and then **remarries** her. Henchard **is** also affected by external forces over which he, like the rest of us, has no control. During the 1840s when the novel **is** set, long-established agricultural practices were being modernized by machines and business practices **were becoming** much more complex. In addition to the forces of industrialization, Henchard, as a wheat trader, is especially vulnerable to natural forces such as the weather. After all, he **makes** his living by predicting the harvest yields. Finally, Henchard is affected by chance and coincidence. It just happens that Farfrae, the man with exactly the skills Henchard **needs, shows** up when he is looking for an assistant manager.

Exercise 20.3

1. The light changed to amber before Oliver reached the intersection.

2. **C** [The agent opening the pool is unknown or unimportant.]

3. Burt completely misunderstood my directions.

4. **C** [The agent adjourning the meeting is unimportant.]

5. Marietta spilled the milk, but she made no effort to wipe it up.

6. **C** [The agents shutting down the site and eliminating the safety hazards are unknown.]

7. **C** [if you want to emphasize Marcia's feelings]

8. After we trimmed and raked the lawn, we weeded the front flower bed.

9. Before setting out to write my exam, I searched for my good luck pen, but I couldn't find it anywhere.

10. **C** [The sentence emphasizes the late delivery.]

Exercise 20.4

1. sisters/are

2. team/has

3. Neither/is

4. **C**

5. Fear/is

6. goldfish/makes

7. **C**

8. jury/has

9. Each/has

10. Nothing/seems

Chapter 21

Exercise 21.1

1. manager/his or her [**Or** all managers/their]

2. immigrant/he or she [**Or** new immigrants/they]

3. daycare worker/his or her [**Or** daycare workers/their]

4. actor/he or she [**Or** actors/they]

5. customer service representative/his or her [**Or** customer service representatives/their]

Exercise 21.2

1. supervisor/his **or** supervisor/her [**Better:** Neither the supervisor nor the employees/their]

2. **C**

3. herd/its/its

4. committee/its

5. Matt/Richard/his

6. government/its

7. group/its [**Or** the hotel]

8. **C** [class acting as individuals]

9. family/its [family acting as unit]

10. Pierre/Antoine/his [**Or C**]

Exercise 21.3

1. Everyone/his or her

2. **C**

3. Each/his or her

4. Neither/his/he

5. **C**

Exercise 21.4 Pronoun Agreement Review

1. writer/his or her [**Or** writers/their]

2. Neither/his

3. **C**

4. No one/his or her

5. **C**

6. Stacey/Veronica/her

7. addict/his or her [**Or** addicts/their]

8. **C**

F4

9. army/its

10. Everyone/his or her

11. **C**

12. Sandra/Brianne/her

13. Neither/his

14. winner/his or her

15. who/his [*Who* is singular because it refers to *man.*]

Exercise 21.5 Pronoun Agreement Review

PowerPoint presenters arrange words and pictures into a series of pages that they project from a laptop computer onto a screen. Each **screen** typically has **a** heading followed by bullet points: six or seven words a line, six or seven lines a slide. Paragraphs and even sentences have too many words for a PowerPoint presentation, so **presenters** must reduce their most complex ideas to little phrases. Of course, the bullet points eliminate the need for transitions, such as *because* or *on the other hand,* that might help a viewer understand connections among these phrases. **Typically, presenters haven't** noticed the absence of transitions. They have been so caught up in the technical features of PowerPoint that they have concentrated on the appearance of the text and the accompanying graphics. Never mind, if there are enough snappy visual aids, neither the viewers nor the presenter may notice that **the** presentation has the intellectual substance of a kindergarten show and tell.

Exercise 21.6

1. We workers
2. He and I
3. than she
4. whom to contact
5. or me

6. or him
7. Adrilla and I
8. Michael, Stephen, and he
9. that she and her sister
10. **C**

Exercise 21.7

1. anyone's
2. Whose
3. yours

4. Theirs
5. its

Exercise 21.8 Review of Pronoun Case and Possessive Pronouns

1. Nigel or me
2. he and his brothers

3. than I that you and she
4. their furniture

F4

5. whose limousine

6. hers

7. Between you and me

8. **C**

9. Dave and I

10. her boyfriend and she

Exercise 21.9

Last February, Peter and **I** decided to get married. We wanted to get married in June, so **there** were four months to plan the wedding. Although our wedding cost only $2000, it turned out beautifully. Here's how we did it.

First we made a list of everything we could do **ourselves. My sister and I** spent two weeks shopping every chance we got in Value Village stores and all the second hand vintage clothing shops. Luckily, I found the perfect dress for just under $50 and my sister found a gorgeous bridesmaid's dress for $100. I didn't mind that **hers** cost twice as much as mine because she said that **she** and her boyfriend might get married **themselves** and she would wear that dress to the wedding. Peter was able to borrow his dad's dark suit, which his dad said looked better on Peter than it did on **him.** Peter's brother Tom had just gotten married, so he had a dark suit he could wear as best man. Having dealt with the clothing issue, we went to a pawnshop and bought two gold rings for $50 each.

Now we had to find a place to get married. We have a friend **whose** parents own a cottage near a local lake. They agreed to lend us **their** place for the weekend. For $200 we could rent canopies and tables to put on the lawn. Then I persuaded my mother to let Peter and **me** raid her garden for lilacs, tulips, and daisies. They made lovely bouquets for all the tables.

Peter's Uncle Ted said that **he** and his friend, an amateur photographer, would take all the photographs. If we supplied the film, which cost about $100, he would print the photos with his own computer.

Now we had to find someone to marry us. We contacted a local marriage commissioner and discovered that the usual gratuity is $50. We had to give her another $50 to cover her travelling expenses. The marriage licence cost $50. So far, we had spent $700.

It's probably not surprising that food and liquor were our biggest expense. Because so many of our guests had allergies or were on special diets, we decided on a simple meal of chili, homemade cornbread, and huge salads, with beer and wine. For dessert, we had soy ice cream and a vegan wedding cake made by my father and **me.** Buying the food and liquor, and renting cutlery, glasses, and dishes cost about $700.

Of course, what's a wedding without music and dancing? No one knows more about the local music scene than Peter and **I,** so we hired a band for $300. We didn't need to provide any of the sound equipment because the band said they would bring **theirs.**

Naturally, there were a few more miscellaneous expenses, but the total cost of our wedding was well under $2000. Between you and **me,** the wedding couldn't have suited **us** thrifty folks better if it had cost $20,000.

F4

Exercise 21.10

1. Experts say
2. when you know your behaviour upsets her?
3. when Nicole told her, "You [or I] didn't get the job."
4. but my efforts
5. the customer service representative said
6. but at the time Giselle didn't know what had caused the problem.
7. The pie crust is tough because Raul added too much water to the dough and beat it mercilessly.
8. but these qualities don't bother his friends.
9. Her actions greatly surprised me.
10. Mr. Carlson ruined the lawn by applying too much weed killer and overwatering the grass.

Exercise 21.11

Vegans do not eat any animal products. This **dietary limitation** means that many of the foods most people enjoy, such as ice cream, mayonnaise, bacon and eggs, even toast with honey, are off limits. Because most prepared foods contain some animal products, eating out can be a real challenge, **so** many vegans cook at home and bring food with them when they go out. Of course, vegan cooking presents its own difficulties. When I became a vegan, I bought a cookbook with lots of delicious-looking recipes, but **these recipes** didn't help. **Each recipe contained so many exotic ingredients** that I had to dash to the health food store before I could begin. Despite these obstacles, I'm glad to be a vegan. Now that **stories about so many diseases carried by cows, fish, and birds are in the news,** who would want to eat meat even if **animals** were killed more humanely?

Exercise 21.12

1. because I never know
2. Even when they are knowledgeable and competent,
3. **C**
4. The owners claim that they can hear [**Or** visitors can hear]
5. because he doesn't want to lose a tooth that can be saved.

Exercise 21.13

You can write this paragraph in either the third person (participants/they) or the second person (you). Both versions are shown below.

F4

367

You will get a more effective workout in your next fitness class if you follow this advice. **If you are new,** position **yourself** near the instructor so you can see and hear clearly. **If you are near the front, you** are also less likely to be distracted by other participants. **You** should give the class **your** full attention, so don't spend your time worrying about whether other people are watching you or whether you put enough change in the parking meter. Although **you** might be tempted to compensate for **your** lack of ability with expensive exercise clothes, don't spend a fortune on exercise accessories. All **you** really need is a T-shirt, shorts, running shoes, and a willingness to devote an hour to **your** own good health.

Participants will get a more effective workout in **their** next fitness class if **they** follow this advice. **Novices** should position themselves near the instructor so **they** can see and hear clearly. **Those** near the front **are** also less likely to be distracted by **others. All participants** should give the class **their** full attention **rather than** worrying about whether other people are watching **them** or whether **they** put enough change in the parking meter. Although **some people** might be tempted to compensate for lack of ability with expensive exercise clothes, **no one needs to** spend a fortune on exercise accessories. All participants really need is a T-shirt, shorts, running shoes, and a willingness to devote an hour to their own good health.

Chapter 22

Exercise 22.1

1. two suitcases, called a cab, and headed for the airport.
2. eye of newt, toe of frog, wool of bat, and tongue of dog.
3. to put the armoire in the master bedroom, the console in the hall, and the pine desk in the study.
4. bread, cheese, cold cuts, fruit, and sodas
5. the meat was underdone, the vegetables were soggy, and the wine was sour.

Exercise 22.2

1. now, for
2. the wall, and David [**Or C**]
3. editor, yet
4. colour, or the house
5. produce, but

Exercise 22.3

1. For example, pizza/groups, but
2. in Calgary, Louis
3. on the tile floor, he

4. High above, the planes

5. No, I don't remember

Exercise 22.4

1. fever, isn't it?

2. **C**

3. However, I always counter, "Look before you leap."

4. no man, if you catch my drift.

5. the savage breast, not the savage beast.

Exercise 22.5

1. Thank you, Mr. Sutherland,

2. **C**

3. Punch Dickins, who won the Distinguished Flying Cross in World War I,

4. python, which hasn't eaten in a month,

5. promised us, however, that

Exercise 22.6 Comma Review

1. Winnipeg, Manitoba?

2. turkey sandwiches, turkey casserole, and turkey croquettes

3. has expired, Mr. Fortino, is not

4. microwave sounded, Ted

5. **C** [no commas]

6. Whenever we go camping, Father always says, "If you don't fish where the fish are, you'll be having hot dogs for supper."

7. opened the window, took a deep breath, and composed

8. The one novel that I didn't read was the basis for the essay question on the English exam. [no commas]

9. Lucy Maud Montgomery, the author of *Anne of Green Gables,* was born in Clifton, Prince Edward Island, on November 30, 1874.

10. Well, you

11. perspective, I

12. Yes, we do

13. Howard would bring the food, Cliff would bring the drinks, and you

14. deep drifts, and icicles

15. Taxes, of course, are

16. Even during the day, light

17. Mr. Ramondo said, "We're a few bricks short of a load, but I

18. **C** [no commas]

19. dark, stormy night I like nothing better than

20. to study engineering because she discovered that

Exercise 22.7

1. astronaut; he

2. jeans; however,

3. door; but, fortunately,

4. family; Erica

5. night; as a result,

Exercise 22.8

1. interpretation, he [semicolon replaced with a comma]

2. use; otherwise,

3. stop, patiently waiting [semicolon replaced with a comma]

4. **C**

5. local band;/comedy act; and

Exercise 22.9

1. choices: "When choosing

2. term: Basic Calculus,

3. convinced—I say this without reservation—that Luke

4. suspects—Winken, Blinken, or Nod—knew

5. companion: he

Exercise 22.10

1. escape: all [**Or** escape—all]

2. **C**

3. Mrs. Christie—you met her last week at the Doyles' party—will

4. furniture—all

5. state: he

Exercise 22.11

1. "Two negatives make a positive," explained Ludwig. "However, two positives don't make a negative."

   "Yeah, right!" replied Noam.

2. **C**

3. proverb, "When money talks, the truth keeps silent."

4. "like" and "basically" [**Or** *like* and *basically*]

5. "The Death of the Moth"

Exercise 22.12

1. "No, I won't move my car!" shouted the irate driver.

2. **C**

3. said, "Give me a firm place to stand, and I will move the earth"?

4. The term "portmanteau word" refers to a word combining the sounds and meanings of two other words. For example, the word "smog" is a blending of the words "smoke" and "fog." [period goes inside the quotation marks]

   [**Or** *portmanteau word/smog/smoke/fog.*]

5. "Dulce et Decorum Est" and Randall Jarrell's poem "The Death of the Ball Turret Gunner." [period goes inside the quotation marks]

Exercise 22.13

1. said, "The acorn never falls far from the oak tree"?

2. "If fifty million people say a foolish thing," noted Anatole France, "it is still a foolish thing."

3. yelling, "We all scream for ice cream!"

4. "chimpanzee"/"gorilla"/"zebra" [**Or** *chimpanzee/gorilla/zebra*]

5. Sam Cooke's "Sad Mood."

Exercise 22.14

1. all-purpose floor covering

2. self-satisfied/twenty-three/equally qualified

3. "workmen"/"mankind"

4. ninety-year-old/weekend

5. ex-boyfriend/compact disks

Exercise 22.15

1. icono-clast

2. cry-baby

3. wrap-ping

4. **C** [no hyphen]

5. **C** [no hyphen]

6. rail-road

7. thrill-ing

8. jim-jams

9. memo-rize

10. **C** [no hyphen]

F5

371

Exercise 22.16

1. Helen's/Stephanie's/year's
2. patrons'
3. Nobody's

4. Men's/women's/store's
5. Anne's/sister-in-law's

Exercise 22.17

1. *u*'s
2. It's/hostess'
3. Mary's
4. Justin's/parents'
5. Someone's

6. children's
7. Don't/*um*'s/*uh*'s.
8. month's
9. Won't/Mildred's
10. book's

Exercise 22.18

1. four 250-page
2. Fifteen percent
3. twenty

4. **C**
5. 1980s **or** 1980's/1999

F5

Index

377

387